About the Author

Marie Carney is Head of the UCD School of Nursing, Midwifery & Health Systems. She was awarded a PhD in Strategic Management from the UCD Michael Smurfit Business School and a Master's of Business Administration from the UCD Faculty of Commerce. The title of her doctoral thesis, which she completed in 2002, was *A Strategic Consensus Model for Not-for-Profit Organisations*. She has developed curricula for Bachelor's and Master's programmes in organisational behaviour, general management, financial management, leadership and strategic management, and lectures in UCD to Bachelor's and Master's students in these subject areas.

She has had careers in nursing, teaching and business. She obtained her Fellowship in Nursing from the Faculty of Nursing & Midwifery, Royal College of Surgeons in Ireland, and the Diploma in Nurse Teaching from UCD and holds professional qualifications in general nursing and midwifery. She worked as a Nurse Tutor in the Richmond Hospital and Beaumont Hospital, Dublin. She was general manager Ireland for the multinational nutritional company, Milupa, for several years.

She has published papers in the Irish and international academic press and has delivered papers at national and international research and management conferences.

She serves on several national and international committees and on various strategy groups for management, research and nursing. She represents UCD at the European networks for the development of advanced nursing practice (TENN). She is a member of several management organisations, including the American Organisation of Nurse Executives, the Irish Management Institute and the MBA Association.

HEALTH SERVICE MANAGEMENT:
CULTURE, CONSENSUS &
THE MIDDLE MANAGER

Marie Carney

Published by
OAK TREE PRESS
19 Rutland Street, Cork, Ireland
www.oaktreepress.com

A catalogue record of this book is
available from the British Library.

ISBN 1 904887 11 2
978-1-904887-11-9

Printed in Ireland by ColourBooks.

CONTENTS

TABLES

FIGURES

For Tom, Deirdre,
Eimear, David & Fiona.

FOREWORD

I am delighted to comment on what I feel is a most welcome addition to the literature within the field of Health Service Management. In contextual terms, I come to review this impressive work having known of Marie's Carney's academic abilities and achievements since she joined UCD as a professional colleague with mutual academic interests. She is highly qualified to write this work. Her fundamental respect for the detail in any endeavour and her decision-making, in both academic and managerial matters, is consistently sound and this shows through repeatedly in this book.

The organisation of the text is notable for its appropriateness to a multi-professional audience and hence its appeal is not restricted to managers. This is principally because of its conceptual generalisability, which makes it equally pertinent to a broad constituency of clinical professionals who need to possess a familiarity with management theory and techniques. The quality of the volume's adaptability is worthy of reiteration, because experience suggests that, wherever they occur, health services comprise a number of professional cultures that are not always mutually complimentary but always require consensus to ensure their smooth governance. This is indeed is why the focus that Marie has chosen is so apt – which also renders the book very applicable outside the Irish context. That so much of the work is evidence-based and derives from her own empirical endeavour also provides added value.

In examining health service management texts on a continuum, it can be seen that they range from the theoretically-robust to others that are more practically-oriented and are akin to workbooks designed for specific groups such as nurses or doctors. This text seems to provide the ideal *via intermedia* between these polar extremes and the approach has some novel features that differentiate it from the more conventional books that are available.

In terms of content, there is a logical consistency throughout the volume. The chapters are discrete entities and can be dipped into individually. At the same time, they are mutually enhancing and thus cohere, so that many will wish to use the book its in its entirety as a study guide and as a valuable aid to understanding management theory and, thereby, to develop their own managerial ability.

This text book is well-presented to give a fluent and comprehensive overview of key propositions to its readership. It draws on appropriate theoretical perspectives and the depth and breadth of its substance is entirely rigorous. Most importantly, and in commending it most highly, the work offers scope for sound description and analysis that make for the articulation of notions that readers will be able to value and to translate for use in their everyday professional work.

Professor Peter Bradshaw
Professor in Health Care Policy
School of Human & Health Sciences
University of Huddersfield

PREVIEW

This book is very timely and addresses the management issues to be dealt with in the health care sector, which is becoming ever more important in Ireland. The book is the first of its kind, written specifically for managers of all levels in the Irish health care system and for students who will pursue careers for health care.

Marie Carney has drawn on her wealth of experience as a professional practitioner, as a manager and as an academic to produce a book that will serve the needs of managers, potential managers and students. The book is research-based and provides extensive and very valuable references to leading research articles from national and international journals and reports.

In particular, the book will be a very valuable source of information for all health care students of management in programmes such as the MBA in health services, the BSc and MSc in nursing and students from other disciplines and non-clinicians who need to understand the job of managing in a health services environment.

The integrative approach taken in the book is very welcome. Topics like leadership, strategic management, change management and motivation are all dealt with very comprehensively. I especially like the emphasis put on the importance of middle managers and on the role of organisational culture and professionalism in achieving managerial effectiveness.

In the increasingly complex and political world of health care, effective managers require an ever-increasing skill-set, which is broadening and deepening all at the same time. Above all, it requires the ability to integrate a wide diversity of knowledge, activities and skills to make good decisions that will result in excellence in health care service. This book will make a major contribution to achieving this, as I hope you will agree when you have had the chance to read it.

Frank Roche
Berber Family Chair of Entrepreneurship
UCD Michael Smurfit School of Business

PREFACE

This book takes a different approach to health service management than heretofore, as it is designed to provide health professionals with an integrated theoretical and empirical approach to strategic management through the incorporation of managerial, behavioural and organisational skills into a consensus model. These concepts are important in health service management from a strategic perspective. The book will provide a holistic approach to health service management through its integrative nature and, in the process, will assist in the strategic management development of health service clinician and non-clinician managers.

HEALTH SERVICE MANAGEMENT will endeavour to provoke and stimulate professionals to examine the behavioural, professional, environmental and structural factors underpinning health care management and, thereby, to adopt a multi-disciplinary approach to strategic management in health service organisations.

CONTENTS

Primary sources from nursing, health service, organisational behaviour and management literature are included. In addition, empirical research undertaken by the author, in the areas of strategic management that incorporate organisational structure, involvement, commitment and culture, and culminating in the strategic consensus model, is included.

The book is organised around 13 major management areas:

♦ Strategic management

♦ The middle manager

♦ Managerial effectiveness

♦ Policy and structure

♦ Professional health service organisations

♦ Inter-professional relationships in health care

♦ Change management

♦ Leadership in health service delivery

- Motivation and the environment
- Strategic involvement
- Organisational commitment
- Organisational culture and values
- Strategic consensus.

A brief outline of the contents of each chapter is presented below.

Chapter 1: Strategic Management Principles

This chapter examines three main subject areas:

- Strategic management principles
- The strategic management process
- Strategy development in for-profit and not-for-profit organisations.

There is little agreement on the definition of strategic management. It is believed that this lack of consistency is due to its multi-dimensional and situational nature. Strategic planning is an on-going decision-making process, the purpose of which is to specify the ideals, goals and objectives required by the organisation in the future. The background to strategic management development varies between the public and private sector; this book focuses on not-for-profit health service organisations.

Chapter 2: The Middle Manager in Health Service Provision

The important role played by the middle manager in health service management and in the delivery of care is analysed. The middle manager in the health service context, defined in this book as a manager who reports to the chief executive officer or to a manager who him/herself reports to the chief executive officer, may be the head of a department or in a functional role in any of the health service management configurations such as clinical nurse manager, clinical director, or service manager, and may be a clinician or non-clinician. The middle manager *versus* the senior management role is explored. In order to reach an understanding of the strategic role of middle managers, it is necessary to trace the evolution of this role, and to determine the level of middle manager involvement in not-for-profit organisations.

Chapter 3: Managerial Effectiveness

Chapter 3 presents an introduction to managerial effectiveness, through incorporating the skills required by health professionals in the delivery of health care. This includes the background to management concepts, the principles and skills of management and strategic management and provides a discussion and analysis of the theories and concepts on which management processes are based. Definitions of management and role requirements are also presented. Management skills required by health service managers include: planning, organising, decision-making and problem-solving, critical thinking, clinical governance and managed care.

Chapter 4: Organisational Policy & Structure

This chapter examines the impact of changing organisational structures on health care managers, including nurse managers. A body of mainly qualitative research and normative theory exists on the relationship between middle managers and organisational performance and this is also explored. Organisations are central to the delivery of the nation's health care service. In order that these organisations can respond to the developing and challenging trends occurring in the health service's strategy, the delivery of health care needs to be efficient and effective. Health care organisations represent a specific form of organisation, although having similar characteristics to many other organisations. Widespread restructuring and redesign of acute care delivery is taking place in many countries. Managers need to be able to respond to the changes brought about by health service restructuring. This chapter relates to the restructuring of the layers of hierarchy and its impact on health service management. Some aspects of the NHS restructuring, components of the US health care system and the Irish health care origins are included. Formal and informal organisational design and future organisational structures and networks are also explored.

Chapter 5: Professional Health Service Organisations

Professional health service organisations are unique. Such organisations have undergone restructuring change that has led to major consequences for health service professionals, particularly middle managers. The reduction in hierarchy, and in layers of management during the previous decade, has led to greater responsibility, a larger span of control and the taking-on of new roles by middle managers that were previously undertaken by those above and below. This resulted in a greater strategic role. The restructuring of middle management that has taken place has provided managers with greater levels of responsibility and decision-making than before. The internal and external environments of professional health service organisations are explored.

Chapter 6: Inter-professional Relations

Successful health care delivery depends, to a large extent, on the types of clinician and non-clinician interactions that occur. If these interactions are of a collaborative and strategic nature, positive benefits will result for both groups of professionals and for patients. Collaboration is defined as clinicians from different disciplines working together co-operatively through sharing responsibility for decision-making, problem-solving, conflict resolution and the co-ordinating of activities. Chapter 6 explores the collaborative and interactive patterns that occur in health care delivery, including how these interactions may be developed and enhanced by educational programmes and collaborative research. The consequences of inter-disciplinary and multi-disciplinary education programmes at pre- and post-registration levels are also explored.

Chapter 7: Change Management in Health Service Provision

In this chapter, the management of change is explored from the individual manager, the strategic and the organisational perspective. In order to manage the changes currently taking place, managers are required to be involved in strategy development.

This chapter explores change management within the health service context and demonstrates how a change management model developed by the author may be used in the evaluation of the change process. This model of change presents the key variables and critical success factors necessary for the successful implementation of change, in addition to a construct tool for measuring successful implementation. The chapter explores shaping change from below, as well as upwards through selling issues and includes models for managing the change process including `The Change Management Model' and `A Model of Preparedness for Occupational Change'.

Chapter 8: Leadership for the Future

Managers require leadership skills that provide direction for health care organisations for the future. Leadership in the delivery of health services is influenced by the changes that are taking place in health care and, therefore, organisations are looking for health care professionals who can provide leadership in the co-ordination of services offered to patients. This chapter explores the important theories and concepts of leadership, including the differences between leadership and management. Particular emphasis is placed on transformational leadership and empowerment. The concept of empowerment in nursing and health service leadership is analysed through existing leadership research. How transformational leadership may be developed in clinicians and non-clinicians is explored.

Chapter 9: Motivation for Health Professional Managers

In chapter 9, motivational theories, the ways to achieve job satisfaction and motivation and an exploration of how managers inspire ordinary employees to do extraordinary things are presented. In addition, clinicians' and non-clinicians' motivational techniques are discussed. This chapter explores the important theories and concepts of motivation and illustrates the important part played by health service managers in ensuring that staff working in the health service environment are motivated to deliver professional care. It is recognised that leadership and motivation in the health services is influenced by the changes that are taking place in health care.

Chapter 10: Involvement in Strategy Development in the Health Service

This chapter explores how involvement in strategy development by clinicians and non-clinicians influences patient care delivery and critically examines the importance of involvement in the development of strategy in health service organisations. The positive and negative outcomes and consequences from involvement and non-involvement of both groups are presented from empirical research. The primary focus of this chapter is on the level of influence that middle managers have in engaging in strategy development, their involvement in the strategic process and their understanding of the strategies developed. How organisational structure impacts on the role of nurse managers is examined and the effect of organisational structure on strategic involvement in the changing, dynamic health service environment is incorporated into the material presented.

Chapter 11: Organisational & Professional Commitment & Its Influence on Health Service Management

This chapter explores commitment to the organisation and professional commitment to the role in the health service context. The importance of involvement and influence in the development of organisational strategy and in the development and maintenance of commitment to the role and to the organisation are critically analysed. Other factors that lead to commitment are also presented. The relationships between organisational commitment and strategic involvement and between organisational commitment and strategic consensus are analysed, as there is limited evidence to show that commitment to the organisation may influence strategic involvement. The literature indicates that the concept of organisational commitment is complex and encompasses many dimensions. Commitment is defined as employees encompassing a complex sense of loyalty that involves a strong belief in the goals of the organisation, congruence with the value system of the organisation and a willingness to serve the organisation through continued membership.

Chapter 12: Organisational Culture & Its Effect on Health Service Management

There is a need for managers to understand the cultural dynamics operating within the organisation and how organisational culture influences health service management. What is evident from the literature is that culture is a multi-dimensional, multi-faceted phenomenon that is not easily reduced to a few major dimensions. This chapter explores the important aspects of organisational culture, including the positive and negative effects of strong organisational culture. Ethical beliefs and values required by health care managers are discussed and the positive and negative outcomes of holding such values are analysed. The importance of socialisation into the role that health service clinicians undergo during their education and training, and the view that an organisation may have more than one culture, sub-culture or cell culture due to the make up of organisational groups, are explored.

Chapter 13: Strategic Consensus of Health Service Strategy

Research on consensus has been related to senior management and, up until 1990, the middle manager was not the focus of consensus research. This chapter critically analyses the role of the manager in the achievement of strategic consensus and follows on to examine the importance of consensus in health service management. It will be demonstrated in an integrative manner that the organisation's structure, manager involvement in strategy development, the manager's commitment to the organisation and the organisation's culture are necessary for consensus of strategy. Researchers have supported the idea that strategy is formulated through consensus building among senior management. However, few middle managers articulate the same goals as their superiors and those who disagree with strategic initiatives can block the implementation of strategy. The consequences of managers blocking strategic initiatives as a result of not being strategically involved and, therefore, not achieving consensus of strategies, are explored. Chapter 13 culminates in the 'Strategic Consensus Model'.

Chapter 14: An Integrative Approach to Strategic Management in the Health Services: The Consensus Model

Chapter 14 summarises the integrative approach to strategic management, through the defining of the consensus model. This is a new concept in strategic management. The consensus model incorporates the management principles, organisational, behavioural and cultural patterns that form the health services' strategic management. Through the use of the strategic consensus model, a higher level of strategic involvement by clinicians and non-clinicians will occur. As a result, patient services will be enhanced, if both clinicians and non-clinicians are willing to take greater responsibility for ensuring that strategic consensus is fostered in health service organisations. It is important for managers to maintain strong organisational culture, thereby ensuring the maintenance of ethical cultural norms such as caring. As both groups are strategically involved, two different perspectives will be obtained through the participation of clinicians and non-clinicians in strategic matters, and in the recognition that both groups have different perspectives in care delivery. The strategic model presented in this chapter will contribute towards improving the quality and effectiveness of health care through the generation of knowledge-based innovation and new ways of thinking. In the future, health service managers must be able to balance the learning and performance organisations through being internally- and externally-orientated and by creating a culture within their organisations that is creative, multidisciplinary and experiential.

CHAPTER 1
STRATEGIC MANAGEMENT PRINCIPLES

INTRODUCTION

Developing and managing strategy is a critical success factor for health care managers, yet the idea of involving managers below the level of chief executive or senior manager in the development of strategy remains underdeveloped. There is little agreement regarding the definition of strategic management and this lack of consistency is often attributed to the multi-dimensional and situational nature of strategic management. Effective strategic planning requires that management possesses sufficient information about themselves and their environment and have the managerial capabilities that allow for effective strategic planning to occur. Strategic action in health care is identified notably by the distinctive competencies required, the phases in strategy formulation, the environmental analysis and the strategic choice evaluation. The purpose of this chapter is to define the strategic process in the not-for-profit health service organisation.

DEFINING THE STRATEGIC PROCESS

Although there is little agreement on the definition of strategic management,[1,2] it is commonly accepted that a positive attitude towards strategic planning results in practical strategy-making and performance outcomes.[3] Strategy is defined as "the pattern or plan that integrates an organisation's major goals, policies and action sequences into a cohesive whole".[4] Strategic planning is an on-going decision-making process, the purpose of which is to specify the ideals, goals and objectives that the organisation will require in the future. The programmes that are necessary to achieve these ends must be developed, and resources and organisational structures must be in

---

[1]   Hambrick (1983).
[2]   Chaffee (1985).
[3]   Glaister & Falshaw (1999).
[4]   Quinn (1995), p.5.

place. The generation and formulation of strategic options, the evaluation of strategic alternatives, and the likely impact of the proposed decisions on others are critical components of the strategic planning process.[5;6]

The strategic management process is described in various ways, emphasising the complex nature of the process – for example, as a rational, analytical and deliberate process,[7;8] as an incremental process involving environmental scanning and evaluation,[9] or where power structures within the organisation reinforce cultural influences on strategy development. Strategy may evolve through political influence where it is developed through the negotiation process[10] or *via* cultural and social processes within the organisation that reinforces cultural influences on strategy development.[11] The process by which organisational strategies are developed is influenced by several factors, including the planning process, incrementalism, and political, cultural or enforced choice.[12]

Bryant, Dobal & Johnson,[13] in a study undertaken in a large hospital in the US, found that collaboration in the strategic process is a critical factor in the development of a strategic plan, and that this collaboration ensures that strategy is understood and supported by the entire organisation. Additionally, senior management in successful organisations expend effort on building induced and autonomous strategic processes in tandem with concerns regarding the content of strategy. A consequence of this integrative process is the development of distinctive competencies in managers that then become part of the new vision of the organisation.[14] Induced strategy ensures that there is a fit with the current organisational strategy, goals and competencies. However, autonomous strategic initiatives are seen as being outside the scope of current strategy and are driven by middle and operational managers seeking to develop new competencies in order to enhance and develop their roles within the organisation.[15] Conversely, unsuccessful organisations are those where strategy-making is hyperactive or inactive,[16] and where formal planning frequently does

---

5   Dyson (1990).
6   Ashmos, Duchon & McDaniel (1998).
7   Quinn (1980).
8   Rowe, Dickel, Mason & Snyder (1989).
9   Quinn (1982).
10 Feldman (1986).
11 Trice & Beyer (1993).
12 Bailey, Johnson & Daniels (2000).
13 Bryant, Dobal & Johnson (1990).
14 Burgelman (1991).
15 Burgelman (1991).
16 Hambrick & D'Aveni (1988).

not occur – as a result, strategies emerge from informal decisions and entrenched values.[17]

STRATEGY IN NOT–FOR–PROFIT ORGANISATIONS

The health care sector consists mainly of not-for-profit organisations. The background to strategic management development varies between the public and private sectors,[18] and some authors argue that the strategies developed for the private sector are not appropriate for the not-for-profit sector.[19;20] In the not-for-profit sector, it is more abstract to describe a service than to plan for a product – thus a change in thinking is required which moves away from product-oriented management to the application of techniques suitable for a service-oriented business.[21] However, the application of the management principles, techniques and tools used in the for-profit business sector has been recognised as necessary for the not-for-profit sector. Even though not-for-profit organisations do not emulate for-profit organisations, many hospital managers have adopted the managerial techniques and systems of the for-profit organisations as a perceived means of improving their operations, thereby enhancing the level of service delivered to patients and clients.[22;23]

There are strategic similarities and orientations, including overlap, such as in the areas of financial management and service quality, between for-profit and not-for-profit organisations but, equally so, there are many differences between both types of organisation. Unlike for-profit organisations, not-for-profit organisations tend to be labour-intensive, to be critically dependent on high quality staff,[24] to require a significant amount of professional input[25] and usually involve layers of managerial hierarchy.[26] Social services, including health, educational, religious and cultural activities, are part of the not-for-profit domain and provide services that are difficult for the user to judge in terms of service and quality. Although most health care organisations fall

---

[17]   Harris (1999).
[18]   Bowman & Asch (1987).
[19]   Wortman (1979).
[20]   Ring & Perry (1985).
[21]   Thomas (1978).
[22]   Oster (1995).
[23]   Wells (1999).
[24]   Oster (1995).
[25]   Perrow (1986).
[26]   Jaques (1989).

within the category of social services, specific differences exist in relation to legal and regulatory rules and regulations, and these differences are more pronounced in the hospital sector.[27] Such differences between for-profit and not-for-profit organisations appear to affect strategy development in several areas, including the planning process,[28] financial and budgetary management,[29] and human resource management practices. [30]

In the developed world, not-for-profit hospitals have had to become increasingly business-like in terms of organisation and management.[31] Consequently, professional clinicians are now involved in new strategic management roles and responsibilities in addition to their clinician practice roles,[32;33] and this has resulted in changes in the traditional self-image, perceptions, values and roles of the individual health professional.[34] In the health service, the emphasis is on a caring approach to health care delivery rather than on the generation of profits for the organisation, and this difference in orientation has contributed to strategic management difficulties in health care organisations.[35;36] The complexity of not-for-profit organisations has also increased due to the hierarchical nature of these systems,[37] the diversity of operations, the competition from for-profit organisations and from similar not-for-profit organisations, and the demands of their clients and their public masters for high quality, efficient services.[38;39]

Evaluating Strategic Competencies in Hospitals

The strategic actions of managers may influence health care delivery positively or negatively, and these actions may be related to the relationships that are developed, externally or internally to the organisation. External relationships may include networks, professional organisations or communications with similar hospitals, while internal relationships may be departmental, multi-professional or inter-professional. The importance of these relationships, and the strategic decisions made by senior and middle executives in such

---

[27]   Wells (1996).
[28]   Bryant, Dobal & Johnson (1990).
[29]   Wells (1995).
[30]   Budhwar (2000).
[31]   Carney (2001a).
[32]   Gavin (1995).
[33]   Jowett (1996).
[34]   Wells (1995).
[35]   Wortman (1979).
[36]   Ring & Perry (1985).
[37]   Jaques (1989).
[38]   Oster (1995).
[39]   Ring & Perry (1985).

relationships, has an impact on organisational performance through the manner in which they position the organisation in its specific sector.[40;41] For example, in the health care sector, if hospitals are perceived as centres of excellence in specific areas, such as cardiology or paediatrics, strategic decisions made by the hospital's executives will influence the future direction and reputation of the organisation. Other strategic decisions that may influence the future direction of the organisation include the formation of national or international strategic alliances with similar hospitals. Such alliances may broaden the range of competencies provided and enhance the hospital's reputation for excellence still further. Partnership arrangements and networking with similar or dissimilar organisations have the potential to extend the strategic capabilities of each organisation,[42] as the pooling of resources provides these organisations with competitive advantages over other similar organisations.[43]

STRATEGIC MANAGEMENT IN ACTION IN THE HEALTH SECTOR

The key players in the strategic management process are the general manager and the middle manager; they are the strategists, the goal-setters, the organisation-builders, the directors and the controllers of operations and, therefore, are responsible, to a large extent, for the survival of the organisation.

The general manager, in consultation with heads of department, will ask pertinent questions, such as, *What business are we in?*, *What is the purpose?*, *Does the mission of the organisation provide a statement as to the service provided for customers?*, *What image does the organisation portray?*, and *What are the distinctive competencies of the organisation over those of similar type organisations?*. The general manager and departmental heads define the mission and the goals of the organisation, set the organisational objectives, develop the strategies, actions and tasks to achieve the goals of the strategy, and control the achievement of objectives.

The mission is defined as a common thread that runs throughout the organisation and to which related activities are identified; it is often defined as the scope of products of the organisation. It is the overriding premise of the organisation that is in line with the expectations and values of the employees and the stakeholders, and

---

40   McGahan & Porter (1997).
41   Hoskisson, Hitt, Wan & Yiu (1999).
42   Douglas & Ryman (2003).
43   Dyer & Singh (1998).

must be broad enough to define the organisation's purpose and scope. However, if factors that are critical to the organisation's success are too broad or are eliminated, this process is then perceived as a paper exercise and becomes meaningless for the members of the organisation.

Goals are general statements of aim or purpose. Initially, objectives are formulated in a general form and, subsequently, expressed in a specific form; they are statements of the organisation's intentions, expectations and plans for the future.

Objectives define the purpose of the organisation in its environment and are more tangible than mission statements because they define the output goals and the service outcomes. The objectives assist managers and decision-makers in co-ordinating decisions and provide standards and quality measures for assessing organisational performance. In order to assess organisational performance, objectives being pursued are quantified and given time weighting and time frames for completion. Priorities for each objective are determined and techniques for measuring objectives are identified. Generally, objectives are defined for a one-year period, but may be delivered within a period of up to five years; the objectives state what the organisation intends to pursue during that time.[44]

The strategic process then continues with the development of strategy, that is, a broad category or type of action undertaken to achieve the objectives, which is implemented through individual or group actions and tasks. Finally, the strategic process is controlled and evaluated through the monitoring of action steps, designed to reinforce the objectives that assess the level of effectiveness of strategies and actions. Modifications and changes to the process are introduced, as required, and rewards for meeting or exceeding objectives should be provided to employees.

There are several levels of strategy, including corporate, business, and functional, each of which involve questions to be answered by managers. While the strategy questions at the corporate-level pertain to what business the organisation is in, at the business-level the questions to be asked are: *How does the organisation compete?* and *What are the specific services or business units provided?*. At the functional-level, the strategy question is: *How does the organisation and its managers support the business-level strategy through its structures, strategies and policies?*. Strategy is formulated at all levels and involves planning and decision-making that ultimately leads to the organisation's goals and objectives being set out in a clear and concise manner and to the development of a specific strategic plan by the managers involved.[45]

---

44   Jauch & Glueck (2003).
45   Daft (2003).

Strategic evaluation is concerned with a number of factors, including an assessment by managers of the suitability of the strategies developed. Suitability refers to the fit or consistency of the strategy with the organisation's mission and objectives and its feasibility; it is also concerned with the strategy's successful implementation and acceptability and is related to the expectations of all of the stakeholders. In addition, the strategic evaluation identifies scope, synergy and distinctive competencies. Scope is determined by the identification of the number and type of products and services offered by the organisation. Synergy refers to the state that is deemed to exist when the organisation's parts interact in unison, producing an effect that is greater than the sum of its parts acting independently. Distinctive competence is the position that the organisation achieves through its scope and synergistic interactions, with reference to its competitors in its industry. An organisation must determine what its distinctive competencies are (what makes it unique in the sector), so that it will be in a position to make decisions as to how it will use these abilities and competencies now and in the future. In addition, in order to face environmental threats to its existence or progress, the organisation must determine if its perceived or actual weaknesses will limit its future growth and how these weaknesses (areas requiring further development) can be overcome.

Phases in Strategy Formulation

The process of strategy formulation consists of four phases:

♦ **Phase one**, which includes trend analysis and forecasting, is based on past performance and future trends. Trend analysis should be carried out at four levels: organisational, business sector, national and international.

♦ **Phase two** involves the identification of future threats and opportunities, including critical threats to the organisation's survival, the opportunities open to the organisation to develop further and the identification of potential allies, opponents and detractors.

♦ **Phase three** entails political and economic analysis; it is concerned with the nature and number of external relationships and network pathways open to the organisation and with the power coalitions that exist both within the organisation and external to it. The prevailing economic climate will either assist or hinder future progress. Structure, strategy, culture and internal political structures, if not managed effectively, will also affect organisational functioning.

♦ **Phase four**, the final phase of strategy formulation, relates to
political strategy formulation; it is concerned with the establishment
of alliances, networks and internal coalitions, and the form of
negotiation and conflict resolution mechanisms in place to assist in
pushing strategy forward.

The strategic plan should address the critical success factors that must
be in place to secure the organisation's future short-, medium- and
long-term success. Key tasks and priorities are set out and the
assumptions underpinning the strategic plan are tested and measured
through the use of one or more planning tools, including financial
plans and budgets, human resource activity and plans and network
analysis or project planning. In addition, controls must be put in place
in the management of physical resources, such as buildings, plant and
machinery; these include security, production controls ˙ and
maintenance systems. While financial controls include budgets,
costing systems and capital investments, the control of resources used
includes stock control and supplier controls over quality, quantity, and
cost. Human resource controls pertain to staff recruitment and attrition
rates, management of key personnel and succession, working
agreements and contracts and leadership succession. There are also a
number of intangibles, often immeasurable – for example, control of
the organisation's image and reputation, how sensitive information is
managed and the tracking and management of the industrial relations
climate within the organisation.[46]

ENVIRONMENTAL ANALYSIS

The strategic management process includes situational analysis – that
is, the analysis of the strengths and weaknesses of the organisation and
the opportunities and threats existing in the environment that have the
potential to harm the organisation in some way. The following
questions assist in clarifying weaknesses or areas that require further
development: *What does the organisation do commendably well?*, *Do these
competencies count and, if so, when and how?*, *In what respect(s) does the
organisation perform poorly, relative to competitors?* and *Do these
weaknesses matter and, if yes, to whom?*.

In determining the organisation's strengths and weaknesses, a
number of sources of information are available to managers, including
internal reports, budgets and financial data, human resource
capabilities, the reputation of its staff for evidence-based practice, and
the organisation's image for excellence in patient care delivery.

---

[46] Johnson & Scholes (2002).

Employees should be surveyed in order to determine their attitudes and satisfaction levels regarding management and strategy implementation perceptions, as a wide range of views are obtained from employees through this inclusive process. After the employees' perceptions have been analysed, changes may be made in the strategic process that ultimately lead to the development of strategies that will most likely lead to the fulfilment of the organisation's objectives. Once identified, this knowledge should then be used to divert resources to areas where they are most needed, particularly, towards the organisation's critical success factors that must be well-resourced and managed. This process should enhance the organisation's capabilities, lead to superior advantages over competitors and allow entry into new service areas. In assessing the threats or potential to harm, sources of information include patient satisfaction surveys, suppliers, friends, associations, professional journals and economic reports. Opportunities are determined in the context of the potential to help the organisation.

Managers should undertake analysis of environmental factors affecting, or likely to affect, the organisation; such factors are a measure of the organisational environment that is external to the organisation's boundaries and that have the potential to affect the organisation. In contrast, the task environment is the layer of the external environment that directly influences the organisation's operations and performance. Chaffee[47] proposes that there are three models of strategy (linear, adaptive and interpretive), each of which depend on the level of complexity that exists in the organisation's hierarchical structure.

It is important to differentiate between the general and the internal environments. The general environment affects the organisation indirectly and includes political, legal, socio-cultural, economic, technologic, and international dimensions. Political and legal factors may concern environmental protection laws, such as incineration, employment laws, EU regulations pertaining to health and safety, or government directives, such as health strategies. Due to the demographic shifts and the changing populations that are emerging within society, socio-cultural factors that impinge on the health sector will require on-going monitoring. Socio-cultural dimensions include the demographic characteristics, as well as the norms, the customs and the values of the population within which the organisation operates. Culture represents unwritten, informal norms that bind an organisation's members together. In the internal environment, which exists within the organisation's boundaries, there is an internal culture that consists of key values, beliefs, understandings and norms which

---

[47]   Chaffee (1985).

members of an organisation share. Factors that have the potential to affect the organisation's undertakings include population demographic analysis, income distribution affecting health care provision, and access to services. Other socio-cultural factors that need to be considered include the social mobility of patients/clients, nutritional and social lifestyle changes, and attitudes to leisure, such as exercise and levels of education.

Economic factors represent the overall monetary health of the country or region in which the organisation functions and will always be a part of health care provision. Numerous factors require close scrutiny by managers due to their potential to destabilise the organisation's financial well-being; these factors include trends in GNP (gross national product) and GDP (gross domestic product), interest and inflation rates, the level of disposable income and unemployment in the catchment area of the organisation. At the internal level, factors that will affect the organisation's economic and financial environment include the capacity or bed utilisation, the competitive position of the hospital *vis-à-vis* its competitors, the methods of reimbursement for services provided, the economies of scale, and the level of integration of delivery systems. In addition, a key economic factor, particularly in times of shrinking government and private sector funding, is support for research funding for health service research, including medical research.

Technological factors will continue to affect health care delivery due to the constant stream of discoveries, new equipment, medicines, and techniques being introduced; these factors may include the costs associated with equipment, including the purchase of, the training of personnel in the use of, and the running costs. The speed of technological transfer will determine the rates of obsolescence of existing equipment and the capital funding that must be put in place in order for the organisation to be in a position to maintain its reputation, expertise and capabilities within the health service sector. The availability and cost of energy are likely to remain critical for health care and, indeed, for industry and government. The continuing government focus on technological effort and industry competitiveness will continue in the health sector as in other sectors of the economy.

A survey of the process of strategy development is presented in **Figure 1.1**.

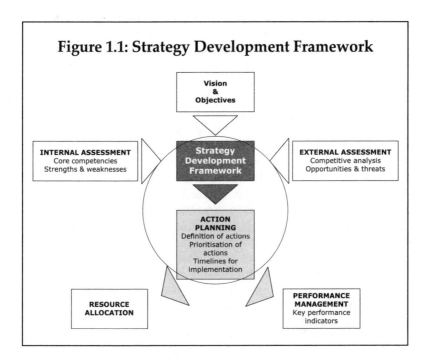

Figure 1.1: Strategy Development Framework

Strategic Choice Evaluation

Strategic choices are evaluated and determined after internal and external environmental analysis has been completed. The basic questions that managers should ask include: *What strategy does the organisation wish to pursue?* and *Are programmes to be discontinued, merged, replaced or new programmes introduced?*.

In order to allow for strategic choices to be made, managers must be able to focus on a few of the alternatives open to them, to illustrate the conditions under which strategy variations could be appropriate and, following this analysis, to make a choice from among these alternatives. Reasonable strategic alternatives result from knowledge of the area, staff proposals and, if necessary, consultant advice.

The purpose of strategic choice is to accomplish objectives; it must remain clear throughout the process. A strategy may be chosen to close the gaps in the organisation's objectives. Miles & Snow's framework, [48] introduced in 1978, defines four postures open to managers: defenders, prospectors, analysers and reactors.

Hospital managers who are classified as *defenders* hold a narrow view of the organisation's capability, guard their positions carefully,

---

[48]   Miles & Snow (1978).

and plan intensively. Although power is held centrally, defenders use limited environmental scanning and therefore, are unaware of the potential opportunities or threats that exist to the organisation. As a consequence of their tight planning and control, defenders are cost effective in terms of service delivery but have a narrow perspective. In contrast, *prospectors* are active managers who use broad planning approaches and decentralised controls; they use extensive environmental scanning to actively seek out new services and products that will match their organisations' capabilities. Prospectors often hold under-used resources due to their 'catch all' approach to management. *Analysers*, the third type of manager posture, are situated in between defenders and prospectors; analysers hold some of the characteristics of the defender and the prospector, whilst analysing all aspects of the business intensively. Analysers must move on from the stage of analysis to planning and implementation. The *reactor*, the final type of manager, operates in "unstable posture mode". Whilst the reactor realises that the organisation's environment is changing, this type of manager appears unable to get the alignment right or into a favourable position that will benefit the organisation through the exploitation of its capabilities.[49]

A number of techniques have been developed to assist managers in making strategic choices. However, Ring & Perry [50] argue that many of the techniques developed for the private sector are not suitable for use in the public sector, due to the different emphasis placed on its operations. Such private market techniques include the portfolio matrix developed by the Boston Consultancy Group that identifies:

♦ 'Stars', that is, leaders in the field that are growing rapidly and require cash for growth.

♦ Low growth-high market share products or `cash cows' that generate large profits

♦ Low growth-low market share products, termed `dogs', that require cash to survive.

Strategic Choice Management

In strategic choice development, power relationships must be actively managed, as politics will play a role in the correct choice being made, even to the extent of influencing the objectives and the manner in which analysis is used. If mistakes result from the strategic choices made, a powerful shift to blame the middle or lower executive will

---

[49]   Jauch & Glueck (2003).
[50]   Ring & Perry (1985).

occur;[51] therefore, middle managers should involve their next-level-above manager in the strategic choice process.

The strategic choices made depend on the type of strategist. *Active* strategists act before they are forced to react to environmental concerns. For example, concerns over health and safety, environmental hazards and patient complaints are vigorously analysed and decisions as to the course of action to take are taken and managed dynamically. In contrast, *passive* strategists react only when forced to do so by the staff or by environmental change.

Strategic choices made by managers in order to ensure the organisation's future financial viability may include the merger of two or more organisations. In health care, mergers are undertaken frequently in order to increase the new reputation, the image, the specialities or the financial well-being of the hospital formed from the merger. As a consequence of the enlarged entity, competition will be reduced and, generally, it is expected that synergies will be achieved from the merger; thus, the profitability and the efficiencies through economies of scale will increase due to the reduction of combined costs of resources. Although it is possible to diversify service lines and to provide a balance or fit between programmes and services, merged operations also produce negative outcomes, such as loss of employment and dissatisfaction amongst remaining staff that may lead to "survivor syndrome".

External retrenchment is a further strategic choice that includes divesture or liquidation of assets; usually, retrenchment is undertaken to reduce costs or assets. Within the health service context, retrenchment may result in the closing-down of a hospital or community care unit or division. Divesture is used as a strategic choice primarily where there is a lack of demand for a service, to reduce the costs of running an unprofitable division, to reduce staff costs, due to social and demographic changes occurring in society, or may be forced by conflicts with the social responsibility of the organisation. Limiting retrenchment strategies include leasing equipment instead of purchasing, contracting out surplus staff or selling off some non-critical-to-operations assets.

In contrast, internal expansion may be the strategic choice made, to expand the current product, programme or service range. Expansion may also be undertaken in order to penetrate new markets with existing products or services to attract new customers – for example, by extending the ante-natal programme to offer post-natal and paediatric services. Internal expansion may add to new markets or services – for example, setting up a diabetic clinic.

---

[51] Jauch & Glueck (2003).

In the future, knowledge of strategic management, the strategic management process and the strategic options open to managers will be required more than heretofore. Therefore, it is important that health service professional clinicians and non-clinicians have an understanding of the language of strategy and contribute to the debate concerning the future strategic planning of their organisations and to the strategic issues concerning health care at the national level. Due to heightened consumer expectations, the restructuring of health care planning, the organisation and the delivery of health care in many countries is often instigated following, for example, White or Green papers in Britain or Health Strategy documents in Ireland. In this way, the need for greater efficiencies and effectiveness in health care delivery has emerged. The further delegation of responsibility from central government to local management requires that professional managers become more accountable for the services that they deliver, for strategic planning and ultimately, for the strategic choices made.

SUMMARY

♦ The key theories that provide explanations for how the strategic management process is managed are centred on strategic planning, environmental scanning and strategic evaluation.

♦ The general manager and the middle manger are the central players in the strategic management process and, it could be argued, are responsible to a large extent for the survival of the organisation.

♦ The background to strategic management development in the public and private sector varies. The health care sector consists mainly of not-for-profit organisations – therefore, strategies developed for the private sector are not appropriate. Although it is possible to plan for a product in the abstract, it is not yet possible to do so, to any extent, for a service, such as health care delivery. Therefore, a change in conceptual thinking is required for strategic management.

♦ Strategic management refers to the set of decisions and actions used by managers to design, implement and evaluate strategies that will provide a good fit or balance between the organisation/hospital and its environment in order to achieve the objectives of the organisation. Elements of strategic management include strategy, strategic analysis, strategic choice and strategy implementation.

♦ There are four phases in the strategy formulation process: phase one involves trend analysis and forecasting; phase two includes the identification of future threats and opportunities; phase three entails political and economic analysis and the final phase relates to the political strategy formulation that is required to assist in pushing strategy forward.

♦ Strategic analysis is guided by factors within the internal environment of the organisation, such as the requirements of customers, suppliers and competitors, and by factors external to the organisation, including technological, economic, social, international, legal and ethical aspects, which are perceived as influencing the organisation's strategy.

♦ Strategic analysis is also influenced by the organisation's culture and value systems and the expectations of its members, in addition to the resources and capabilities of the organisation.

♦ Strategic choice is concerned with the identification of strategic options, the evaluation of these options and the subsequent selection of strategy.

♦ Strategy implementation is concerned with planning and allocating resources to fulfil strategic plans. The organisation's structure will also influence the success of the strategic plan; an unwieldy or hierarchical structure will militate against its success. The management of strategic change is also necessary for successful strategy implementation.

♦ The purpose of strategic choice is to accomplish objectives. This purpose must remain clear throughout the process; otherwise, strategic dissonance will occur.

CHAPTER 2
THE MIDDLE MANAGER IN HEALTH SERVICE PROVISION

INTRODUCTION

Chapter 1 explored management of strategy and the strategic process. This exploration included an evaluation of the strategic choices open to managers in not-for-profit health service organisations. Chapter 2 is about the middle manager, who may be either a general manager or head of department and is a key player in the strategic management process. The general manager, in consultation with heads of department, will ask questions pertinent to the organisation's strategic direction, after which they will define the mission and goals of the organisation, set organisational objectives, develop strategies, actions and tasks to achieve strategy and to control objective achievement. As strategy is developed through collaboration, the role of the middle manager in this process is critical to its successful development and implementation. The objective of this chapter is to define the role of the middle manager and to place the middle manager in the organisational context and in strategy development. This chapter will identify how middle managers attempt to formulate broad strategies for new business and service activity by gaining access and selling issues to senior management, and in boundary-spanning, thereby achieving strategic orientation.

THE MIDDLE MANAGER

The middle manager is defined as a manager who reports to the chief executive officer or to a manager who him/herself reports to the chief executive officer.[1] The middle manager usually has significant supervisory responsibility, and a high degree of responsibility in relation to other positions. It is the size and complexity of this responsibility that are important in determining their role and function within the organisation.[2] Within the hierarchy of the organisation, the

---

[1]   Wooldridge & Floyd (1990).
[2]   Dopson & Stewart (1990).

chief executive officer is situated at the apex and the middle manager is located below him/her. The operations manager concerned with the delivery of services may be one layer, or several layers, below the middle manager. The middle manager is responsible for the aggregate performance of the workers who report to him/her, thus, providing this group of workers with an organisation-wide perspective.[3] Major influences on the middle manager's role include the reduction in organisational hierarchies, which has resulted in middle managers behaving as risk-taking entrepreneurs, responsible for measuring performance in terms of efficiency and effectiveness.[4;5;6]

In the last decade, research on middle managers has focused on the future of the middle manager in downsized organisations, centring on the process of staff reduction or on the image of the middle manager survivor.[7;8] The image portrayed is of a group of managers with low morale who are motivated either by a fear of redundancy[9] or a fear of senior management.[10] The complexity of changes affecting the role and responsibility of middle managers in the public and private sectors is now more challenging and fulfilling than in the past;[11] the role has become more, rather than less, important.[12] This recent change is due to the downsizing in organisations, which has resulted in middle managers now functioning in changed roles that confer devolved decision-making on them.[13]

The Role of the Middle Manager in Strategy Development

Middle managers are reluctant to become involved in strategy development due to insecurity in their role.[14] Empirical research has revealed different reasons and consequences for this lack of middle manager involvement. A British study involving 52 middle managers, undertaken by Goffee & Scase, found that middle managers were insecure in their role and were mainly concerned with career development. This focus on career development resulted in reduced

---

3   Freidson (1976).
4   Carney (2004a).
5   Goffee & Scase (1986).
6   Goffee & Scase (1986) undertook this study in six large, public and private British organisations. The sample consisted of 323 male middle managers, therefore the lack of gender balance in the study should be borne in mind.
7   Ebadan & Winstanley (1997).
8   Thomas & Dunkerley (1999).
9   Peters (1992).
10   Caulkin (1995).
11   Dopson & Stewart (1990).
12   Dopson & Stewart (1993).
13   Millman & Hartwick (1987).
14   Floyd & Wooldridge (1992a).

effectiveness that, in turn, produced too many "unwillingly plateaued managers" in the "middle management trap".[15] Supporting this view, Floyd & Wooldridge's study, which involved American managers in mainly for-profit organisations, found that middle managers were unsure of their role and potential and were unable to articulate successfully their potential contribution to the organisation.[16;17] In a study of 365 middle manager clinicians and non-clinicians in 55 health service not-for-profit organisations in the Republic of Ireland, Carney found that middle managers were mainly satisfied with their strategic role and were dissatisfied with this role only if they perceived that their expertise and contribution to the organisation were not appreciated or recognised by other middle managers or by senior managers.[18]

The image of the middle manager portrayed above contrasts with the traditional representation of the middle manager. The traditional approach, found mainly in large organisations, considers strategic sense-making as the responsibility of top management alone and views senior managers as bringing together and interpreting information for strategic planning.[19] The origin of the traditional approach is related to the idea that it is seldom below the level of top management that middle managers have sufficient information of the organisation to enable them to contribute meaningfully to the strategic process,[20] that senior managers naturally assume environmental scanning and strategic planning roles[21] and that decision-making within large organisations should be limited to senior management in order to avoid an overwieldy process.[22] Within these roles, strategic planning is viewed as a "top down" system, with middle managers portrayed as providing the upward flow of information that senior managers require in order to manage strategy formulation.[23;24;25;26;27]

---

[15] Torrington & Weightman (1987), p.88.

[16] Floyd & Wooldridge (1996).

[17] Floyd & Wooldridge (1996) undertook this study in the United States, involving 259 American managers, in 25 mainly for-profit organisations.

[18] Carney (2002a).

[19] Daft & Weick (1984).

[20] Dutton & Ashford (1993).

[21] Leifer & Delbecq (1978).

[22] Westley (1990).

[23] Burgelman (1983a).

[24] Shrivastava (1986).

[25] Nonaka (1988).

[26] Burgelman's (1983a) study, which provided insights into the strategic process that resulted in the consensus model outlined in this book (**Chapter 14**), was based on previous research findings and on insights from Chandler (1962) and Bower (1970), and attempted to stimulate further empirical and theoretical research in the area of strategic management.

However, the following quote from Floyd & Wooldridge challenges this view:

> Any individual who is regularly involved in, or interfaces with, the organisation's operations and who has some access to upper management has the potential to be a strategic middle manager.[28]

It appears that the realisation that strategy contains more elements of knowledge generation than of formal planning has yet to be recognised universally by senior managers in organisations. The middle manager needs to be involved in strategic decision-making, in addition to acting as a conduit for information-processing. In order to achieve strategic effectiveness, middle managers combine a specific, strategic-oriented knowledge base, involving the integration and application of specific strategies with operating knowledge.[29;30]

The strategy-structure debate has influenced the strategic role of senior and middle managers, beginning with the study of the historical development of major American industrial firms during the period 1919 to 1959,[31] and the recognition of multiple layers of management in the strategic process. Although the influence of middle and operational level managers in the strategic process was recognised then, this process was viewed as an exclusively top management activity.[32] However, other authors have emphasised that managers, other than senior managers, are aware of the opportunities available to the organisation, and of the subsequent development of corporate strategy.[33;34] Following this, strategy development was viewed as a

---

[27]   Although these studies relate to strategic planning and contribute to the existing body of knowledge, they were all undertaken in for-profit organisations, mainly using case study approaches to theory development, with the exception of Bower (1970), and focused on the role of senior rather than middle managers in strategy development.

[28]   Floyd & Wooldridge (1996), p.xi.

[29]   Floyd & Wooldridge (1996), p.xi.

[30]   Floyd & Wooldridge (1992a) used a large-scale survey design of 259 middle managers in 25 organisations, in order to test inferences that would be relevant to a wider variety of industries. This research provided empirical support for prior theoretical arguments related to middle manager strategic involvement and to the earlier clinical work of Burgelman (1983b).

[31]   Chandler (1962).

[32]   Burgelman (1983a).

[33]   Bower (1970).

[34]   Bower's (1970) carefully designed, landmark study of strategic process in the management of strategic capital investment projects provided a rich description of the process through which middle managers become champions of strategic alternatives.

bottom-up approach by strategic process-oriented researchers,[35] with the recognition that senior management's role was not necessarily critical to the process, and that strategy development should be viewed as a bottom-up and top-down multi-layered process.

HOW MIDDLE MANAGERS ACHIEVE STRATEGIC ORIENTATION

Middle managers attempt to formulate broad strategies for new business and service activity, and then endeavour to convince senior management of the importance of supporting them by linking service/market level strategy to corporate strategy and, in the process, develop new strategic process models for their hospitals.[36] This model requires the intertwining of middle manager strategic initiatives with experimentation of these process and implementation models and, finally, the selection, at top manager level, of the most appropriate model for the organisation,[37] in consultation with, and the involvement of, the middle managers. What is required for successful involvement in strategic planning is the understanding and support of senior management,[38,39] as a higher level of involvement occurs when consultation takes place.[40] Middle managers should also be involved in the selection of policy and the designation of priority decisions.

Middle managers become champions of strategic alternatives and frequently become organisational champions for initiatives developed at the operating level,[41] thus allowing them to become key players in setting the organisation's strategic agenda.[42,43] Benefits, therefore, are conferred on the organisation, including enhanced service delivery that results from the use of the middle manager's superior operational knowledge,[44] which is due, in part, to middle managers having their

---

[35] Cyert & March (1963).

[36] Burgelman (1983a).

[37] Bower (1970).

[38] Bryant, Dobal & Johnson (1990).

[39] Carney (2002a).

[40] Chadderton (1995).

[41] Burgelman (1983b).

[42] Dutton, Ashford, O'Neill, Hayes & Wierba (1997).

[43] *Re* access to top managers, Dutton *et al.* (1997) conducted a two-part study, in a regional telecommunications organisation in the US, on how middle managers sell issues to senior managers, and concluded that the process is placed in context by middle managers in terms of access to top management. This study has merit, even though the sample, which included interviews with 30 middle managers and a survey of 118 middle managers, was relatively small.

[44] Carney (2001b).

hands on the pulse of the organisation.[45] The crucial role of the middle manager involves conceptualising new strategies, supporting initiatives generated at operational levels and combining these initiatives with the organisation's strengths.[46] Middle managers become organisational champions of strategic thinking, affecting how issues are interpreted, and resulting in the fostering of flexible organisational arrangements that, in the process, align the organisation's activities with top management strategy.[47;48;49] However, this strategic thinking and initiative is not just the domain of senior management; in large complex organisations, such as hospitals, managers from middle and operational levels are also involved in strategic activities.[50] Thus, synergy develops between the provision of information to senior management by middle and operational management and the crucial influence that this information has on the strategic agenda of the organisation.[51]

Therefore, before middle managers can become involved in the strategic process, they must have access to senior management. This access to top management is one of the key determinants in deciding to sell an issue to senior managers, as the diagnosis of strategic issues occurs at the top level of the organisation but emanates from activities occurring at multiple levels in the organisation, including the level of middle manager.[52;53] Schilit[54] found that middle managers frequently participated in strategic decisions, and that the number of years working for the same superior increased their potential to influence strategic involvement. The level of upward strategic influence demonstrated by managers has varied from little influence[55] to strong influence.[56;57;58] The manager's position influences individual levels of

---

[45]   Moss Kanter (1983).

[46]   Carney (2002a).

[47]   Dutton & Duncan (1987).

[48]   Floyd & Wooldridge (1992a).

[49]   *Re* strategic issues, Dutton & Duncan (1987) presented a theoretically-, but not empirically-, based two-step model of how decision-makers interpret strategic issues.

[50]   Carney (2002a).

[51]   Dutton & Duncan (1987).

[52]   Schilit (1987a).

[53]   *Re* strategic decision-making, empirical research, undertaken by Schilit (1987a), involved 60 middle managers in 57 public and private sector organisations, in which middle managers were asked to maintain a personal diary relating to the number and type of strategic decisions they were involved in during a two-month period. The group categorised 352 influence attempts, which represented 329 distinct strategic decisions.

[54]   Schilit (1987b).

[55]   Hutt, Reingen & Ronchetto (1988).

[56]   Dutton, Ashford, O'Neill, Hayes & Wierba (1997).

strategic upward influence, and managers weigh the benefits that may accrue to them before attempting to influence strategically their next-level-above-manager. Strategic awareness increases with organisational level and, conversely, there is a decline in strategic awareness at descending levels of the managerial hierarchy.[59] This awareness has implications for the strategic management required to build the requisite organisational values into everyday management practices, and to provide excellence in the provision of service delivery.[60]

Contemporary Organisations

In contemporary flattened organisations, management layers have been eliminated and middle managers now assume a greater strategic role, often without line management responsibility, which means that, at present, they must cope with the difficulties of their position, while justifying why their positions exist at all.[61] This has implications for organisational effectiveness, hierarchical reporting,[62] and for excellence in the provision of patient services.[63] Staehle & Schirmer[64] found that a tendency toward decentralisation would relieve the burden of senior management and enlarge the tasks and responsibilities of middle management. In an international study involving 63 middle managers, Wooldridge & Floyd[65;66] found that 16% of middle managers were one level below senior managers, 66% were two levels below, and 17% were three levels below. However, middle managers still looked to hierarchical career progression, even though their organisations were facing flattening and restructuring.[67] In hospitals, the effectiveness of strategic decision-making is constrained by the existing routines of the organisation,[68;69] and by the habitual response patterns to strategic

---

[57] Levine (1986).

[58] Using the same data set of strategic decision-making and upward influence as in Schilit (1987a), and this time involving 47 middle managers, Schilit & Paine (1987) explored the underlying dynamics of strategic decisions that are subject to upward influence activity and concluded that middle managers regularly influenced their superior to take a particular course of action.

[59] Schilit & Paine (1987).

[60] Lebor & Stofman (1988).

[61] Moss Kanter (1986).

[62] Goffee & Scase (1986).

[63] Lebor & Stofman (1988).

[64] Staehle & Schirmer (1992).

[65] Wooldridge & Floyd (1990).

[66] This study by Wooldridge & Floyd (1990) examined the organisational charts of 25 organisations.

[67] Thomas & Dunkerley (1999).

[68] Ashmos, Duchon & McDaniel (1998).

issues already existing in the organisation,[70] such as rituals, routines, policies and guidelines.

Boundary-spanning

Middle managers, who work in boundary-spanning roles that cross several disciplines within the organisation, have a distinct advantage over other managers who are not in these positions, as they have higher levels of strategic involvement and influence.[71] The championing role of middle managers is enhanced by the fact that middle managers use a specific strategic knowledge base[72] that allows them to integrate strategic and operational knowledge and, as a result, to achieve strategic effectiveness.[73] Middle managers working in boundary-spanning positions report higher levels of strategic influence due to the opportunities available to them for moderating between the internal and external constituencies of the organisation. Innovative middle managers who champion or promote new initiatives demonstrate higher levels of upward influence and strategic involvement than those who do not.[74;75] This group of managers demonstrate upward influence on strategic decisions through regular interaction with their direct supervisor, thereby influencing their superior to take a particular course of action.[76] Middle managers successfully intervene in strategic decisions and the impact of these interventions extends beyond their departments.[77;78] Thus, there is a need for timely information generation, achieved through upward influence, whereby senior management creates the vision for the organisation and the middle managers create and implement concrete concepts by which to realise the vision.

---

[69] This study by Ashmos, Duchon & McDaniel (1998) was undertaken with 164 middle managers in 55 non-academic hospitals in Texas and examined the direct and indirect effects of how strategic issues are interpreted during the process of strategic involvement in decision-making.

[70] Hamel & Prahalad (1994).

[71] Floyd & Wooldridge (1997).

[72] Moss Kanter (1983).

[73] Floyd & Wooldridge (1996).

[74] Floyd & Wooldridge (1997).

[75] *Re* strategic type, Floyd & Wooldridge (1997) explored the relationship between middle manager strategic involvement and the Miles & Snow (1978) typology of middle manager strategic type.

[76] Schilit & Paine (1987).

[77] Guth & Macmillan (1986).

[78] *Re* strategic decision-making, a study by Guth & Macmillan (1986), of 90 middle managers undertaking part-time business degrees, produced further support for middle manager strategic involvement. In this study, middle managers provided 330 written descriptions of decision issues they were involved in.

RESISTANCE BY MIDDLE MANAGERS TO THE STRATEGIC PROCESS

Nevertheless, middle managers are often cited as being important and recurrent sources of resistance to employee involvement. If middle managers perceive that they are being excluded from the strategic process, they will be a recurring source of resistance to the development of new organisational strategy,[79] thereby blocking new strategy initiatives developed by, or being taken to, top management. Middle managers, if excluded from the strategic process, will accept the strategies perceived by them as being imposed by senior management, but will then erect barriers in order to prevent their implementation.[80] Few middle managers articulate the same goals as their superiors, and those who disagree with strategic initiatives proposed by senior managers will block the implementation of strategy.[81] These blocking mechanisms take many forms. During strategic involvement, a range of alternatives are exercised, including cooperation and competition.[82] Middle managers are often dissatisfied with the quality and level of communication with their next-level-above-manager, who is often perceived to be unresponsive to two-way influence, and with the level of "tight control" exercised on them by senior managers, and this dissatisfaction occurs in both bureaucratic and "innovative" organisations.[83] Control by senior management produces adverse effects on organisational efficiency and responsiveness,[84] with the result that middle managers respond by impeding the implementation process.[85] This form of perceived powerlessness results in negative consequences for the organisation, such as avoidance in formal planning and mistrust in senior manager's motives for initiating the procedure. This mistrust is often due to a fear of failure,[86] which consequently results in reluctance by middle managers to provide inputs into the strategic process[87] and in extensive dissatisfaction with the role.[88] This level of exclusion varies

---

79 Fenton-O'Creevy (1998).
80 Carney (2001c).
81 Floyd & Wooldridge (1994).
82 Longest (1990).
83 Westley (1990).
84 Izreali (1975).
85 Nonaka (1988).
86 Lyles & Lenz (1982).
87 Nonaka (1988).
88 Fenton-O'Creevy (1998).

across organisations, suggesting that exclusion and its consequences can be reduced.[89]

Disagreement exists regarding the level of inclusion that is advisable. For example, while Kelley[90] argues that inclusion in the strategic process may lead to inefficiencies and unresponsiveness, conversely, Izreali[91] argues that exclusion will lead to de-motivation and proposes that what is required is a greater level of understanding of the concept of inclusion and of the reasons for perceived exclusion. The success or failure of employee involvement is influenced by the form of the employee involvement process in place in the organisation and by contextual variables,[92] in addition to the strategy development process occurring.[93] Strategic involvement by middle managers results in higher levels of motivation and job satisfaction than would occur if strategic involvement were not permitted.[94,95]

It is evident that middle managers contribute significantly to strategic development in health service organisations and it appears that their role and function is often misunderstood. If middle managers are permitted to become involved in strategy development, in a meaningful and timely manner, their contribution is capable of steering the organisation's direction positively into the future, but conversely, if excluded from the strategic process, these managers may be a recurring source of resistance to strategies developed by the senior managers.

SUMMARY

♦ Strategic management is an important component of organisational functioning.

♦ It appears that for-profit and not-for-profit organisations function differently at the strategic level, therefore the role of the middle manager in these organisations may differ.

♦ Middle manager strategic involvement is not universally understood or accepted by senior management, therefore middle managers are often dissatisfied with the quality and level of communication with their next-level-above-manager

---

89   Westley (1990).
90   Kelley (1976).
91   Izreali (1975).
92   Cotton (1993).
93   Bailey, Johnson & Daniels (2000).
94   Carney (2002a).
95   Carney (2002a) undertook this study, through 25 interviews with clinicians and non-clinicians in Ireland.

♦ Middle managers who perceive that they are being excluded from the strategic process will be recurring sources of resistance to strategy development.

♦ Middle managers are often reluctant to become involved in strategy development, due to insecurity in their role, thereby excluding themselves from the strategic process. However, contemporary middle managers are taking a greater part in the strategic management process than heretofore.

♦ Strategic involvement by middle managers in the strategic management process results in higher levels of motivation and job satisfaction than would occur if strategic involvement were not permitted.

CHAPTER 3
MANAGERIAL EFFECTIVENESS

INTRODUCTION

Strategic management and the middle manager are key components of health service delivery. Health service middle managers are typically heads of department or functional heads. Successful health care delivery is dependent, to a large extent, on the managerial effectiveness of health care professionals and the types of interactions occurring between different individuals and groups of clinicians and between clinicians and non-clinicians. Therefore, the success, or otherwise, of managerial effectiveness is dependent upon the collaborative process.

Chapter 2 noted how the middle manager influences strategic management in health care planning and delivery. How this occurs will be explored in this chapter. In addition to managing others and themselves, managers must be able to manage organisations; this chapter will demonstrate how managerial effectiveness is achieved. The focus will be on five different perspectives, or ways to make sense of reality, used by the effective manager. Ten managerial roles are presented, in addition to the management, leadership and administration skills required by professional clinicians in preparation for professional practice. Contemporary management effectiveness techniques are identified, including research-based management skills and techniques that are perceived by practising managers as useful to practice and that add value to clinical practice management. Chapter 3 concludes with an exploration of how decision-making responsibility and clinical reasoning enhance management effectiveness.

MANAGERIAL EFFECTIVENESS

The effective manager requires a variety of skills and behaviours or "mind-sets" in preparation for, and in order to fulfil, the managerial role. The world of the manager is complicated and confusing and making sense of it requires the ability to synthesise insights from different mind-sets into a comprehensive whole.[1;2]

The bounds of management are sandwiched between collaborative action to get work done and analytic reflection on this action and involve five managerial mindsets or ways to make sense of reality, including reflective, analytic, worldly, collaborative, and action. The development of a *reflective* mind-set involves managing the self, through reflection on past experiences and learning from these experiences in order to achieve a greater understanding of how organisations work. The *analytic* mind-set is achieved by analysing the cultural values underpinning the working of the organisation, and then probing deeper, until a greater understanding of how the organisation actually functions is achieved. The *worldly* mind-set is needed to manage context, and this must be managed well; it is achieved through recognising the existence of many different worlds and perspectives on life, and on how work may be achieved, and involves opening up minds to diverse worlds and learning from them. Managers must also be able to manage relationships by developing a *collaborative* mind-set, which means learning to manage the relationships that exist between employees through engaging continually with them, finding out what they need in order to do their work, and then putting in place the structures, processes and conditions to assist them. Finally, managers must possess an *action* mind-set in order to be able to manage change – that is, to be able to harness the physical and emotional energy of employees. The action mind-set requires an understanding of the motives and aspirations of staff, in addition to holding a steady course, or steering a new course when necessary, in order to achieve organisational goals.[3]

In assessing the effectiveness of the manager, pertinent questions should be asked of the individual, including, for example, the level of conformity to rules the manager/supervisor requires and the degree of responsibility that they feel they are given. The emphasis that the manager places on standards of performance, and how often rewards and praise for work well done are provided in comparison to the frequency of punitive measures when something goes wrong should

---

[1]   Gosling & Mintzberg (2003), p. 54.
[2]   Gosling & Mintzberg's (2003) article, 'The five minds of a manager', published in *Harvard Business Review*, is recommended as one approach to management.
[3]   Gosling & Mintzberg (2003).

also be assessed, as well as the degree of organisational clarity within the department and the level of team spirit. The good manager, as indicated by the level of morale within the department, helps employees to feel strong and responsible for their actions, ensures that organisational goals are clearly defined and understood, and that individuals know what is required of them. In this way, a good team spirit is fostered within the department. Good managers care about organisational power but use their personal power wisely to stimulate their employees to be more productive and effective.[4]

Management & Leadership Concepts in Managerial Effectiveness

The dual concepts of managing and leading often cause confusion as to their individual meaning. *Management* encompasses a large number of ever-expanding concepts, and prescribed principles and practices, each of which is open to differing interpretations.[5] Successful management is achieved through not always willing others, whereas *leadership* is mainly concerned with influencing, persuading and leading others towards a mutually desired outcome, through enlisting enthusiastic, willing followers.[6,7] Both leadership and management skills are required of professionals, as evidenced in recently published government strategies. The principal message emanating from recent strategy documents is one of co-operation and quality provision of services at individual hospital level,[8,9] and in sharing best practice between institutions.[10] Additionally, in the future, academic institutions will be required to prepare professionals with transferable and complementary skills. Multi-professional education in such diverse areas as management, leadership, quality assurance, risk management, communications and advanced life support will also be required.[11]

---

[4] McClelland & Burnham (2003).
[5] Moss Kanter (1989).
[6] Burns (1978).
[7] Kouzes & Posner (1995).
[8] Department of Health (UK) (2000a).
[9] Department of Health & Children (2001).
[10] Department of Health & Children (2001).
[11] Calpin-Davies (2003).

Similarities in Management, Leadership & Administration

There are many similarities in the management, leadership and administration knowledge and skills required by each professional clinician, but they vary in content, context and depth and are dependent upon experience, level of education and the clinical demands of the role. Health service professionals have borrowed management theory from the business literature and follow the work of authors, such as Fayol, Mintzberg and Drucker, all pioneers of management knowledge.

Fayol, early in the 20th century, described the functions of planning, organising, directing, and controlling that are required by the manager.[12;13] In the early 1970s, Mintzberg identified 10 managerial roles, including disseminator, disturbance handler, entrepreneur, figurehead, leader, liaison, monitor, negotiator, resource-allocator and spokesperson.[14;15] Mintzberg's model has been used to study health care professional managers' perceptions of the management skills required by them. Some pertinent areas of research include hospital middle managers,[16] research and development in health care managers,[17] physical therapist managers and educators[18] and nurse managers in the areas of learning disability[19] and general nursing.[20] Over the course of these studies, at least eight additional roles were added to Mintzberg's original model, including technical expertise,[21] communications, financial control, interpersonal relations, operations and strategic assessment,[22] clinical competence[23] and planner.[24]

Further research suggests that, for example, physical therapists are deemed to require 178 management, leadership and administration

---

[12]   Fayol (1949).

[13]   Fayol's (1949) research, first published in France in 1916, was the first to describe the concept of managerial work. His work contrasts with that of Fredrick Taylor who, in 1911, published the principles of scientific management, which focused on individual workers rather than on the manager's work.

[14]   Mintzberg (1973).

[15]   Mintzberg's (1973) study, undertaken in the US with five chief executive officers from five different industries, involves the development of a model that identifies managerial functions.

[16]   Roemer (1996).

[17]   Pavett & Lau (1985).

[18]   Schafer (2002).

[19]   Power (2001).

[20]   Cody (2000).

[21]   Pavett & Lau (1985).

[22]   Roemer (1996).

[23]   Cody (2000).

[24]   Power (2001).

skills in order to prepare them for professional practice,[25;26] and that the most important skills required by new physical therapist graduates are communication, professional involvement, ethical practice, delegation and supervision, stress management, budgeting, time management and health care industry scanning.

Professional competence and ethical value systems were also identified by Irish health care middle managers as critical success factors in management.[27;28] Despite the increasing importance of financial management and strategic management in health care delivery, these skills were ranked in the bottom five in several studies.[29;30;31] This finding indicates that managers have yet to perceive the significance of such skills in their work and that, according to Carney,[32] this "knowledge gap" will prevent their involvement in strategy development in their organisations and consequent consensus of this strategy.

Financial management is also a critical component of strategic management; capital projects financing and budgeting are now essential components of the health care manager's role. Power[33;34] found that leadership skills were ranked in the median management categories, which again suggests that health care managers do not perceive leadership to be of significant importance in their work.

Contemporary Management Effectiveness Techniques

In the past decade, there has been much discussion related to the notion that management knowledge, ideas and techniques have been subject to the whims and perceived requirements of modern business and managers who introduce "new" techniques into their businesses only to discard these ideas when a newer, more fashionable

---

[25] Lopopolo, Schafer & Nosse (2004).

[26] Conducted by Lopopolo, Schafer & Nosse (2004) in the US, this research was a Delphi study that involved 34 physical therapist managers, from which the authors developed the LAMP components required by this group of professional clinicians.

[27] Carney (2002a).

[28] Carney (2002a) undertook this study amongst 365 heads of department working in acute care hospitals in Ireland.

[29] Lopopolo, Schafer & Nosse (2004).

[30] Cody (2000).

[31] Cody's (2000) study of managerial competencies was undertaken for the partial fulfilment of the MSc (Nursing) in University College Dublin.

[32] Carney (2002a).

[33] Power (2001).

[34] Power's (2001) research was undertaken in partial fulfilment of the MSc (Nursing) in University College Dublin.

management technique comes along or when the techniques do not meet their outcome expectations. Examples of such management techniques that have been superseded include total quality management (TQM), continuous quality initiatives, quality circles, as well as human resource management practices including measurement practices, business process re-engineering (BPR), excellence principles, Six Sigma and several cultural and change techniques.[35;36;37] This process of decline includes idea invention, dissemination of information concerning the idea, acceptance of the idea or technique and, finally, following a period of time, abandonment of the idea.[38]

It was Abrahamson, in the early 1990s, who first mooted this management fashion-setting notion.[39] Abrahamson's theory is that management knowledge is actively produced by a number of "experts" for general fashion-setting managerial consumption, and therefore, as a consequence, is not fully researched or formed. According to Abrahamson, this form of management was personified by "management gurus" and does not necessarily conform to the rigours of academic research.

There is now a demand for research-based management skills and techniques that are perceived by practising managers as useful to practice and that add value to clinical practice management. Therefore, academics must move faster in identifying current business problems and in meeting this demand through research.[40] Karen Legge[41;42] argues that the actor-network theory, which she identified, is perpetuated by the networking activity of management consultants, whom she believes are *par excellence* systems of persuasion. Health service management has also contributed to this management persuasion, and it may be time to stand back, and reflect on the new management techniques and practices that managers and practitioners are being asked to introduce into health service management on a fairly regular basis. It is important to determine whether such

---

[35]   Clarke (2004a).

[36]   Clarke (2004b).

[37]   Clark (2004). This paper by Tim Clark, editor of the *Journal of Management Studies*, was inspired by the work of Karen Legge, an expert in management and organisational management, and discusses the controversies and continuities in management studies over this period.

[38]   Gill & Whittle (1993).

[39]   Abrahamson (1991).

[40]   Clarke (2004a).

[41]   Legge (2002), p.80.

[42]   Karen Legge was editor of the *Journal of Management Studies* for over 25 years and has recently retired.

techniques will assist patient care management, education and clinical practice in a meaningful way, or in the case of a "new technique" being proposed, whether it will solve all of the health service management problems. A starting point should be systematic research in health service management, drawn from tried and tested research.

The question that is often asked is: *Does self-knowledge lead to improved managerial effectiveness?*. It is possible to change managerial style through training and education, if the manager, following identification of their management styles and subsequent behaviours, is prepared to make changes in order to improve their management skills. A manager might decide to move into another area of work if unable to make the required changes that were identified during management development workshops. Or a manager may decide to modify their management style through becoming more approachable, less coercive and more positive to their staff. Others may delegate more and encourage their employees to take on higher levels of responsibility.[43]

Clinical Reasoning by Professionals

Decision-making responsibility enhances management effectiveness. Decision–making by professionals may differ in relation to the focus of the problem. Clinical reasoning is a form of decision-making that remains a relatively under-researched subject in health care delivery.[44] Clinical reasoning refers to the thinking behind the decision-making processes used in clinical practice; it is the process in which the clinician interacts with the patient, assisting the patient in choosing health goals for their future health management. During the interaction process, the clinician uses clinical information and professional knowledge that has been stored in his/her memory from previous experiences. Professional judgement originates from the professional role and previous training. This process results in the identification of future strategies, based on previous information and experience.[45]

But should senior managers care about management theory? Christensen & Raynor[46,47] think so, and advise managers to use three stages in theory-building:

---

[43]   McClelland & Burnham (2003).

[44]   Edwards, Jones, Carr, Braunack-Mayer & Jensen (2004).

[45]   Edwards, Jones, Carr, Braunack-Mayer & Jensen (2004).

[46]   Christensen & Raynor (2003).

[47]   Christensen & Raynor's (2003) article, 'Why hard-nosed executives should care about management theory', published in *Harvard Business Review*, debates the merits and demerits of management theory.

♦ First, to seek an explanation from employees as to what caused a particular outcome.

♦ Then, through the process of categorisation of the problem, the employee moves from tentative understanding of the existing problem to making reliable predictions of the future.

♦ The third stage emphasises the importance of studying why failure occurred, gaining understanding of the dynamics involved in the failed situation and thereby building future good theory and reliable work practices.

Managing for Increased Productivity

Managing time in order to be productive is necessary. Many managers look busy, yet they are under-achieving in the work situation. Managers spend time delivering care, and in the decision-making and problem-solving necessary to deliver this care. Managers rush from meeting to meeting, spend time on the telephone or at their computers, all of which is undertaken at a fast-moving pace with little time for reflection on action. Bruch & Ghoshal[48;49] refer to this as "spinning of wheels" of unproductive busy-ness or active non-action; they report that only one in 10 managers is purposeful – that is, highly-focused and energised – with the remaining nine managers squandering time in ineffective activities. Successful managers achieve a high level of focus through concentrating on important goals and then taking deliberate action to achieve these goals. Some one in three managers suffer from procrastination. Managers who procrastinate fail to prioritise actions or take initiative, and lack both energy and focus, and thus proceed in a passive state of learned helplessness. Approximately one in five managers are easily distracted from the task in hand, fall into the disengaged category of manager characterised by denial and burnout and are easily overwhelmed by unexpected events or crises. Managers who take effective action have focus and energy; focus is concentrated attention that permits the individual to concentrate on a critical task and to complete this task in a designated time frame. Fast decisions are made regarding which distractions to ignore. These managers pick their goals and battles with greater care than other managers do.

---

[48]   Bruch & Ghoshal (2002).

[49]   Bruch & Ghoshal (2002, p.63) present their findings in the Focus-Energy Matrix, now accepted as a management tool.

MANAGING ORGANISATIONS

Managers must be able to manage organisations in addition to managing others and themselves. Gosling & Mintzberg[50] proposed two ways to manage: heroic and engaging. *Heroic* management is based on hierarchy, bureaucracy, top-down management and an emphasis on profits, while *engaging* management is based on collaboration. Heroic, collaborative management means that managers assist employees in doing the important work of the organisation and view the organisation as an interacting network rather than a hierarchy. The network or team develops and implements strategy through collaboration with senior managers. In this way, employees are encouraged to solve their own problems and to become involved in future organisational planning. The manager's role in collaborative management is to bring out the positive aspects of employee's mind-set; this is achieved through inspiring, engaging and leading employees forward. In this way, the organisation becomes a better place for all staff to work in[51;52] and employees perceive that senior managers appreciate their contributions, values, expertise, corporate knowledge and work ethic.[53;54]

In conclusion, corporate knowledge is viewed by managers as the experiences and expert knowledge of employees, achieved through hospital experiences over many years. Carney[55] found that clinician and non-clinician heads of department perceived that they contributed significantly to the establishment of the hospital's reputation as a centre for excellence in the delivery of patient care. In today's fast-changing health service environment, collaborative management is the way forward for managers, the staff and the patients they serve. As stated by Krueger-Wilson & Porter-O'Grady, "the new health care management paradigm demands a finely-honed interpersonal adeptness".[56] Additionally, as Senge[57] notes, managers must be willing to abandon what does not work, as abandonment precedes innovation.

It is managers who act, not organisations. It is the managers who set the context from which all future work emanates, including the

---

[50] Gosling and Mintzberg (2003), p.61.

[51] Gosling and Mintzberg (2003).

[52] Gosling & Mintzberg (2003, p.61) presented this view in an article entitled 'The five minds of the manager' in *Harvard Business Review*.

[53] Carney (2002a).

[54] Carney's (2002a) study of 55 acute care hospitals in Ireland pertained to the perceptions of heads of department *re* cultural norms in health care delivery.

[55] Carney (2004a).

[56] Krueger-Wilson & Porter-O'Grady (1999), p.275.

[57] Senge (1998).

way that work is defined, limits to responsibility and accountability,[58] and the organisation's cultural value system.[59] Middle manager strategic inputs are likely to be superior to those developed solely by top executives and, consequently, confer benefits to the organisation and to the clients in terms of expertise and a positive value system that has excellence in care delivery as its core value. However, for benefits to be sustainable, all managers need to accept the health service focus on cost-effectiveness and excellence in care delivery.

SUMMARY

♦ The effective manager requires a variety of skills and behaviours or "mind-sets" in preparation for, and in order to fulfil, the roles required of them in an innovative manner.

♦ The bounds of management are sandwiched between collaborative action to get work done and analytic reflection on this action. It is possible to use five different perspectives or managerial mind-sets to achieve this aim.

♦ Developing a worldly mind-set is a perspective that must be managed well. This is achieved through recognising that there are many different perspectives on life and involves opening up the mind to diverse worlds and learning from them.

♦ Successful management is achieved through not always willing others, whereas leadership is primarily concerned with influencing, persuading and leading others towards a mutually desired outcome.

♦ Many skills of management and leadership have been identified, such as decision-making and change management. Professional competence and ethical value systems have recently been added as critical success factors in management. Nevertheless, it is prudent to evaluate "old" techniques for outcome expectations before discarding them for newer, more fashionable management techniques.

♦ Clinical reasoning is a form of decision-making that remains relatively under-researched in health care delivery.

♦ Professional judgement originating from the professional role and previous training of the clinician is a valuable process that frequently results in the identification of future strategies, based on previous information and experience.

---

[58] Krueger-Wilson & Porter-O'Grady (1999), p.269.
[59] Carney (2004a), p.321.

♦ If the organisation is viewed as an interacting network, rather than a hierarchy, the network or team develops and implements strategy in collaboration with senior managers. In this way, employees are encouraged to become involved in future organisational planning through a collaborative process.

♦ In order to ensure that organisational and client benefits will be sustainable, managers need to accept the health service focus on cost-effectiveness and excellence in care delivery.

CHAPTER 4
ORGANISATIONAL POLICY & STRUCTURE

INTRODUCTION

Organisations are central to the delivery of a nation's health care service, which must be efficient and effective in order for health care organisations to respond to the developing and challenging trends occurring in the health services. For this to occur, organisational strategy needs to be accepted and understood by all levels of management. Despite having characteristics similar to those of many other organisations, health care organisations represent a specific form of organisation.

Chapter 1 showed that, in defining the strategic process in not-for-profit health service organisations, the critical success factor of successful health care managers was the development and management of strategy. **Chapter 2** demonstrated that the middle manager is the strategist and is critical to successful development and implementation of strategy. **Chapter 3** further demonstrated that the bounds of management are sandwiched between collaborative action, required to get work done, and reflective analysis of such action, and that the success (or otherwise) of managerial effectiveness is dependent upon this collaboration. Therefore, if the organisation is viewed as an interacting network, rather than a hierarchy, the network develops strategies and then implements these strategies through collaboration with senior managers.

This chapter will explore organisational structures and forms from the perspective of restructuring and the introduction of functional, matrix and virtual organisations, and the effect that these factors have on employees. In addition, the effects of restructuring on health service organisations and health professionals will also be explored. As a result of these changes, new ways of organising and doing work is now occurring through knowledge workers, project teams and cross-departmental groups. Professional judgement originating from the clinician's previous training and professional role is a valuable process that should not be under-estimated, as it frequently results in the identification of future strategies, based on previous information and experience.

ORGANISATIONAL STRUCTURE & FORM

"Organisations are a human enterprise", as Drucker[1] states, whose highest purpose is "to make the strengths of people effective and their weaknesses irrelevant". Despite the fact that organisations get work done, various authors are writing of the end of organisations. However, Drucker[2] contends that the end of the organisation "is one thing we can predict with certainty will not happen";[3] he argues that, due to the turbulence, ambiguity, flexibility and variations in current organisational work practices, what is actually being described is "a changing organisation".[4] This change and turmoil requires clarity about the organisation's mission, goals and strategy and on how to most effectively balance long and short-range goals, to define results, and to identify the person ultimately responsible for decision-making and command in crisis situations. Therefore, according to Drucker, the most consistent and persuasive argument put forward regarding the absence of organisations in the future has a flaw, which is "that it does not work".[5]

One of the common criticisms of hierarchical organisations is that they are outmoded, too slow and unwieldy for the turbulent modern world; yet some have survived, as they have remained flexible and responsive to the changing environment by incorporating new practices, management techniques and technologies. Leavitt[6] proposes that these organisations have survived because they introduced three new waves of innovative management:

♦ The first wave was the human relations movement, envisioned by a small group of academics in the US in the early 1960s. It emphasised a people-focused approach to management, which involved the introduction of industrial democracy and employee-centred participation in decision-making. Paradoxically, the human relations movement actually strengthened hierarchies, as its principles were applied more to managers than to employees, thereby widening the gap that existed between the two. The participative component eventually reached the lower levels of the organisation with the introduction of quality circles and teams in Japanese organisations, which were also the first to advocate participative management.

---

[1]   Drucker (1997).
[2]   Drucker (1997), p. 5.
[3]   Drucker (1997), p. 4.
[4]   Drucker (1997), p. 4.
[5]   Drucker (1997), p. 4.
[6]   Leavitt (2003).

♦ The second wave was introduced in the early 1970s and involved the introduction of mathematical statistical management – that is, the rational, analytical, fact-finding school of management in which problem-solving was characterised by the introduction of computer technology. Again, this form of management reinforced the hierarchical management culture, as project managers crunched the numbers and wrote the business plans, thereby securing their hierarchical positions within their organisations.

♦ In the 1970s, the third wave of management focused on task groups that delivered results and which ignored the hierarchical structure of the organisation, worked in semi-autonomous work groups and, in turn, were ignored by their hierarchical managers. However, eventually, large organisations, such as IBM and others, adopted this approach and continue to use it, due to the appeal of its flexibility and speed of results.

Contemporary Organisations

As indicated above, although organisations are changing shape and form, many contemporary organisations remain hierarchical.[7] Inherent dangers to hierarchy are usually due to power and authority. Management has power over employees of lesser rank, as is evident in the forms of communication used within the organisation and in the cultural values exhibited by managers, both of which may limit involvement in decision-making. In hierarchies, communication must flow upward and downward with the lower level manager expected to report upward and, despite the use of participative management, which empowers and encourages the middle manager, he or she must remain alert to everyday operational and tactical matters.[8] Thus, the delicate balance of the authoritarian hierarchical style of management is fused with the flexible, participative empowering management style, resulting in a greater level of strategic involvement, commitment and consensus than the traditional, authoritarian hierarchical management style generates.[9]

Hierarchies do have merit – for example, they provide employees with symbolic rewards such as larger offices and indicators of how fast the corporate ladder is being climbed. In addition, hierarchies provide psychological feedback to employees, offering reassurance and providing employees with self-esteem, a badge and an identity. Generally, hierarchies appear to value employee contributions to the organisation, provide stability and add structure to the employee's

---

[7]   Drucker (1988a).

[8]   Leavitt (2003), p. 98.

[9]   Carney (2002a).

work life as the nature of the work is guided by routines, rules, regulations, duties, responsibilities and protocols. Leavitt notes that "hierarchical organisations seduce us with psychological rewards like feelings of power and status".[10] Drucker, in discussing managing during great change,[11] maintains that hierarchies will survive as a modern organisational form because they are the best type of structure for complex work. Thus, it is important that modern management understands the merits and the demerits of organisational hierarchies and develops ways to reduce the negative aspects, whilst promoting their positive characteristics.

Hierarchy & the Middle Manager

Hierarchy also influences how the middle manager functions within the organisation. Health service organisations remain strongly hierarchical in nature and several layers of middle management may be arranged in a hierarchical fashion in these bureaucratic organisations,[12,13] resulting in ambiguity in the nature and role of middle managers.[14] This ambiguity poses difficulties in terms of the level of manager involvement occurring, as the influence that middle managers command is important to organisational effectiveness and strategy development. It is evident that layers of management create complexity in reporting structures,[15,16] and that shorter hierarchies ensure that middle managers are closer to senior management and to the strategic policy arena.[17,18]

Mintzberg & Quinn[19] argue that parallel administrative hierarchies often arise, characterised by bottom-up, democratic approaches for professionals, and top-down for support staff. A study by Dopson, Risk & Stewart[20,21] of the changing role of the middle manager in Britain, which attempted to provide an explanation for this phenomenon, found more resistance to change by middle managers in public sector organisations, such as the National Health Service (NHS),

---

[10] Leavitt (2003), p. 102.
[11] Drucker (1988a).
[12] Mintzberg (1998).
[13] Wells (1999).
[14] Mintzberg (1998).
[15] Yasai-Ardekani & Haug (1997).
[16] Mintzberg (1998).
[17] Dopson & Stewart (1990).
[18] This study was undertaken by Dopson & Stewart amongst 26 middle managers working in organisations in Britain.
[19] Mintzberg & Quinn (1992).
[20] Dopson, Risk & Stewart (1992).
[21] Dopson, Risk & Stewart (1992), in their study of the changing role of the middle manager in Britain.

and related this opposition to the distinctive sense of professional identity among such managers. Further, these authors stated that industry and commerce have few examples of the professional identity found in the NHS. Therefore, if permitted, middle manager professionals can influence the management of the organisation by having an impact on the policy formulation process.

Strategy, Structure & Systems

In the 1920s, in an effort to improve organisational performance and efficiency, Alfred Sloan introduced the "3S" doctrine of strategy, structure and systems.[22] During the last decade, organisations have concentrated on "what they did" and this has resulted in re-organisation to make "what we do" better but, often, without achieving the expected results. Although the widespread malady of "structuritis" *per* Hammer[23] resulted in the issuing of yet another new organisational chart, the benefits of such restructuring have been hard to achieve and, often, suitably-aligned structures have not achieved the cost efficiencies desired by management. As Champy[24] states, focusing on cost reductions alone leads to downsizing with no visible improvements in organisational effectiveness. Restructuring may be couched in the language of seeking improvements in service, through return in investment, enhanced shareholder value or organisational realignment. Champy[25] further argues that, during restructuring, difficulties arise regarding the fundamental question of "what is the business of a hospital whose future has yet to be clearly defined", and proposes that the answer to this question will require "much more than the re-engineering of a company's processes",[26] and that such change will require that managers anticipate challenges and breakdowns and re-invent the organisation in such a way that it will be able to cope with future change and challenges in an agile manner. The foundation of any future change should be that the organisation remains capable of maintaining client and staff loyalty and retention.[27] One way to accomplish this is through the clear articulation of, and strong adherence to, organisational values.[28;29] Evidence indicates that it is more difficult to duplicate an organisation's culture and *modus*

---

[22] Oxman & Smith (2003).
[23] Hammer (2001), p. 136.
[24] Champy (1997).
[25] Champy (1997), p. 12.
[26] Champy (1997), p. 10.
[27] Duques & Gaske (1997).
[28] Duques & Gaske (1997), p. 36.
[29] Carney (2006a).

operandi than its structures and work processes;[30] therefore, organisational culture, organisational capabilities and employee competencies are increasingly becoming critical success factors for organisational success.[31]

An organisation is a human society and, like all societies, it exhibits a particular form of culture – that is, a "company culture", through which the organisation's purpose is nourished by the organisation's history, including myths and legends[32] and "the way we do things around here" thinking.[33] Loyalty to the organisation, as a cultural artefact, in many instances has been replaced by commitment to business success, as employees are responsible for results and not for effort. This shift in cultural emphasis has arisen as organisations offer employees the educational opportunity for personal growth, and in return, expect employees to exercise initiative and skill in creating value for clients and shareholders. In some public organisations, there remains a sense that employees continue to avoid blame or responsibility, and treat colleagues as competitors rather than as collaborators with the same mission and purpose.[34] However, Carney[35] found that adherence and commitment to organisational values and ethics remain strong in health service organisations, particularly in hospitals, where the key organisational value is the provision of excellence in service delivery.

New Organisational Forms

Talk of the virtual organisation, the networked organisation and the boundary-less organisation abound with presumptions that these new organisational forms will change the much-maligned hierarchical organisation.[36] Nevertheless, the need for organisations remains unquestioned due to their very nature of being – that is, of being a human enterprise.[37] New forms, such as organisational expansion and vertical integration, arose because employers wanted to have more control over work processes, employees and decision-making. However, Pfeffer[38] argues that these are not new forms, but are similar to the manner in which organisations were arranged over 100 years ago, and that managers have not learned from past successes and

---

30   Pfeffer (1997).
31   Carney (2002a).
32   Conger (1997).
33   Deal & Kennedy (1983).
34   Conger (1997), p. 28.
35   Carney (2006b).
36   Pfeffer (1997).
37   Hesselbein, Goldsmith & Beckhard (eds.) (1997).
38   Pfeffer (1997).

mistakes nor from the strengths and weaknesses of recent organisational forms and, consequently, the hidden costs of new organisational forms and structures are not known. The counter-argument is that advances in modern technology have permitted cross-functional communication, cross-boundary co-ordination and the achievement of higher levels of integration to a much greater level than ever before. This ability to manage and communicate across boundaries is a real advantage that leads to organisational efficiencies. In support of this view, Galbraith[39] recommends the "reconfigurable organisation", an organisational type resulting from the formation of three capabilities:

♦ The first capability requires that the organisation reconfigure through the formation of specially constructed teams, which cross boundaries, therefore necessitating extensive internal networking.

♦ The second capability, the co-ordination of multiple teams, is achieved through clarity in organisational procedures and in processes.

♦ The third capability requires that the organisation form external partnerships and external networking in order to acquire the skills and competencies that its employees do not possess. Additionally, assignments may be cross-functional, thus permitting employees to develop new competencies and new internal and external relationships and, thereby, to contribute to developing the organisation's present and future networking capabilities.

However, in order to be successful, reconfiguration takes time and effort in employee training and development and requires a "communication-intense form of organisation".[40]

Consequences of Functional, Matrix-type & Virtual Organisations

The introduction of functional, matrix-type, and virtual organisations has resulted in professional employees losing their jobs, and the emergence of the "survivor syndrome". Survivor syndrome refers to those employees who remain in the organisation and exhibit a loss of morale and a lack of loyalty and commitment to their organisation. A consequence of this lack of commitment is that middle managers become dedicated networkers, renewing their membership to professional organisations where they interact and share ideas. Professional organisations are filling the roles previously undertaken

---

[39] Galbraith (1997).
[40] Galbraith (1997), p. 96.

by managers, many of whom have left their organisations due to restructuring. The traditional organisational chart allowed for the implementation and control of functions and for the separation of duties with top-down management control and the management of communication flow through a cascading effect. However, due to current technology, such as e-mail, internet access and instant messaging, more efficient and effective communications with less interpretation problems have emerged.

Reconfigured Organisations

New ways of organising, and doing work, are now occurring through knowledge workers, project teams and cross-departmental groups. Knowledge workers, with clearly-defined career pathways, have made hierarchical managers almost redundant.[41] In addition, the focus on people, processes and rewards enhances employee motivation and commitment levels, thereby increasing organisational productivity and efficiency. Today, in many organisations, skills and knowledge, rather than seniority, ensures career progression. In such organisations, team-based, flatter organisations are now the "norm", while formal structures and processes are perceived as the cause of conflict.[42] However, successful cross-departmental, matrix-type and reconfigured organisations require intense and sustainable investment in human resources management. The management of conflict is also necessary, as these forms of organisation have the potential for unresolved conflict, due to the absence of the traditional management and hierarchical means of conflict resolution. Discussions can degenerate into lengthy internal negotiations and internal friction, with unresolved conflict having the potential to redirect employee energies away from clients and to become internalised.[43]

The outsourcing of work processes is a characteristic of the reconfigured organisation; it continues at a pace never before encountered. Normally, outsourcing of core capabilities or core competencies is introduced in order to achieve downsizing and cost savings. Many health service organisations now "contract out" or "buy in" core tasks, consequently returning their core competitiveness edge over their competitors back to the competitors or to the market place.[44] The contrasting argument to this form of organisational denudation is that reciprocity is overlooked; that it is not possible to obtain employee loyalty and commitment from employees, unless the organisation is

---

[41] Oxman & Smith (2003).
[42] Oxman & Smith (2003).
[43] Galbraith (1997), p. 96.
[44] Pfeffer (1997), p. 50.

willing to offer reciprocity in return.[45] According to Pfeffer,[46] reciprocity is not achieved through contracting out or outsourcing.

Health Service Organisational Reforms & Restructuring

The 1980s and 1990s were characterised by frequent health service reforms and the restructuring of hospitals around the world. The country in which the most significant changes occurred in the effort to modernise health service delivery was probably Britain. A summary of the reforms and restructuring that have occurred in Britain, and in Ireland, highlighting the complex nature and effect of these changes on employees is presented in **Chapter 5**. The aim of this change was to strengthen the strategic approaches to management, by putting in place devolved budgets and line management and introducing national performance indicators to measure clinical activity, financial management and health service staffing.[47] Further changes, made in health service delivery in Britain, to improve clinical practice, included a greater emphasis on the quality of service improvement through quality audit, as first set out in the 1989 White Paper *Working for Patients,* and evidence-based practice. However, not all of these quality improvements were successful, due to the somewhat haphazard manner of their introduction.

In the first years of the 21st century, the health service in Ireland, not unlike other health care systems, also underwent a period of change,[48;49] but not to the same extent as in Britain. However, as in Britain, the main cause of problems with service delivery emerged as being due to structural difficulties and the interface that exists between organisations, which resulted in deterioration in the interventions made by health service professionals, the quality delivered, and the outcomes of these interventions.[50] The problems encountered in the Irish health services are best summarised in the comment that it is not primarily the system of funding existing but rather the way the services are planned, organised and delivered that is at fault.[51]

---

[45]   Carney (2006a).
[46]   Pfeffer (1997).
[47]   Audit Commission (2000).
[48]   Department of Health (1994).
[49]   Department of Health & Children (2004).
[50]   O'Hara (1998).
[51]   Department of Health (1989).

Health Professionals' Perceptions of Restructuring

Significant changes occurred in health professionals' perception of their work and their organisations due to the processes of restructuring and re-organisation. Many of the restructuring changes occurred due to decreased spending on health, the introduction of more effective treatment methods, new technology, shorter hospital stays for patients than before and higher patient turnover.

A study undertaken in Sweden,[52] following restructuring that resulted in a 20% reduction in staff and the relocation of a further 10% of staff to other departments, found several significant outcomes, including an enduring distrust of the employer, whereby the perception of nurses was of ever-growing job demands and concurrent challenges in which they were being taken advantage of.[53] The drain of competencies and skills that followed these redundancies, particularly the loss of assistant nurses, was another perceived outcome of the restructuring that provoked anger[54] and professional ambiguity. A major cause of stress amongst nurses pertained to their desire for collaboration, particularly with doctors. This stress was perceived as being due to the "deference-dominance" "doctor-nurse relationship",[55] which was present in the restructured organisations and militated against equal/parallel collaborative patient care.

In a study undertaken in the US and Mexico, involving physician-nurse collaboration, it was found that renewed efforts by professional nurses to gain some measure of control in the workplace was perceived as necessary in order to gain influence in what was perceived as a hierarchical, male gender-related, doctor environment. In less hierarchical hospital settings, a greater degree of nurse-doctor collaboration was evident.[56] A high degree of ambiguity, due to the perceived changes, also occurred in a study that explored the perceptions of registered nurses following restructuring in Sweden.[57] [58]

Although organisations have undergone a period of downsizing and restructuring, the general consensus amongst researchers is that organisational performance has not improved and that the long-term

---

[52] Hertting, Nilsson, Theorell & Satterlund Larsson (2003).
[53] Siegrist & Peter (2000).
[54] Greenglass & Burke (2000).
[55] Malterud (2001).
[56] Hojat, Nasca, Cohen, Fields, Rattner, Griffiths, Ilbarra, Alcorta de Gonzales, Torres-Ruiz, Ilbarra & Garcia (2001).
[57] Hertting, Nilsson, Theorell & Satterlund Larsson (2004).
[58] This study, by Hertting, Nilsson, Theorell & Satterlund Larsson (2004), undertaken in a large hospital in Sweden, was a qualitative study of 14 registered nurses, who were interviewed and followed up twice more, which explored their perceptions following the restructuring that occurred between 1995-1997.

effects have been negative.[59;60] Chadwick, Hunter & Walston,[61;62] in a study of US hospitals, found that downsizing, restructuring and reengineering of work processes was generally not successful and failed to deliver the expected benefits, such as cost savings. However, some hospitals were more successful than others, probably due to the human relations management undertaken during the restructuring. Lundgren & Segersten[63] argue that it is important that registered nurses focus on patient-focused care delivery in organising nursing care in medical-surgical wards, particularly following restructuring, as this results in greater efficiencies and more focus on nursing activities. New structures are required that encourage flexible, innovative thinking and a continuous, dynamic flow of upward, downward, internal and external communication. Relationship-building, collaborative practices and interactions and networking will determine the success of changed organisational structure.

FUTURISTIC HEALTH SERVICE ORGANISATIONAL FORMS

Futuristic forms of organisational communication structures are emerging, including informal networks, network-mapping, boundary-spanning, central connectors and social network analysis. Cross & Prusak,[64;65] who analysed informal networks in the US, found that hierarchies function through personal contacts and informal networks, and that work progresses through such contacts. However, many senior executives regard informal networks as ungovernable and outside the scope of modern management scientific techniques. As informal networks and groupings are powerful political tools, the senior or middle manager needs to develop ways of managing communication emanating from and entering such groups, by focusing on a number of key internal group leaders.

---

[59] Cascio (2002a).
[60] Krueger Wilson & Porter-O'Grady (1999).
[61] Chadwick, Hunter & Walston (2004).
[62] Chadwick, Hunter & Walston (2004), in a study of the effectiveness of downsizing in the US hospital industry, by combining information from two archival data sources, between 1996-1997, in hospitals with greater than 100 beds.
[63] Lundgren & Segersten (2001).
[64] Cross & Prusak (2002).
[65] Cross & Prusak (2002) analysed informal networks in more than 50 large organisations in the US between 1995 and 2000.

Social Network Analysis

A powerful technique, known as "social network analysis", was developed by social scientists to recognise and manage informal networks.[66] Senior or middle managers may use this tool in hierarchical organisations. However, in using the tool, managers should first identify the network function, the process or the activities where connectivity is required, and then collect information that is then mapped. This information identifies sets of relationships existing within key areas, such as employees and other managers that they talk to regularly and the existing information flows. This information is then used to create network maps that graphically present, through computer technology, the relationships existing between the members of the various networks and sub-groups. For example, an incoming line or arrow may indicate that a group member is being sought out by an associate for information, and an outgoing arrow indicates that a group member is looking for information from another group member. Lastly, each network member is interviewed to determine whether his or her communication role has been accurately described, and whether he or she plays more that one role in the network.[67]

Network connectors often spend a considerable amount of time each day guiding and providing information to other executives and in assisting in problem-solving. Often this information flow is not recognised, understood nor rewarded by the organisation; and this lack of recognition of effort and expertise may lead to demoralisation.[68]

Central Connectors

Although most central connectors link colleagues together in a positive way, some may create bottlenecks that hold up the work of the network due to various reasons, including political or financial motives, the pursuit of power and control within the network, or the pressure of work. A bottleneck is recognised when complaints of poor communications or of lowered productivity are reported by network members and, therefore, the group is not working as efficiently as it should be. In such cases, organisational interventions may be necessary, such as moving an individual to another area of work, redesigning or rotating roles, changing the make-up of a project team, educating members who are having difficulty maintaining their work output and productivity, allowing an individual to make more decisions, or by reducing the work load of an individual who is

---

[66]   Krackhardt & Hanson (1993).
[67]   Krackhardt & Hanson (1993).
[68]   Cross & Prusak (2002).

overburdened. Overburdening may occur due to too many group members seeking out an individual for information and assistance.

A solution to such overburdening is the development of the "circular organisation", through which flexible, fluid management structures are created and, in which, employees have the opportunities to be creative and their expertise and accomplishments are valued. To achieve this organisational form, managers must manage the mission, manage for innovation and creativity and for diversity, whilst simultaneously, employees make changes wherever they are, and at every level in the organisation, through collaboration, cooperation and partnerships.

Boundary-spanning

A further extension of the informal network is boundary-spanning. Boundary-spanners are roving ambassadors who communicate with the wider community.[69] This communication may occur within the organisation, external to the networks that already exist or external to the organisation and such information may be strategic or professional in nature. The boundary-spanning role can be invaluable to the organisation in terms of the information, the specialised knowledge and the contacts that the boundary-spanner may make. Similar to the network connector, the role of the boundary-spanner may be overlooked or deemed to be unimportant to the organisation. The boundary spanner has particular significance within external professional networks in maintaining professional knowledge and research related to best practice that, in turn, may be introduced to the other members of the network.

The organisation may assist individual members in building better internal and external relationships through social network analysis and boundary-spanning. This assistance may involve an analysis of where, and how often, the individual seeks out other executives from within or outside their functional work areas, in order to determine whether the hierarchy is hindering such relationships being developed, or if planning is required to develop such relationships. Managers with personally-satisfying networking and boundary-spanning roles are more satisfied in their jobs, they remain more committed to the organisation and stay longer with the organisation than managers not in these roles, thereby boosting organisational productivity and knowledge generation.[70] Additionally, they are motivated to act on behalf of the group,[71,72] as part of an individual's

---

[69] Floyd & Wooldridge (1996).
[70] Cross & Prusak (2002).
[71] van Knippenberg (2000).

self-concept stems from membership of social groups, and this involvement contributes to the individual's increased feelings of respect and pride,[73;74] thereby contributing to greater job satisfaction. Carney[75] found that managers involved in the development of strategy in their organisations were more committed to the organisation and perceived that their expertise was appreciated and acknowledged by senior managers.

Whatever form of structure the organisation chooses to adopt in the future, it must have, as its central philosophy, the recognition and development of its employees' core competencies, and the recognition that core competencies are different to core business. While the core business of hospitals is the delivery of health care, the core competencies reside in its employees and are built on the knowledge and expertise of the employees. Therefore, the delivery of health services should be built around the core competencies of its employees, who then deliver the required services desired by its patients and clients. Thus, relationship skills are essential to the future of the organisation in order to ensure successful outcomes.

SUMMARY

♦ In the 1920s, Alfred Sloan introduced the "3S" doctrine of strategy, structure and systems in an effort to improve organisational performance and efficiency.

♦ The widespread malady of "structuritis" has identified that restructuring benefits have been hard to achieve and have not resulted in the expected cost efficiencies.

♦ Hierarchical organisations have survived because they have remained flexible and responsive to their changing environments and generally appear to value employee contribution to the organisation.

♦ In future change, the organisation should remain capable of maintaining client and staff loyalty and retention. Staff loyalty is retained through maintaining the clear articulation of, and strong adherence to, organisational values.

♦ It is more difficult to duplicate an organisation's culture and *modus operandi* than its structures and work processes, and therefore

---

[72] van Knippenberg (2000). Predictors of social identity in the organisational context was researched in a study of 515 German school teachers.

[73] van Dick, Wagner, Stellmacher & Christ (2004).

[74] Carney (2004a).

[75] Carney (2002a).

organisational culture is becoming increasingly critical to
organisational success.

♦ The introduction of functional, matrix, and virtual organisations
resulted in professional employees losing their jobs and produced
the "survivor syndrome", resulting in the loss of morale and a lack
of loyalty and commitment to their organisations.

♦ New ways of organising and doing work now are occurring
through knowledge workers, project teams and cross-departmental
groups; however, many senior executives regard these informal
networks as ungovernable and outside the scope of the modern
scientific techniques of management.

♦ Focus on people, processes and rewards to enhance employee
motivation and commitment levels will increase organisational
productivity and efficiency, and relationship-building and networking will determine the success of changed organisational
structure.

♦ In Ireland, health care is managed and delivered through a
combination of various groups, all of which exercise varying
degrees of influence and power.

♦ As a result of health service restructuring and re-organisation,
significant changes have occurred in health professionals'
perceptions of their work and their organisations.

♦ Futuristic forms of organisational communications structure are
emerging, including informal networks, central connectors and
social network analysis.

♦ Social network analysis identifies sets of relationships existing
within key areas that may be between employees and other
managers with whom they talk regularly, as well as the information
flows that exist.

♦ A further extension of the informal network is boundary-spanning,
which involves individuals as roving ambassadors who
communicate with the wider community.

♦ Managers with personally-satisfying networking and boundary-
spanning roles are more satisfied in their jobs, remain more
committed to the organisation and stay longer with their
organisations than managers not in these roles, thereby boosting
organisational productivity and knowledge generation.

♦ Managers involved in the development of strategy in their
organisations are committed to the organisation and perceive that
their expertise is appreciated and acknowledged by senior
managers.

♦ Core competencies reside in the organisation's employees and are built on the knowledge and expertise of the employees.

♦ Managers must remain tuned into the opportunities available to the organisation due to environmental change.

CHAPTER 5
PROFESSIONAL HEALTH
SERVICE ORGANISATIONS

INTRODUCTION

Previous chapters demonstrated that organisations are central to the delivery of health care, that the middle manager holds a pivotal role in such organisations, and that the bounds of management are sandwiched between collaborative action required to get work done and reflective analysis of such action. The effects of restructuring on health service organisations and health professionals were explored, as well as the resulting new ways of organising and doing work. The advantages and disadvantages of hierarchical organisations also were identified. Despite the criticism that hierarchical organisations are too slow and unwieldy for the turbulent modern world, it was shown that hierarchies have survived because they have remained flexible, innovative and responsive to their changing environments. Various forms of organisational structure have evolved over the past decade, such as matrix-type, boundary-less and cross-functional forms, but, nevertheless, the delivery of health services should be developed around the core competencies of employees, who will then deliver the required services desired by its patients and clients.

This chapter presents a critical exploration of professional organisations. Competition for health services has resulted in the introduction of managed care, in order to produce efficiencies in health care delivery, through controlling costs and by improving quality. New public sector management is explored, with emphasis on the new management changes currently being introduced in several countries, and the controlling effects of such changes on professional practice and work processes. In addition, creating reliable and efficient hospitals through knowledge workers and knowledge economies is considered, in the context of the culture of excellence in "magnet" hospitals. Next, this chapter explores work-based stress and its negative organisational and individual consequences, including silence. Finally, it explores the responsibility of health care managers to develop new ways of becoming more knowledgeable about health care policy that affects their patients and their professions.

PROFESSIONAL ORGANISATIONS

Each hospital should assess and gain an understanding of its strategic position within the health care sector, thereby evaluating its strategic importance and potential competitive advantages.[1] During the past decade, in many countries, changes have occurred in the general hospital structure; a significant change has been the introduction of managed care in order to produce efficiencies in health care delivery by controlling costs[2] and improving quality.[3] A consequence of this change has been the creation of large purchasers of health care, whereby health care is purchased from the hospitals that provides the most cost-effective services. Due to the competitive forces that these purchasers generate, the shift in purchasing power has resulted in major changes in the health care sector,[4] as a result of which, in both public and private hospital sectors, purchasing power and hospital rivalry have become the two most important competitive forces reshaping the health care industry in many countries, including the US, Britain and Australia. In addition, over time, declining ratios between payments for health care by health insurance companies and the costs of providing such health care have resulted in downward pressure on hospitals' revenue and profits. Therefore, as a consequence of individual hospitals being required to control costs and to increase operational efficiency while continuing to provide high quality care, the pressure that clinicians and non-clinicians are placed under when delivering patient care has increased.[5]

Rivalry in Health care Delivery

Rivalry for patients has also increased, due to competition in the health sector since the introduction of managed care. Even though there are conflicting industry results,[6] it appears that a consequence of this rivalry is higher rather than lower costs, probably due to the introduction of new expensive services and technology as hospitals attempt to differentiate themselves in order to survive.[7] In the future, the ability of a local hospital to survive will depend on its capability to develop superior services or competencies and to provide value and

1   Douglas & Ryman (2003).
2   Burns, Gazzoli, Dynan & Wholey (2000).
3   Dranove, Simon & White (1998).
4   Teisberg, Porter & Brown (1994).
5   Douglas & Ryman (2003), p.338.
6   Robinson & Phibbs (1989).
7   Rivers & Asubonteng (1999).

rareness in the services offered to its patients relative to its competitors.[8]

The type of service, and the manner in which it is offered to patients, depends upon the expertise and capabilities of the clinician delivering the service, as the production of the service and the delivery of the service to the patient occur simultaneously.[9] Therefore, unlike the provision of a product, there is no time for the clinician to improve on or to enhance the manner in which the service is delivered, if it is initially perceived as unsatisfactory by the patient. This situation is called "strategic competencies"; it refers to the excellence of the service delivered to patients, which the patient perceives as being superior to that offered by another hospital or as being excellent.[10] Thus, over time, distinctive strategic competencies will allow a hospital to attract more patients and a higher calibre of professional clinicians than similar hospitals, thereby further enhancing its reputation for excellence and sustaining its competitive advantage over other similar hospitals.

New Public Sector Management

During the last decade, the hospital sector has undergone changes in its organisation that have centred on making health care delivery more efficient and effective. The important component of this change is a quality-focused culture, which as Hoggett[11] says, wants to "get more for less". Health service professionals, particularly nurses as the largest single professional grouping, have attracted considerable management attention during this time. Bolton[12,13] argues that the control of health care professional work is now firmly in the hands of hospital management, with the health service organisational culture now oriented towards a customer service ethos.

The recent National Health Service (NHS) reform programmes in Britain have involved senior nurses, at line management level, in the role of the "modern matron", signalling the nurse as the coordinator of quality-focused care delivery.[14] The post-modern NHS and, in Ireland, the Department of Health & Children (DOHC)[15] are promoting a

---

[8]   Barney (1995).

[9]   Bowen & Ford (2002).

[10] Douglas & Ryman (2003), p.333.

[11] Hoggett (1996).

[12] Bolton (2000), p.319.

[13] This qualitative study by Bolton (2004) is part of a longitudinal study carried out in a large North West NHS Trust hospital in Britain, which charts the changes that occurred in the nursing work process over the period from 1994 to 2000.

[14] Department of Health (UK) (2000a).

[15] Department of Health & Children (2001).

participative management style, whereby health care professionals are deemed to be empowered to undertake their roles in a quality-focused manner. In Britain, senior nurses are now being seen as the mediators between operational and strategic management.[16,17] Nonetheless, in Ireland, although Carney[18,19] found that senior nurses were involved in strategic management and planning at the highest levels of their organisations, thereby shaping the organisations' cultural change,[20] this sense of involvement is not fully inclusive, as the perception of some managers is that "lip service" is being paid to professionals by non-clinicians and senior management, and that the invitation to become part of the strategic management process comes too late to allow for meaningful input and results.[21]

Hoggett[22] describes the new management changes being introduced in Britain as "simultaneous centralisation and decentralisation" and argues that this is an apparent combination of bureaucratic and non-bureaucratic organisational structures. Others argue that this structural combination succeeds by controlling the work processes of health service professionals[23,24] through the tight control of finances, clinical budgeting, work measurement, target-setting and performance indicators.[25] Practice protocols, that provide step-by-step detail on how nursing tasks should be carried out, are in evidence in one UK Trust hospital and appear to indicate that, in this particular hospital, managers and not health care professionals control the day-to-day activities of care delivery,[26] and that the essence of nursing, the caring role, can easily be broken down into quantifiable tasks. However, this is clearly not possible.[27]

Nurses are a costly occupational group, due to their large numbers, and, because they are at the front line of health care delivery, they have been the main focus of this change.[28] The focus on nurses' work has resulted in an attack on the nurses' occupational autonomy[29] – for

---

[16]   Lapsley (1994).
[17]   Loan-Clarke (1996).
[18]   Carney (2002a).
[19]   This study by Carney was undertaken with 365 health service professional managers at head of department level in Ireland, of which 43% were senior nurse managers.
[20]   Oroviogoicoechea (1996).
[21]   Carney (2002a).
[22]   Hoggett (1996), p.17.
[23]   Harrison & Pollitt (1994).
[24]   Webb (1999).
[25]   Pollitt (1993).
[26]   Bolton (2000).
[27]   Ackroyd (1998).
[28]   Hewison (1999).
[29]   Keenan (1999).

example, in management determining the number of patients that nurses should take care of in a given time and particular situation, and in the increase in patient turnover without a corresponding increase in the number of nurses delivering this care.[30] However, it is also acknowledged that the nurses' work involves rapid, autonomous decision-making that puts the nurse firmly in the work role of *knowledgeable doer*.[31;32]

Evidence of the success of management in controlling the work processes of nurses and other health service professionals is difficult to define or quantify, particularly when structures and management strategy vary across hospitals.[33;34] Therefore, the hospital management of the future, is likely to rely on the traditional autonomy of nurses in relation to how health care is delivered by them, and that, even though nurses may resist some of the management demands placed upon them in their roles, they are likely to accommodate many of these demands.[35] Carney[36] argues that this compliance results from the nurses' professional sense of putting the patient first and their perceived conciliatory role in health care partnership. This professional sense has allowed nurses to develop their own ways of interpreting the wishes of management. It is important that co-operative relations are maintained between management and health care professionals, as the objective of both groups is the same – that is, the provision of quality care to patients.

The key factors in successful care delivery include ongoing, negotiated discussions of costs, efficiency and quality between management and clinicians, the accommodation of both perspectives and the recognition, by hospital management, of the clinician's expertise and professionalism.[37] In order to do this, it is necessary for hospitals to be efficient and reliable in patient care management. However, the debate continues as to whether professionalising improves patient care or provides additional power to the professional group, such as medicine or nursing.[38;39]

---

[30] Bolton (2000).
[31] Robinson (1992).
[32] Witz (1995).
[33] Grimshaw (1999).
[34] Adams, Lugsden, Chase, Arber & Bond (2000).
[35] Bolton (2000).
[36] Carney (2002a).
[37] Carney (2002a).
[38] Oakley (1998).
[39] Davies (1995).

CREATING RELIABLE & EFFICIENT HOSPITALS

Hospitals should be classed as knowledge economies, as the core assets of health service organisations are housed in the commitment, capabilities, skills and knowledge of its employees, and not in the modern buildings in which some hospitals are located. This classification largely does not occur, as demonstrated in **Chapter 4**, as health care continues to be delivered and managed by hierarchies within bureaucratic organisations. Small management teams of executives, built on top of such hierarchies, determine governance. Although authority has been pushed downwards, with employees having more authority and greater autonomy than previously, the major strategic decisions of the organisation continue largely to be made by this small group of executives.[40] It is questionable whether the organisation's knowledge expert workers are consulted to any great extent. A consequence of this lack of involvement at top level is distrustful employees.[41] Manville & Ober[42] contrast the ancient Greek type of governance with today's hierarchies, exploring this limited authority through the eyes of citizens and building citizenship that, in the process, goes beyond the empowerment of the individual to take account of the organisation's needs. These authors argue that individual needs, beliefs and actions should determine the manner in which the organisation is governed, and that knowledge workers must be able to grow from their own aspirations and initiatives. Therefore, the key to success is participatory structures for decision-making and dispute resolution, which contain clearly defined procedures, as this structural form permits employees with expertise to come forward when their particular skills are required.

Moral reciprocity provides the link between *What is in this for me?* and *What is in this for us [the organisation]?*, whereby the individual, through involvement in participatory decision-making, is provided with the opportunity to grow and to develop their talents and skills further. Individuals owe the organisation their best efforts and, in turn, the organisation is obliged to provide the individual with the opportunity to fulfil his or her potential. This type of system would be capable of combining structures, values and practice. Reciprocity, from the organisational perspective, was explored in **Chapter 4**. The purpose of any organisation, particularly a professional organisation, is to serve its customers and employees. The mission of the organisation must be crafted in such a way that the organisation's objectives are met. Members join the organisation for various

---

[40] Bolton (2000).
[41] Carney (2004a).
[42] Manville & Ober (2003).

purposes, the chief of which is to serve their own interests[43] (for example, career progression), while others may join for altruistic reasons, such as to serve the common good or from a sense of providing an important service. Unless the organisation permits and provides a valued exchange of ideas in return for the services provided by the employee, over time, the members of the organisation will not serve it well. Therefore, exchange and reciprocity are necessary for organisational viability, reliability and patient-centred focus.

"Magnet" Hospitals' Expertise

How may exchange and reciprocity be assured? An American project involving a study of hospitals perceived by patients and health service provider organisations to deliver consistently excellent patient care is worthy of note. This important 1982 study conducted by the American Academy of Nursing[44] identified 41 characteristics in nurses who consistently delivered excellent care to patients and involved "magnet" hospitals – that is, organisations that were perceived by staff as being good places to work. In 2002, the findings of Kramer & Schmalenberg's[45] 20-year study of the culture of excellence at magnet hospitals were presented in a report entitled *Magnet Hospitals Revisited*. These authors compared the experiences of nurses working in magnet hospitals with those working in non-magnet hospitals, and presented eight attributes which nurses perceived as essential to the delivery of quality patient care:

♦ The first pertained to the provision of organisational support for nursing education, in the form of study leave and funding.

♦ The second and third attributes involved the recognition of competence at the Bachelor of Science in Nursing level, and of working with clinically-competent nursing colleagues in hospitals.

♦ The fourth attribute related to the presence of positive nurse-physician relationships – that is, collaborative and collegial relationships that promoted and encouraged an equal distribution of power.[46]

♦ The remaining four attributes related to autonomous nursing practice, which involved the nurses having the knowledge and education to maintain control of their profession and of their own practice; working within a hospital culture that valued the patient and promoted quality-focused care, with adequate staffing levels in

---

43 Scott (2004).
44 Kramer & Schmalenberg (2002).
45 Kramer & Schmalenberg (2004).
46 Kramer & Schmalenberg (2003).

order to provide quality care and consistent nurse-manager support in the work environment.

The magnet hospital staff perceived the collegial nurse-physician relationship as the key to quality patient-care. Kramer & Schmalenberg[47;48] noted that, even though the physician-nurse relationship in their study was mainly collegial, there was also evidence of adversarial relationships in a study undertaken with physicians in the US,[49] which indicated that adverse physician-nurse relationships contributed to nurses leaving the profession, resulting in nursing shortages.

Negative Organisational Consequences

Work and stress has been associated with negative organisational and individual consequences.[50] Empirical evidence indicates that nurses and doctors report higher levels of stress than other health care managers.[51;52] Schulz *et al.*[53] suggest that organisations need to accept that work-related stress exists and to manage this stress in an appropriate manner. Rodham & Bell[54;55] found that junior health care managers suffer stress, and that this group was generally unaware of potential work stressors or of the effect of work stressors on their own health and performance or on that of other employees. These authors suggest that there is an inherent culture of acceptance of workplace stress and, consequently, an inability to proactively manage work stress.

Management of stress should be an organisational concern and individual staff should be encouraged to manage stress in the workplace and to develop coping strategies. Indeed, there is evidence to suggest that many organisations, including health care organisations, off-load their employee relations to external consultants and, in the process, lose the capacity to develop their staff. Organisations rely on temporary staff to manage wards and

---

[47]   Kramer & Schmalenberg (2004).
[48]   Kramer & Schmalenberg (2004) reported that 13% of magnet hospital nurses perceived the relationship to be hostile and adversarial. This figure rose to 23% in magnet-aspiring hospitals and to 34% in other hospitals.
[49]   Rosenstein, Russell & Lauve (2002).
[50]   Morath & Turnbull (2005).
[51]   Anderson, Cooper & Willmott (1996).
[52]   Lipley (1998).
[53]   Schulz, Greenby & Brown (1985).
[54]   Rodham & Bell (2002).
[55]   This study by Rodham & Bell (2002) was undertaken amongst a group of six managers working in a large NHS Trust hospital in Britain, through critical incident diaries and semi-structured diaries.

administration on the pretext that this practice offers the organisation flexibility. Peter Drucker[56] argues that, in doing so, organisations make non-employees out of individuals who have continued to work for the organisation in a temporary capacity for months, and in doing so, avoid many of the costs associated with permanent workers. In addition, Drucker asserts that employers now claim that people are their greatest liability and are no longer chanting the old mantra that people are their greatest assets. In the US, hospitals frequently seek their required specialist professionals from a specialist outsourcer. Consequently, some hospital workers are now temporary, on short-term contract or are employees of the outsourcer or provider, and this splintering makes it is difficult to view the organisation in its entirety and to recognise its responsibilities to the staff and to the patients. Organisations must take responsibility for all of the people whose productivity and performance it relies on to deliver the highest standards of care required by its clients. Therefore, it is important for organisations to pay more attention to its employees' health, welfare, performance and productivity than it did 50 years ago. As Drucker argues, the knowledge-based economy of today is health care's future and this knowledge base will generate capital and ensure the organisation's survival.

Knowledge Workers

In the traditional workforce, the worker served the system; in contrast, in the contemporary health service, the knowledgeable workforce is staffed by a majority of knowledge workers and, thus, the system must serve the worker.[57] Senior managers do this by challenging the employees' limits, spending time developing their talents, and discussing their expectations. Knowledge workers require mentoring, coaching and encouragement as motivation, satisfaction, professional development and performance all require the attention of senior managers in order for the employees' knowledge-based capital assets to be realised for the benefit of both the organisation and the individual. This shift in orientation away from the traditional performance appraisal methods will require new measurement systems, new goals and policies and a new set of cultural values that recognises talent and individual worth.[58]

---

[56]   Drucker (2002).
[57]   Drucker (2002), p.77.
[58]   Kiluchi (2005).

The Spiral of Silence

Scott[59] talks of the "spiral of silence" that is common in today's health care organisations, noting that health service professionals often perceive silence as being the best way to avoid conflict and, thereby, to preserve relationships within the organisation. However, Scott argues that silence allows deviant behaviour to become the norm and results in unresolved issues and unstable system processes, as remaining silent in the face of conflict generates feelings of anxiety, resentment, discontent, anger and loss of trust in management amongst the silencer and the silenced health care professionals.[60;61] Therefore, leaders who are not afraid to speak out when conflict presents must emerge from the health service ranks. Leaders must have the courage to create new organisational processes that encourage communication, involvement and collaboration amongst the organisation's members and, in effect, move the health care organisation from a hierarchical model towards a socio-cultural and consensus model.[62] As noted in **Chapter 4**, hierarchy is structured, ordered, reliable and generally efficient and operates to maximum levels of effectiveness and efficiency if the organisation remains in a stable state.[63] However, today, few health care organisations remain in a stable state for long, due to challenging environmental, financial and technological changes.

A socio-cultural health care system is required that offers its members the choice to change the structured mind-set of the organisation by promoting participation, involvement and collaboration in the delivery of health care rather than competition. Weick & Sutcliffe[64] identify organisational characteristics that, if pursued, will result in system regeneration, including the importance of identifying major and minor incidents that have a negative effect on health care delivery and then, through collaboration, changing the processes that permitted those lapses to occur. These authors further recommend that a culture of commitment to resilience be promoted in the organisation, which means that the organisation's members develop the "ability to recover from or adjust easily to misfortune or change".[65] This resilience is achieved through awareness of difficulties and problems that are likely to occur,[66] that have caused system

---

59   Scott (2004).
60   Carney (2004b).
61   Scott (2004).
62   Carney (2002a).
63   Leavitt (2003).
64   Weick & Sutcliffe (2001).
65   Merriam-Webster Online. Available at: http://www.m-w.com/home.htm. Accessed 21.9.2003.
66   Carney (2004b).

problems in the past, and of the preventive measures that may be put in place before serious harm occurs. Preventive measures are undertaken in the spirit of interaction, collaboration and team communication.[67] Finally, expertise rather than hierarchy and seniority is recognised and acknowledged in decision-making.[68] Expertise may be obtained through informal networks, professional organisations and team collaboration. In this way, members become truly integrated into the decision-making processes of the organisation.

Developing Political Acumen

In today's challenging environment, where significant changes are occurring, health care managers have a professional responsibility to develop new ways of becoming more knowledgeable about health care policy. In addition, managers have a responsibility to become more involved with the policy issues that affect their patients, the wider population and their professions. Collectively, health care professionals are the largest hospital grouping holding a critical voice in the development of patient services and in patient outcomes and, as such, must develop political skills so that they may influence health policy.[69] This includes involvement in health policy discussion at all levels, from the Department of Health & Children downward to the local hospital level, and involvement should include meaningful participation in the development of strategy and in the implementation and evaluation of policies.

There is nothing new about the importance of health care professionals developing political acumen. However, health policy, as a separate entity subject, receives scant attention at undergraduate or postgraduate levels;[70;71] consequently, health care professionals do not view politics and public policy in health care as their responsibility.[72] [73] Public policy needs to be introduced early in the undergraduate curriculum for all health care students, so that socialisation into the subject occurs; similar to the process of socialisation into the role and profession that takes place during professional discipline-specific training. Each professional has a duty to become familiar with the policies that concern their future patients. Professionals need to think policy and politically, because if this group is not interested or involved in the development of health service strategy, they will not be

---

[67] Scott (2004).
[68] Oxman & Smith (2003).
[69] Faulk & Ternus (2004).
[70] Brown (1996).
[71] Murphy (1999).
[72] Carney (2002a).
[73] Faulk & Ternus (2004).

capable of acting as successful professional advocates for their patients.

There are, however, some concerns as to the extent that public policy knowledge and skills should be incorporated into undergraduate education. Reutter & Williamson[74] advocate that undergraduate students require knowledge on public policy in order to extend their practice beyond the individual focus, so that they are able to ask health care managers questions relating to policy and the implementation of policy. Pertinent areas that professionals should be familiar with include policy formation, the economics of health care delivery, financing, supply and demand, regulatory agencies influencing policy and ethical and legal issues in health care delivery. The ultimate aim of such a programme is to stimulate knowledge and to develop new voices to express this knowledge on behalf of the patient. This knowledge will allow the professional to access, evaluate and use information and to wield influence on behalf of their patients and clients.

SUMMARY

♦ Major changes have occurred in the general hospital structure during the past decade, most significantly, the introduction of managed care in order to produce efficiencies in health care delivery.

♦ Rivalry for patients has increased due to competition in the health sector. A consequence of this rivalry appears to be higher costs, probably due to hospitals attempting to differentiate themselves from others in order to survive.

♦ Individual hospitals are required to control costs and to increase operational efficiency while continuing to provide high quality care. This increases pressure on clinicians and non-clinicians.

♦ Health service professionals, particularly nurses as the largest single professional grouping, have attracted considerable management attention and this has resulted in the control of the health care professionals' work now being placed firmly in the hands of hospital management.

♦ The purpose of any organisation, particularly a professional organisation, is to serve its customers and employees; therefore, the mission must be crafted in such a way as to enable these objectives to be met.

---

[74] Reutter & Williamson (2000).

♦ Magnet-hospital staff perceived collegial nurse-physician relationships as the key to quality patient-care.

♦ Nurses and doctors report the highest levels of stress within health care managers, and therefore, organisations need to accept that work-related stress exists and to manage this accordingly.

♦ Health service professionals often perceive silence as being the best way to avoid conflict and, thereby, to preserve relationships within the organisation. However, silence allows deviant behaviour to become the norm and results in unresolved issues and unstable system processes.

♦ Resilience in the work place is achieved through awareness of difficulties and problems, that are likely to occur, that have caused system problems in the past, and of the preventive measures that may be put in place before serious harm occurs.

♦ Public policy needs to be introduced early in the undergraduate curriculum for all health care students.

CHAPTER 6
INTER-PROFESSIONAL
RELATIONS

INTRODUCTION

Chapter 5 showed that the introduction of managed care has been a consequence of competition for health services, and that managed care has had the effect of controlling professional practice, inter-professional relationships and work processes. However, an analysis of "magnet" hospitals (recognised centres of excellence) demonstrated that professionals working in these hospitals perceived collegial nurse-physician relationships to be the key to quality patient care, thus emphasising an integrative approach to health care delivery. This chapter identifies the collaborative and interactive patterns that occur in health care delivery, including how these interactions may be developed and enhanced by educational programmes and collaborative research. The consequences of inter-disciplinary and multi-disciplinary education programmes at pre- and post-registration levels are also explored.

INTER-PROFESSIONAL COLLABORATIVE RELATIONSHIPS

Successful health care delivery depends, to a large extent, on the types of interactions that occur. If these interactions are of a collaborative and strategic nature, positive benefits will result for clinicians, non-clinicians and patients. Collaboration is defined as clinicians from different disciplines working together co-operatively through sharing responsibility for decision-making, problem-solving, conflict resolution and the co-ordination of activities.[1] In health care strategic planning, the involvement and committed collaboration of professional clinician and non-clinician managers results in strategic consensus on health service strategies and in excellence in health care

---

[1]   Boyle & Kochinda (2004), p.61.

delivery.[2;3] However, the positive benefits of collaboration are often negated or reduced by the presence of power groupings and by inter-professional rivalry and discord.[4;5] Recent research has shown that it is possible to enhance collaborative communication between different groups of clinicians. For example, a study undertaken in the US by Boyle & Kochinda[6;7] amongst nurses and physicians working in acute care settings, particularly Intensive Care Units (ICU), indicated that positive benefits accrued for staff and patients from different disciplines using purposeful intervention techniques in the management of patient care. However, intervention techniques remain relatively rare in enhancing collaboration amongst professionals in health care settings. Collaboration, particularly important in ICU settings, is deemed to be a key outcome of care.[8;9] If collaboration occurs, there is a positive association between increased nurse-physician collaboration and reduced risk of patient re-admission to ICU.[10;11] Additionally, collaboration results in positive outcomes for nurses, including more satisfaction with the role, less turnover of staff and an enhanced professional relationship between nurses and physicians. Physicians reported similar outcomes and enhanced research utilisation. The collaborative model used by Boyle & Kochinda incorporates the dimensions of leadership, communications, co-ordination, problem-solving, conflict management and teamwork.[12] These authors found, albeit in a small study, that when the ICU environment fosters a culture of teamwork and trust, collaboration increased between both disciplines, but recommends further research in collaborative intervention in order to determine whether patient

---

[2]   Carney (2002a).
[3]   Carney (2002a) found, through quantitative research, that collaboration in strategic management occurred in a group of 365 professional clinicians and non-clinicians from 11 health care disciplines, in 21 different hospital departments, in Ireland.
[4]   Carney (2002a).
[5]   Carney (2002a) undertook a qualitative study through semi-structured interviews with 25 managers, of which almost an equal number were clinicians and non-clinicians, working in acute care hospitals in Ireland.
[6]   Boyle & Kochinda (2004).
[7]   This study by Boyle & Kochinda (2004), undertaken in two ICUs in the US, reported that positive benefits accrued from purposeful intervention techniques. These researchers used a pre-test-post-test measure of the Analytic Model for Studying ICU Performance and developed a conceptual model to assess collaboration between physicians and nurses.
[8]   Baggs, Schmitt & Mushlin (1999).
[9]   Knaus, Draper, Wagner & Zimmerman (1996).
[10]   Manojlovich (2005).
[11]   Baggs, Schmitt & Mushlin (1999).
[12]   Boyle & Kochinda (2004).

care outcomes improve as a result of intervention techniques. Knaus *et al.*[13] reported that, in ICU, poor collaboration between physicians and nurses resulted in poor leadership and an almost 2% increase in patient mortality, therefore future research in this area is necessary. However, it is important that inter-professional collaboration occurs in all settings in which clinicians work and not just between nurses and doctors/physicians. Collaboration is required between all professional clinicians who are involved in patient care delivery,[14] for example physiotherapists and occupational therapists.[15]

Interaction Patterns with Patients/Clients

Communication practices between professional clinicians and patients will determine the success, or otherwise, of health outcomes for the patient. For example, communication practices considered most helpful in assisting patients with chronic or progressive diseases are those that support the individual in living with the disease, including helping the individual to manage pain and fatigue and to assist them in living as normal a life as possible. It is through these interaction patterns that health care professionals, including physiotherapists and occupational therapists, are in the important position of making a difference to the lives of individuals.[16;17] Interactions between health care clinicians and patients may often be complicated if the symptoms presented by the patient are inconclusive or vague. In order to obtain the care that they require, patients often seek out several different health care professionals. The communication interaction includes the provision of information concerning the illness and active involvement in the ongoing process of problem-solving; these factors are commonly recognised by patients as offering maximum support in assisting them to cope with their illness and in providing "normalcy" for them. If pain is perceived as intolerable, a patient may feel patronised or dismissed by the professional, often re-acting with fury and anger to the professional who appears to doubt the authenticity of the illness. Therefore, it is necessary for health service educationalists in academia and in management to ensure that professional clinicians are educated and trained for the role that they are required to undertake in health services delivery. Education programmes may take place through the

---

[13] Knaus, Draper, Wagner & Zimmerman (1996).
[14] Carney (2006b).
[15] Baggs, Schmitt & Mushlin (1999).
[16] Thorne, McGuinness, McPherson, Con, Cunningham & Harris (2004).
[17] This Grounded Theory study by Thorne, McGuinness, McPherson, Con, Cunningham & Harris (2004), undertaken in British Columbia, included 11 patients suffering from a chronic condition and was part of a larger study.

traditional single discipline or the modern forms of duo-discipline, or multi-disciplinary, educational approaches.

DEVELOPING INTER–PROFESSIONAL EDUCATION

A debate is currently taking place concerning the place of inter-professional education amongst health care professionals. Although there have been some positive reports concerning some aspects of the process of inter-professional shared learning, negative aspects have also been identified. Modern health care services require that professionals work together collaboratively so that patient care may be delivered through a seamless process.[18] During the past decade, there has been much discussion concerning the sharing of learning amongst professional clinicians. Inter-disciplinary sharing of knowledge, through shared education programmes, has been around for almost 30 years,[19] and is viewed, by some managers, as a panacea for solving the ills of the health care systems. Inter-professional education is advocated as the way forward in breaking down the professional and educational barriers that exist in health care.[20;21]

However, Barr [22] suggests that there are important distinctions to be made between inter-professional and multi-professional shared learning. Inter-professional education centres on professionals working together and has the objective of professionals interacting together and understanding each other's roles. In contrast, multi-professional education is concerned with professionals sharing learning without any emphasis on professional interaction or team working, and the basis for shared learning is the content of the education programme rather than the collaborative process.[23;24] As teamwork and collaboration are important goals for health and social care, with inter-professional communication viewed as the vehicle to achieve this aim,[25] it is important that these differences in approach and orientation, inherent in inter-professional and multi-professional shared learning educational programmes, are understood and acted upon by educationalists. If this does not occur, inter-professional and

---

[18]   Cullen, Fraser & Symonds (2003).
[19]   Glen & Reeves (2004), p.45.
[20]   General Medical Council (1997).
[21]   Department of Health (UK) (2000b).
[22]   Barr (1996).
[23]   Barr (1994).
[24]   Vanclay (ed.) (1997).
[25]   Morison, Boohan, Moutray & Jenkins (2004).

multi-professional education will remain blurred, resulting in the terms "inter-professional" and "multi-professional" remaining as concepts only. However, the question remains whether this form of education delivery should become the norm in the education of various clinician disciplines.

Pre-Registration Inter-disciplinary Education Programmes

Pre-registration education should be the first step in assisting students to learn about the professional roles and responsibilities of other health and social care service professionals.[26] Although awareness of each discipline's role is achieved through teamwork and collaboration during programme delivery,[27] governments, professionals and third level colleges are unclear as to how this aim may be achieved. Pre-registration education programmes leading to professional qualification are generally separate, although there may be shared learning through a multi-disciplinary approach in a limited number of areas – for example, in the teaching of physical sciences or occasionally in the social sciences. Shared learning is also viewed, by some managers in the National Health Services (NHS), as the way forward in creating a generic professional, who will deliver health care through a flexible approach, and as a means of reducing the current fragmentation in health care delivery.[28;29] Generally, shared learning across disciplines occurs at post-registration levels, in areas such as primary health care,[30] community mental health,[31] advanced nurse practitioner, or in the physical sciences at Bachelor's and Master's degree levels.[32] During the next decade, shared learning is expected to increase in frequency and in content.[33;34] In one British university, medical, nursing and obstetric students now share learning with other student groups during the early part of their education programme.[35] Furthermore, the NHS states that inter-professional pre-registration education is the path to improving collaboration between professional groups.[36;37] Although Glen & Reeves question whether this aspiration

---

[26] United Kingdom Central Council for Nursing, Midwifery & Health Visiting (2000).
[27] United Kingdom Central Council for Nursing, Midwifery & Health Visiting (2000).
[28] Department of Health (UK) (2000b).
[29] Department of Health (UK) (2001a).
[30] Long (1996).
[31] Reeves, Leiba, Freeth, Glen & Herzberg (2002).
[32] Carney (2004c).
[33] Freeth, Hammick, Koppel, Reeves & Barr (2002).
[34] Koppel, Barr, Reeves, Freeth & Hammick (2001).
[35] Cullen, Fraser & Symonds (2003).
[36] Department of Health (UK) (2001b).

is "mission impossible",[38] due to the logistical, cultural, educational and organisational problems inherent in achieving this aim, on reflection these authors conclude positively. However, Walshe,[39] in discussing nursing in inter-professional pre-registration education, appears to disagree, as she argues that inter-disciplinary education fails to acknowledge the uniqueness of nursing knowledge, which consequently marginalises the profession of nursing. Walsh suggests that shared educational initiatives must take into account the evolving nature and substance of nursing knowledge and the context in which nursing operates, as opposed to, for example, the well-established knowledge base, philosophy and cultural norms of medical education and practice. This is also true for other evolving health care disciplines, which, due to their recent origins in academia, have not yet had the opportunity to develop the discipline's knowledge base, philosophy and cultural ethos. In addition, the logistical and registration difficulties inherent in the delivery of such educational programmes to different disciplines must be addressed.

Difficulties in Collaborative Inter-disciplinary Pre-Registration Programmes

There are inherent difficulties in collaborative inter-disciplinary pre-registration education programmes and those that have been identified to date address the logistical problems faced by universities and higher education in delivering such programmes. These difficulties include timetabling incompatibility across colleges and schools,[40;41] the content and context of clinical placements, discipline-specific curricula and curricula design,[42;43] and the learning process itself.[44] Professional clinical placements in environments where there is expected to be competition for placements between disciplines, and where overlap currently occurs, will require dedicated clinical practitioner assistance and commitment. In addition, securing joint or single professional validation from regulatory bodies, such as nursing, medicine, dentistry or physiotherapy is of concern.[45] In such a practice scenario, professional collaboration following registration will be necessary and it is acknowledged that this form of collaboration and

---

[37] Glen & Reeves (2004).
[38] Glen & Reeves (2004), p.45.
[39] Walshe (2003).
[40] Pirrie, Elsegood & Hall (1998).
[41] Morison, Boohan, Moutray & Jenkins (2004).
[42] Pirrie, Wilson, Harden & Elsegood (1999).
[43] Harden (1998).
[44] Parsell & Bligh (1999).
[45] Glen & Reeves (2004).

the proposed substitution of career pathways will tax the current professional regulatory bodies in terms of the registration of each discipline. Loosening the rigid professional designation that exists for each profession will also be a challenge for these regulatory bodies and there is much evidence to suggest that the blurring of professions and professional roles creates tensions between professions.[46;47;48] Therefore, it is very likely that there will be resistance from these same bodies, individual professions and the trade unions.

Inter-professional Education for Professionals

Currently, in Britain, collaborative inter-professional projects are taking place, including, the Jump Project and New Generation Initiative. These projects are expected to identify the positive and negative aspects of collaborative programmes and the desirability of such programmes from the standpoints of education and clinical practice.

There are two schools of thought on when it is best to introduce inter-professional education for professionals. One school states that collaborative, inter-professional education should be introduced post-registration, when students have developed the maturity and confidence to study alongside other allied professions.[49] The other favours the pre-registration level,[50] when students have not yet been socialised into a role or profession and, therefore, will be less likely to harbour negative perceptions of other professionals or their roles. However, Pryce & Reeves[51] advise that, even in year one of an inter-professional programme, nursing, medical and dental students have already developed stereotypical attitudes toward the other professions. Consequently, these students question the purpose of shared learning and the relevance of the subject matter to their profession. Resistance to collaborative learning activities occurs when professional groups do not perceive designated teaching and learning activities as suitable to the needs of their specific discipline.[52;53] Therefore, educationalists must ensure that students in such education programmes are encouraged to gain greater understanding and acceptance of each other's discipline and roles in the delivery of health services.

---

[46] Brown, Crawford & Darongkamas (2000).
[47] Finch (2000).
[48] Barr (2000a).
[49] Dombeck (1997).
[50] Tope (1996).
[51] Pryce & Reeves (1997).
[52] Reeves & Freeth (2002).
[53] Fraser, Symonds, Cullen & Symonds (2000).

Multi-professional Education

Indeed, in a study undertaken with midwifery and medical students, in a multi-professional education programme, it was found that feelings of antagonism and professional rivalry between both groups of students occurred when the programme was delivered early in the education programme. In addition, the experience of multi-professional education was deemed to be ineffective in creating a shared learning climate.[54]

A further study, in the University of Nottingham, is developing inter-professional collaboration between midwifery and medical students with the aim of enhancing opportunities for inter-professional collaboration in education and research.[55;56] In the delivery of this programme, teamwork is facilitated through structured discussion, interaction and communication sessions. Furthermore, care is required and taken, in as far as it is possible, to ensure that the topics chosen for class discussion do not reinforce the professional stereotyping that exists from an early stage in the socialisation process in both professions.[57;58] Stereotyping, if present, prevents team-building from occurring.[59] Results, thus far, from this project are positive, with both groups of students agreeing that the initiative assisted them in breaking down professional boundaries through enhanced team working and a greater understanding of each other's role.

Higher education colleges will be required to develop a clear definition of the term "multi-professional education",[60] in order to develop requisite educational and curriculum approaches, and to ensure that imbalances in student numbers, across the disciplines, does not occur, as this will lead to domination by one discipline.[61] The timing of shared inter-disciplinary education appears to be important. If undertaken in year one, students in various disciplines will not have yet developed a sense of professional identity;[62] by year four,

---

[54] Miller, Ross & Freeman (1999).
[55] Cullen, Fraser & Symonds (2003).
[56] Cullen, Fraser & Symonds (2003) discuss the processes involved in implementing an inter-professional education strategy in a recently established School of Human Development at the University of Nottingham. To further this aim, inter-professional team objective structured clinical examinations (OSCE) for midwifery and medical students were developed.
[57] Freidson (1970).
[58] Freidson (1984).
[59] Cullen, Fraser & Symonds (2003).
[60] Barr (2000a).
[61] Funnell (1995).
[62] Horsburgh, & Lamdin & Williamson (2001).

professional identity is firmly established[63] and individual cognitive maps are established.[64] Attitudinal differences concerning shared learning in the area of communications are evident even between junior and senior medical students.[65] The development of professional identity and a sense of belonging to the chosen discipline are important and must be fostered and developed.

Advantages of Inter-disciplinary Education

Advantages identified to date of inter-disciplinary education programmes include evidence of students having greater knowledge of each others' discipline[66;67] and positive attitudes toward understanding and collaborating amongst disciplines in primary or secondary care settings.[68;69] Glen & Reeves[70] recommended that much more research is required into all aspects of the education programme, inter-disciplinary collaboration and outcomes for patient care delivery.

These aims were used in a recent, exploratory study in Northern Ireland, to determine whether it was possible to anticipate the problems, if any, likely to occur in an inter-disciplinary education (IPE) pre-registration programme involving the Sick Children's branch of nursing and medical students undertaking a paediatric module.[71;72] Both groups of students perceived that learning about team work and professional roles were important, and both had a keen sense of their own professional role, but indicated that, if IPE hindered their professional education and development, this would be viewed as disadvantageous to their professional development. Although the preference of both groups was for a discipline approach to learning, the medical students were particularly aware of their professional boundaries. The medical students perceived that they required a higher standard of education than nurses and questioned the need for shared learning with nurses. It appears that the seeds of medical dominance over nurses had already been sown at this stage in the medical students' educational development. Indeed, as Horsburgh *et*

---

63   Morison, Boohan, Moutray & Jenkins (2004).
64   Hall & Weaver (2001).
65   Reeves & Pryce (1998).
66   Green, Cavell & Jackson (1996).
67   Virgin, Goodrow & Duggins (1996).
68   Barr (2000b).
69   Reeves (2001).
70   Glen & Reeves (2004).
71   Morison, Boohan, Moutray & Jenkins (2004).
72   Morison, Boohan, Moutray & Jenkin's (2004) exploratory study was undertaken in a Belfast university. A modified version of the readiness for inter-professional learning scale (RIPLS) was used in a convenience sample of 20 fourth-year medical students and 10 third-year nursing students.

al.[73] found, medical students had already developed a strong professional identity by the end of year one of their programme.

These issues will require careful consideration in the future, if IPE is to be successful in achieving its aims. Therefore, further research is required into the advantages of inter-disciplinary education, and a sound evidence base is required.

RESEARCH COLLABORATION BETWEEN ACADEMICS & PRACTITIONERS

It has been demonstrated that educational collaboration, through shared teaching and inter-disciplinary and multi-disciplinary approaches to educational delivery, has the potential to enhance inter-disciplinary relations. A further form of collaboration is through research. Research collaboration is possible between academics and professional health service practitioners or clinicians. There are many areas of each professional clinician's work that may be researched from a multidisciplinary perspective. Patients and professionals alike will benefit from research collaboration. Currently, shared research occurs mainly within medicine and involves a nurse researcher who may, or may not, be mentioned as a joint researcher or joint author. Since health care is delivered through a multidisciplinary or an inter-disciplinary approach, research projects and the dissemination of research findings through publications also needs to be multidisciplinary, with all participants in the research acknowledged. This sharing approach will lead to greater research collaboration in the future. However, non-sharing of research knowledge amongst health care professionals is not unique.

In the business world, sharing of research information and acknowledgement of participation in the research process, by practitioners and academics, does not occur to any large extent, even when practitioners have been involved in the process. A study of manuscripts presented to the *Academy of Management Journal* for publication found that just 20% of submitted articles appeared to reflect collaboration between academics and practitioners, even though more than double that figure had direct contact with practitioners during the course of the research process.[74,75] As a result

---

[73]   Horsburgh, Lamdin & Williamson (2001).
[74]   Rynes, Bartunek & Daft (2001).
[75]   Rynes, Bartunek & Daft's (2001) study involved an examination of manuscripts submitted to the US *Academy of Management Journal* and attempted to determine the extent of academic-practitioner research collaboration and relationships.

of this finding, Rynes, Bartunek & Daft[76] stress that, since academics and practitioners could learn from each other, the transfer of knowledge between professional clinicians and academics should take place. Given the potential for both positive and negative effects from research collaboration, further exploration of the practice-science-academic areas is required.

A further possible cause of conflict exists between academic researchers and clinical practitioners in health care. Organisational research findings and management practices often vary.[77] Even when each group studies the research findings of other groups, and despite the fact that research techniques have become more sophisticated, collaborative research has become less useful in solving the practical problems encountered by professionals.[78] Academics and practitioners or users of research often belong to different worlds and hold different values. Consequently, a gap exists between the research culture and ideology of both groups and this has impeded or prevented research use by professionals.[79] This gap now exists in nearly all fields in which there are both researchers and practitioners,[80] and is thought to be due to the different frames of reference regarding the type and purpose of the information required by both groups,[81] the goals the groups seek to influence, the social systems they operate in and the time frames for addressing technical or practical problems.[82]

A further complication relates to the corporate interests that are evident in health care products. Therefore, the importance of ethical collaboration between practitioners and corporation researchers or academics/practitioners is important in view of the cultural differences that exist.[83] These differences may relate to only commercially-profitable projects being pursued[84] and may include restrictions on publishing findings[85] and precedence of corporate interests.[86;87] The commercialisation potential and implementation of research in the physical sciences research is greater than that in the organisational sciences.[88]

---

[76]   Rynes, Bartunek & Daft (2001).
[77]   Rynes, Bartunek & Daft (2001).
[78]   Hambrick (1994).
[79]   Beyer & Trice (1979).
[80]   Rogers (1995).
[81]   Shrivastava & Mitroff (1984).
[82]   Powell & Owen-Smith (1998).
[83]   Hyde, Lohan & McDonnell (2004).
[84]   Murphy & Saal (1990).
[85]   Rynes & Trank (1999).
[86]   Cohen, Florida, Randazzese & Walsh (1998).
[87]   Press & Washburn (2000).
[88]   Pfeffer & Sutton (2000).

Links between scientific research and practice require further development, particularly between clinicians and academics. It is evident that medicine has developed its research capability and collaboration but that other health care professionals have not done so to the same extent. Nursing and allied health care professionals require greater research collaboration. A recent study by Offermann & Spiros[89;90] found that collaboration between academics and practitioners existed and that the flow of knowledge was generally two-way. Therefore, further research collaboration between academics and practitioners requires good social relations between both groups, free from cultural or values conflicts that may hinder progress. Team-building and trust-building activities are considered to be important in this process.[91;92]

Evidence of lack of knowledge transfer between academics and practitioners exists and therefore learning from each other is limited.[93] Clearly-written research findings containing interpretation of data and a summary that is then followed by discussion of the data with particular relevance to practice are required.[94] Academics and practitioners learning together is important for future research collaboration, implementation and dissemination of research knowledge in order to overcome barriers. Collaboration will require that groups listen to each other and discuss practice problems and potential solutions. Social and learning activities that merge ideas are important ways to bridge the academic-practitioner research-practice gap and thereby ensure enhanced patient care delivery.

Meeting Modern Health Care Demands through Education

When government initiatives that produce competency-based skills through inter-professional shared education are introduced during a period when fewer students are entering professions, including nursing, they may be viewed as an attempt to produce a multi-skilled generic workforce that is flexible in meeting the demands of modern health care.[95;96] Fears have been expressed, in the case of nursing, that the process of multi-professional education will cause a blurring of

---

[89] Offermann & Spiros (2001).
[90] This study involved 245 team developers (59% practitioners, 41% academics) from the Organisational Development & Change Division of the Academy of Management, and examined the current state of team development practice.
[91] Amabile, Patterson, Mueller, Wojcik, Odomirok, Marsh & Kramer (2001).
[92] Mohrman, Gibson & Mohrman (2001).
[93] Rynes, Bartunek & Daft (2001).
[94] Mohrman, Gibson & Mohrman (2001).
[95] Department of Health (UK) (2001b).
[96] Walshe (2003), p.526.

nursing roles with those of other professional clinicians, resulting in the loss of the particular caring essence of nursing and the danger that nursing knowledge, practice and, indeed, the profession will experience disempowerment.[97]

Much has been written about medical dominance over other professions[98] and particularly over nurses.[99;100] Studies undertaken amongst Australian, British and Irish nurses suggest that medical dominance is perceived as causing work place dissatisfaction.[101;102] Medical dominance is regarded as a structural failure of the health care systems in many English-speaking countries.[103;104] Dominance is perceived in many ways, including control over patients,[105] and over other professions.[106]

However, on a more positive note, in a study undertaken in Scotland in the area of elderly care, it was found that lower than expected levels of medical dominance occurred.[107;108] In this study, dominance by the consultant, though found in certain areas of team discussion, was perceived by the team members to be reduced due to strong consensus amongst team members as to the aims of geriatric care and to the strength of the team.[109] Gair & Hartery[110] found that reducing the level of medical dominance in a team encouraged all team members to participate and thus enhanced patient care.

Dominance by one group over another is reduced by team members demonstrating expert knowledge of the care required, avoidance of the learned helplessness mode, and through collaboration and consensus in approaches taken to patient care. Additionally, each discipline must demonstrate, through word and action, respect and acceptance of each other's role in the team. Through mutual recognition of each other's expertise, competencies and complementary team-based roles, excellence in patient care delivery will be further enhanced.

---

[97] Walshe (2003), p.528.
[98] Bates & Lapsley (1985).
[99] Katavich (1996).
[100] Kenny &. Adamson (1992).
[101] Adamson & Kenny (1995).
[102] Carney (2002a).
[103] Freidson (1970).
[104] Willis (1989).
[105] Phillips (1996).
[106] Bates & Lapsley (1985).
[107] Gair & Hartery (2001).
[108] This study by Gair & Hartery (2001) was undertaken in Scotland in a geriatric assessment unit, to explore whether medical dominance over other team members occurred.
[109] Gair & Hartery (2001), p.3.
[110] Gair & Hartery (2001), p.6.

SUMMARY

◆ Communication practices between the professional clinician and the patient will determine the success, or otherwise, of health outcomes for the patient.

◆ Collaboration is defined as clinicians working together co-operatively, with shared responsibility for decision-making, problem-solving, conflict resolution and the co-ordination of activities.

◆ Clinician and non-clinician involvement and collaboration in strategic planning will result in strategic consensus. However, the presence of power groupings and inter-professional rivalry and discord reduces collaboration in the strategic process.

◆ Enhanced collaborative communication between nurses and physicians in the management of patient care is possible when both parties use intervention techniques, such as the Collaborative Model, which incorporates the dimensions of leadership, communication, co-ordination, problem-solving, conflict management and teamwork into the collaborative process. Collaboration results in positive outcomes for clinicians, including more satisfaction with their role, less staff turnover and enhanced professional relationships.

◆ Inter-professional education is advocated as the way forward in breaking down the professional and educational barriers that exist in health care. Inter-professional education has the objective of professionals understanding each other's roles and interacting together, whereas multi-professional education is concerned with professionals sharing learning and, therefore, the content of the education programme is the educational goal.

◆ Pre-registration education should be the first step in assisting students to learn about the professional roles and responsibilities of other health and social care service professionals.

◆ There is much evidence to suggest that the blurring of professional roles, and of professions, creates tensions between professions. Therefore, shared educational initiatives must take into account the evolving nature and substance of professional knowledge and the context in which different professional disciplines operate.

◆ To date, the effectiveness of multi-professional education remains unclear, and such educational programmes have been deemed ineffective in creating a shared learning climate. Therefore, each discipline must demonstrate, through word and action, respect and acceptance of each other's role in health care delivery.

♦ Research collaboration will bridge the gap between education and practice and knowledge transfer in health services delivery, thus ensuring that patients will also benefit from this collaboration.

CHAPTER 7
CHANGE MANAGEMENT IN HEALTH SERVICE PROVISION

INTRODUCTION

Previous chapters demonstrated that clinicians and non-clinicians are central to health care delivery in hospitals and that managerial effectiveness, in such organisations, is dependent upon the collaborative process undertaken through interacting networks and involvement in future organisational planning. This chapter explores the management of change from the individual manager, the strategic and the organisational perspectives. It also considers shaping change from below upwards through selling issues and presents models for managing the change process, including the Change Management Model and a Model of Preparedness for Occupational Change.

CHANGE THEORIES

Theories on the nature of change management continue to grow and include the processes and procedures that contribute to introducing change.[1] Various views exist concerning change implementation and the debate regarding the processes to adopt to ensure successful change implementation from the perspective of the individual employee, organisational manager and organisation is ongoing. Although change is a constant in the health care field, currently it is faster and more complex than it has ever been before.[2] Health care managers may not always accept change, but they must learn to manage it and, indeed, the ability to manage change has become an essential skill for all managers.[3] Poggenppoel[4] suggests that change may lead to real innovation, providing abundant opportunities for creating a better way forward.

---

[1] Carnell (1995).
[2] Mannion (1994).
[3] Zukowski (1995).
[4] Poggenppoel (1992).

Bradshaw & Mulholland have highlighted the profound changes taking place in the British National Health Service (NHS) during the past decade,[5,6] and health service strategies introduced by the Irish Health Service demonstrate that similar change is occurring in Ireland. This prolonged process of change, which many health services are undergoing, is characterised by a long period of transition from a relatively stable environment to one where cost control, efficiencies in health care delivery and value for money are paramount. Therefore, health care professionals should be concerned with organisational change. The effective manager needs insight into change theories[7] in order to take up the challenges offered through constant change. Poggenppoel[8] suggests that health care managers should view change as a challenge and manage it pro-actively, innovatively and creatively and, through this introspective process, to look upon change as an opportunity to create processes that will offer a better standard of care to patients.

There are many ways of managing change. Few organisational changes are complete failures, and few are entirely successful.[9] The management of change draws from psychological, behavioural, political, social and cultural dimensions, many of which may be conflicting.

A realisation that change is the result of competition between driving and restraining forces is evident in much of the literature. Lewin[10] noted some forces drive change whilst others resist change. A change agent is required to facilitate change, to manage the restraining forces, and to drive change through. The agent is required to understand change as a phenomenon, identify the key emotional reactions associated with change, such as resistance, and know how to manage change in a positive manner. Kotter[11] contends that both leadership and management skills are required to effectively and positively manage change, particularly in a volatile environment. He further argues that the change process is deductive; it is about managing complexity and is often undertaken in order to prevent a more chaotic reality than that presently in force. If change is approached with a certain level of excitement and enthusiasm, it will create opportunities that will make patients lives better.[12] However, change is often introduced without due regard for the realities of

---

5   Bradshaw (1995).
6   Mulholland (1994).
7   Limo-Basto (1995).
8   Poggenppoel (1992).
9   Kotter & Schlesinger (1979).
10   Lewin (1951).
11   Kotter (1990).
12   Muller (1992).

individual areas of health care practice. Some managers may not have an insight into the effects of the change on the lives of individuals or a realisation that even minor change may have unintended consequences for the individual and the organisation.[13] Most resistance to change occurs not because of the proposed change, but as a result of individual perceptions of expected outcomes due to the change and on how this is likely to impact on their lives. Therefore, an accurate assessment of the environment, both internal and external to the organisation, is required prior to the change, thus preventing negative consequences for individuals.

Selling Issues to Senior Managers: Shaping Change from Below

Change is often portrayed as a discrete event, whereby a system is unfrozen, moved, and then refrozen.[14] However, this is not the reality as people, processes and organisations are dynamic, evolving entities in a constant state of change. The reality is that managers often compete with, and complement, each other's ideas, whilst simultaneously pushing their own issues upward to top management for their attention, where they are either accepted or rejected.[15] This process may be termed continuous change.[16]

The implementation of change is assisted through managing issues or issue selling. Issue selling is the process by which individuals affect others' attention to, and understanding of, the events, development, and trends that have implications for organisational performance.[17] Some authors have explored the social-psychological processes that middle managers use when deciding to sell an issue or not.[18] Dutton & Ashford[19] built the initial framework for thinking about issue selling and the moves made. Moves are actions that are informed by, and are expressive of, practical knowledge.[20] These moves are grouped into four categories:

♦ Packaging or framing the contents moves.

♦ Type of involvement moves.

♦ Choice of channel moves.

---

13 Kotter & Schlesinger (1979).
14 Lewin (1951).
15 Dutton & Ashford (1993).
16 Brown & Eisenhardt (1997).
17 Dutton & Ashford (1993).
18 Ashford, Rothbard, Piderit & Dutton (1998).
19 Dutton & Ashford (1993).
20 Pentland (1992).

♦ Formality moves, or the level of formality/informality undertaken in selling the issue.

Dutton, Ashford, O'Neill & Lawrence[21;22] then explored the moves made when selling issues. These moves consisted of the presentation of the issue, mainly through the logic of the business plan and by using charts and graphs. The next move, termed the "bundling move", was characterised by employees' attempts to connect the issue, in some way, with other issues or goals familiar to them – for example, with patient services or to a valued hospital goal, in the belief that this connection would enhance its success rate. Continuous proposal-making or raising the issue many times over a period of time was a further move undertaken; individuals presented issues as if they were incremental changes and, therefore, issues may not have been presented all at once. Other matters to be considered, in relation to selling issues, include making decisions regarding the individuals to be involved in the issue-selling process and the nature, context and timing of involvement moves.

MANAGING CHANGE THROUGH THE USE OF MODELS

Carney[23] developed a change management model to evaluate the change process. The model explores how well change is being managed, or retrospectively, has been managed. When a model is used to guide change, consistency in approach can be achieved, as the model serves to direct, guide and make sense of the change process.[24] Carney also developed an evaluative measurement construct tool that provides change agents with a structured, objective tool to measure managing change.[25] The measurement construct tool, designed to assist in the evaluation of the change process, is used in conjunction

---

[21]   Dutton, Ashford, O'Neill & Lawrence (2001).
[22]   Dutton, Ashford, O'Neill & Lawrence (2001) explored the process of selling issues, and highlighted the importance of selling issues to middle and top management through the process of shaping change from below and, thereby, gaining the attention of management. The study was conducted through an examination of 82 accounts of issue-selling undertaken by employees in a not-for-profit hospital of 2,683 employees, attached to a university centre, in a rural north-eastern town in the US.
[23]   Carney (2000).
[24]   Pearson, Vaughan & Fitzgerald (1996).
[25]   Carney (2000), p.265.

with the change management model.[26] The model identifies four elements that contribute to the successful implementation of change:[27;28]

♦ Communication during the change process.

♦ Change dynamics, which include resistance or acceptance of change.

♦ Management of the implementation stage

♦ Management of the evaluation stage of the change process.

Each element consists of key factors. The success of any change is determined by a number of critical success factors that should be in place or present before success can be guaranteed, and that must be managed well to ensure that change is successful. By concentrating on key factors success is more likely to occur. The key factors identified include:

♦ Commitment.

♦ Motivation

♦ Professional judgement in decision-making.

♦ Understanding of the need for change.

♦ Communication skills.

♦ Desired high quality outcome to change.

Managing the Transition Stage of Change

Management of the transition state of change is of vital importance. Therefore, the change agent should set up facilitation mechanisms and education programmes to ensure that each individual remains aware of each phase of the change process. Constant communication with staff concerning the change will defuse anxiety and reduce resistance to the change and deal with the fears and concerns that individuals may hold or anticipate.

---

[26] The change management model is published in the *Journal of Nursing Management* and was adapted by Carney from an idea in Clarke & Garside's (1997) Maturity Matrix.

[27] Carney (2000), p.266.

[28] Carney's (2000) model was tested on 18 health care management students who piloted the models to evaluate change in situations that they had recently encountered. All of the participants found a positive correlation between their individual experiences and the model scoring system, as the means of evaluating the change mirrored their subjective opinions of the change.

The communications process consists of several key variables including:

♦ Consultation.

♦ Education.

♦ Participation.

♦ Assertiveness.

♦ Negotiation.

♦ Understanding of change dynamics.

♦ Democratic decision-making.

During the initial assessment stage, these key variables are managed through involving staff in the assessment and diagnosis of what needs to be changed and in the design of the proposed change. This involvement may occur through creative workshops or interactive brainstorming and focus groups. It is necessary to identify the possible early adopters of the change and the potential resistors to the change and to realise that some individuals will engage more fully at this stage than others.[29] Managers or facilitators should stress that involvement at this time is voluntary but, equally, involvement in the change process may be sought through invitation to become change agents and to join project groups or development teams.[30] A facilitator, with relevant proven experience in managing similar projects, external to the organisation, may be appointed at this time.

Mechanisms for dealing with self-doubt must be managed during the transition stage and will include the facilitation of problem-solving and individual re-assurance of task or process capability. During the transition stage, regular progress reports, encouragement and recognition of individual effort are necessary. The transition period is a time for remembering the past, then moving on quickly to the future and the "desired new state". The recognition of the past permits the change to be implemented faster and more successfully. The transition period is one of low stability and high stress, where undirected energy may lead to the de-railing of the change process and where conflict and rumours abound with frequent references to the "good old days". Thus, it is important that the transition period is well-managed and that the change agent has a clear understanding of the conflicting opinions and the needs that exist.

---

[29] Carney (2002b).

[30] Office for Health Management (2003).

Key Variables Determining Success or Failure in Change

The level of acceptance or resistance to change is determined by a number of the key variables. These variables include acceptance of change, involvement and understanding of the proposed change and the impact of the proposed change on the lives of individuals. Further variables are the development of a project team, managing resistance and identification of the driving and restraining forces involved in the change process. Thus, managing resistance to change is one of the most important parts of the change process. Often, resistance arises because individuals prefer the old way of doing things and fear the consequences of change on their lives or, in some instances, individuals may hold a different view of the world to those seeking to implement change and, as a result, may not see the rationale behind the proposed change and, consequently, resist it.[31]

During the transition phase, between the completion of the change when new structures or processes or teams are in place and the change process, individuals undergo psychological processes that often include resistance to the change, before coming to terms with the change.[32] Therefore, resistance needs to be managed and this includes dealing with defensive routines, such as political manoeuvring and diverting resources[33] that hinder new organisational learning around the change.[34] Thus, to counteract such defensive behaviour, a climate of openness, transparency about the change and its likely impact, and building up trust in the need for change will limit resistance. This is achieved through team-work, collaboration, face-to-face communications,[35] and actively seeking out resistance and responding to it,[36] appropriately and speedily.

Carney[37] identified the key variables that determine the success or failure of the change implementation process. These variables involve prior research and include mapping the change, setting out clearly for staff the parts that will change and those that will remain the same following the change. This requires resilience, tolerance and patience, and persistent attention by managers or facilitators.[38] The next element of the model, identified by Carney, includes the use of process tools, such as the project management techniques of defining, planning and scheduling the major and minor phases of the change, and the

---

[31] Carney (2002b).
[32] Bridges (1995).
[33] Buchanan & Boddy (1992).
[34] Argyris (1990).
[35] Kotter (1995).
[36] Buchanan & Boddy (1992).
[37] Carney (2000), p.266.
[38] Office for Health Management (2003).

individual and collective tasks required to bring about the change. Project team interaction will cover such areas as clarification of costs and benefits, an outline of the advantages and disadvantages to making the change and of remaining in the same position. An essential part of managing change is mapping the stakeholders by endeavouring to show each individual what the future change will mean to each in the new structure and includes setting out clear inputs and outputs required of, and from, each person. If the change is organisational or involves crossing boundaries, effort will be required to develop cross-discipline working relationships, such as cross-sectoral or inter-disciplinary work groups, particularly for clinicians, who frequently work independently or in clinician groupings. The change agent should consistently reinforce the benefits that are likely to accrue to patients as a result of the change.

The evaluation element is the final key variable in Carney's model and includes recognition of the need to evaluate the change process at various stages in order to take necessary action and to provide feedback and recognition of staff contribution during the process.[39] Constant evaluation of the resource implications, during each phase of the change, is also necessary, otherwise funding "over-runs" may occur that may lead to premature abandonment or reduction in the level of urgency of the change, thus resulting in loss of motivation for the change amongst staff.[40]

Model of Preparedness for Occupational Change

Schyns developed a model of preparedness for occupational change.[41;42] Preparedness for change is defined as the wish to acquire higher task demands. This refers to tasks requiring a greater degree of complexity than were present before the change. The core concepts of this model are self-efficacy and leadership. Bandura[43] defines self-efficacy as "belief in one's capabilities to organise and execute the courses of action required to manage prospective situations". Self-efficacy influences how prepared the individual is for change in relation to initiating behaviour concerning the change, and the amount of persistence and effort the individual puts into the change during the various stages of the change process. Persistence may be required when obstacles occur during the change process and when persuasion and confidence-building is needed. Therefore, leadership is required.

---

[39] Iles & Sutherland's (2001) review of organisational change in the NHS explores different approaches to change management.
[40] Kotter (1996).
[41] Schyns (2004).
[42] Birgit Schyns undertook this work in the Netherlands.
[43] Bandura (1995).

The leader may be a change agent, colleague, supervisor or manager. Schyns' model assumes that perceived leadership, by any of those mentioned, influences self-efficacy through the mastery of the new skill. This is achieved through the supervisor allowing the employee to practice the skill under supervision and to take responsibility for the new skill. The second component of the model, vicarious learning, is achieved by coaching. Finally, the leader demonstrates the ability to persuade the individual that the change is necessary and that it will prove beneficial to him or her.

However, there are some limitations to the use of a change model and measurement tool, because successful implementation of change is mainly judged subjectively by the individuals involved, and may be viewed differently by each person. Also, views will be influenced by the achievement of personal goals, desired outcomes or perceptions on how the change will affect the social, cultural or economic aspects of the individuals' lives. However, the use of a model should assist in reducing subjectivity associated with any change.

MANAGING STRATEGIC CHANGE

Strategists, who may be middle or senior managers, must manage a number of factors during the process of executing change. A significant factor is the management of that part of the organisation's culture that is concerned with cultural artefacts, "those sets of attributes, objects and behaviours that help definitively to characterise one organisation as opposed to another".[44] If strategists do not manage existing cultural artefacts, such as key values, norms, rituals, ceremonies, language systems, myths about the organisation's successes or failures, and the use of physical design and space, the management of change will be unsuccessful as the existing strategy is fostered and nourished by current cultural artefacts.[45]

New organisational strategy will require a different cultural mind-set from its members. For example, if health service senior managers are introducing a new, organisation-wide strategy, and if the existing organisational culture is one of lack of involvement and non-recognition of clinician or non-clinician expertise, managers must provide employees with a renewed climate in which to work.[46,47] This will include a sense of purpose, clarity of mission and clear alignment of the new strategy with the goals, norms and values that the

---

[44] Higgins & McAllaster (2004).
[45] Shrivastava (1986).
[46] Carney (2004a).
[47] Carney (2004b).

organisation wishes to promote in the future. Engendering a sense of responsibility, accountability and commitment in each individual to the new strategy, through increased involvement in strategy development and in developing communication pathways to enhance consensus, often through different structures or processes, will assist the change process. This is particularly so in periods of turbulence.[48;49]

Through this process, cultural artefacts will be managed. It may be necessary to change cultural artefacts in order to provide greater accessibility and improved patient service delivery, but at a reduced financial cost to the organisation. The change management process in this situation will require a balancing of quality and cost-effectiveness that will allow health care professionals to view excellence in care delivery and cost-effectiveness as complementary to each other.

Values in Change

This change process will involve changing values-based cultural artefacts through an education programme that promotes excellence and cost-effectiveness in care delivery.[50] This process should not compromise individual existing values and norms, such as excellence, caring, integrity, trust and so on, but should reinforce the fact that it is possible to achieve health care efficiencies and effectiveness in tandem with high quality, best practice health care delivery. However, it is not possible to change strong value-laden organisations where clinicians and non-clinicians often see excellence in care delivery and cost-effectiveness on two ends of a care delivery continuum and, thus, culturally incompatible. Therefore, in the management of patient care, change is achieved through the recognition of the importance of the organisation's existing values and norms. In addition, through communication, group participation, leadership and education, managers should introduce the new strategy that will complement existing cultural artefacts, whilst also promoting the need for financial independence, efficient management and cost-effective care delivery.

---

[48]   Reilly, Brett & Stroh (1993).
[49]   Carney (2000).
[50]   Carney (2004b), p.15.

HOW MANAGERS PERCEIVE
ORGANISATIONAL CHANGE

Due to the large number of redundancies, de-layering and structural changes that have occurred in recent years, it is to be expected that managers' perceptions of change are likely to cause uncertainty and to produce adverse effects on individuals, on some more than others, and subsequently, on organisations.[51] As a result, resistance to change and failure to adapt to the change occurs.[52]

Redundancy causes fear and uncertainty in the individuals concerned and on the survivors who retain their jobs.[53] During the last decade, restructuring and de-layering has occurred, to a large extent, in British and US companies in a climate of cost-cutting and cultural change,[54] and has mainly affected "white collar workers and middle managers" in what Cascio[55] calls "the planned elimination of positions or jobs". In such cases, redundancy has had injurious effects to those who have lost their jobs and to the survivors of the redundancy programme. Therefore, those reduction-in-staff programmes have not delivered the expected results,[56] and many have resulted in the "survivor syndrome", which Littler, in a study of downsizing in three countries,[57] argues is related to a number of factors, such as workplace morale, commitment, motivation and job security and perceived future promotional prospects. A study undertaken on the effect of restructuring on employee's attitudes demonstrates that, if redundancy or re-structuring is imminent, employees become more interested in their future personal development than in loyalty to the organisation.

In an effort to study the impact of organisational change on managers, Worrall, Parkes & Cooper[58;59] undertook a survey of 830 British managers in order to determine whether various levels of managers perceive change in different ways and whether change affects the managers' perceptions of the organisation they work in. The findings of this research confirmed that managers did experience

---

[51] Ashford & Saks (2000).
[52] King & Anderson (2002).
[53] Kets de Vries & Balazs (1997).
[54] Worrall, Parkes & Cooper (2004).
[55] Cascio (2002b).
[56] Worrall, Parkes & Cooper (2004).
[57] Littler (2000).
[58] Worrall, Parkes & Cooper (2004).
[59] This study, undertaken in 2000, was based on the data of a four-year University of Manchester Institute of Science and Technology (UMIST)/Chartered Management Institute (CMI) research programme.

significant organisational changes; however, the directors viewed change in a more favourable light than the managers who were not directors. Managers also perceived that decision-making in the organisation slowed down, and were uncertain as to whether improved organisational performance followed the change. In addition, a culture of blame and harassment resulted and led to low morale and deterioration in the employee-employer relationship. The authors concluded that restructuring erodes the skill and knowledge base of organisations. However, following restructuring, tasks were cascaded down to lower level managers, who were unprepared for these new roles, but nevertheless were expected, often without training, to take on those roles and tasks. The authors further argued that human resources management is not practised to the extent it should be in redundancy or restructuring situations. Effective communication, that is open and honest, is necessary during the change initiative, and the processes and outcomes clearly communicated and understood by all staff.[60] Abrahamson[61] talks about "avoiding repetitive change syndrome" and advises that employees who have to live through repeated organisational change suffer most, in terms of low morale, cynicism, burn-out, initiative overload and change-related chaos. He also states that loss of trust in the organisation and poor working relationships occur and, therefore, that managers should continually monitor for these effects in the remaining workforce.

Managing Organisational Change

Employees are constantly being confronted with changing task demands as a result of changes occurring in the organisation. These changes may be structural in relation to hierarchy, or due to reduction in layers of management or to technological advances. Changes may also occur as a result of the introduction of new services and processes that require the employee to learn new skills or processes. Many studies related to organisational change have concentrated on how the manager or supervisor adapts to these change processes.[62,63]

Schyns[64] proposes that three main areas of occupational change are identifiable:

♦ Organisational change.
♦ Job change.

---

[60]   Tizard (2002).
[61]   Abrahamson (2004).
[62]   Armenakis, Harris & Field (1999).
[63]   Judge, Thoresen, Pucik & Welbourne (1999).
[64]   Schyns (2004).

♦ Task change.

Organisational change occurs with the restructuring of the organisation and is due to radical causes, such as environmental.[65] *Job* change requires a change in location, career change or simply a change within the existing organisation to a new position. *Task* change, the most frequent type of change, requires the learning of new tasks or skills. When organisations are contemplating change, they require employees who are willing to learn new skills and to adapt to changed tasks, technology or new ways to deliver innovative services. The employee must be willing to learn new skills, otherwise they will be left behind in terms of promotion or, at best, side-lined for career prospects following the change. Therefore, the employee must be prepared to learn a new skill,[66] as this influences and prepares them for the adaptation required, during and following the implementation of the change.[67;68]

Additionally, there are several measures that may be taken to influence the change process positively, and which help to promote a sense of ownership of the proposed change. These measures are centred on team-building, feedback techniques, integrating activities, such as workshops, process-consultation activities, symbolic leadership activities and enhanced interpersonal skills. The importance of participation, negotiation, education, facilitation and coaching during the process should be recognised.

Good practice examples for managing change, from previous change situations, define the establishment of a steering group involving clinicians and non-clinicians, who are perceived by colleagues as credible and trustworthy, to manage the change process. The support of senior organisational management is necessary to demonstrate to the workforce that the organisation is behind the successful implementation of the proposed change and is willing to devote considerable resources, including time and effort, to the change process. Emphasis on the adoption of an inclusion strategy that engages the widest range of employees possible, in addition to an open and transparent process that accepts all views uncritically, and where clarity regarding decision-making is evident, will ensure that communications are maintained throughout the process, thus leading to early adoption of the change by a "critical mass".[69;70]

---

[65]   Audia, Locke & Smith (2000).

[66]   Bandura (1977), p.193.

[67]   McDonald & Siegall (1992).

[68]   McDonald & Siegall (1996).

[69]   Office for Health Management (2003).

[70]   From the report, *Good Practice in Leading & Managing Change in Health Service Organisations*, based on 11 case studies and developed for the Office for Health Management, Irish Government, Dublin.

Support systems to support problem-solving may be needed, as well as active facilitators to map out, for managers and staff, the desired, possible and eventual change patterns that are emerging. Organisations should also be prepared to assist and educate their employees to take on new tasks, roles and processes and, thus, to increase self-efficacy.[71]

Following the introduction of the change, employees must be willing to adapt to, and cope with, the new change.[72] However, as Brodbeck & Rendisch[73] point out, leaders are themselves affected by organisational change, and their tasks may also change. Therefore, managers must ensure that all employees are prepared for the change.

HEALTH SERVICE CHANGE & MODEL EFFECTIVENESS

Health service change should encompass a whole system approach and should focus on staff working in health care organisations, on patients, and on the general public, who are the consumers of health care resources. Above all, introducing change process models that are deemed to be fashionable at the time should be avoided.

Models, such as the Content, Context and Process Model,[74] which is based on eight interlinking concepts, found that health care organisations were able to manage change, depending on the context in which the change was being introduced. However, when introduced in the health service, there was little evidence of a cause and effect relationship between the eight links. The Total Quality Management Model[75] found little evidence of empowerment or health status changes when introduced in the health services. The Business Process Re-engineering Model demonstrated that the top-down approach to re-engineering by management has not been successful in the health service culture. All of these models have been used to introduce change in health care, at various times, with limited success.[76]

Therefore, having a strategic vision for change is the cornerstone of change in an organisation. It is necessary for managers to create a

---

[71] Bloom & Sheerer (1992).
[72] Schyns (2004).
[73] Brodbeck & Remdisch (1993).
[74] This model is discussed in Pettigrew, A., Ferlie, E., & McKee, L. (1992). *Shaping Strategic Change*, London: Sage Publications.
[75] This model was evaluated by Joss, R. & Kogan, M. (1995). *Advancing Quality: Total Quality Management in the NHS*, Milton Keynes: Open University Press.
[76] Office for Health Management (2003), p.12.

vision of the future both for, and with, individuals. Effective change requires clearly-articulated values and a common purpose. Structured implementation planning with specific, realistic time frames and identifiable milestones, throughout the period of change, with a focus on outcomes, is necessary, as well as a clear human resource strategy, allied to investment in leadership and management training. Developing staff capability and then developing the technology required to implement organisational change, in addition to the dissemination of information related to quality control frameworks will assist the change process. Ensuring that system-wide controls are in place will guarantee that service improvements are achieved, monitored and maintained.

In addition to the identification of change agents required to facilitate the change process, central organisational leadership during the change process is also necessary, so that local ownership of the change is promoted. This will also serve to sustain change within local areas. Clarity in relation to focusing on improvements and innovative practices and on the outcomes expected will ensure that the changes have resonance and meaning for all involved.[77]

Management of Major Structural Change in the NHS

A study on the management of major structural change in the NHS[78] explored how learning from UK experiences can assist in strategic planning and organisational development in the context of the Irish health service. The authors found that local training and development programmes are required to assist staff with the technology changes being introduced, or in new process changes; therefore, considerable financial investment is necessary. There is a strong need for practical support from managers and change agents throughout the change process and recognition from them that individual effort is appreciated. The change process will benefit from priority targeting of key change areas and the transparent communicating of each step in the process.

The human resources aspects of the change must be actively managed, including the training of staff in order to ensure the development of future managers and leaders, and to encourage local ownership of the change being introduced. Leadership programmes that place emphasis on action-oriented approaches to learning, and that encourage working in inter-professional and multi-disciplinary teams, will assist the change process. It is important to promote the desired norms and practices expected, whilst simultaneously shifting

---

77   Office for Health Management, April 2003.
78   Office for Health Management (2003), p.15.

old practices to the side; however, there is also a need for local interpretation of change and time frames, within acceptable boundaries. Outcomes expected from the introduction of change need to be consistently reinforced, otherwise the focus remains on the process of change, rather than on desired outcomes.

The recognition that different groups of staff require different levels of development is necessary. Some staff will require specific skills training delivered through task-specific facilitation groups, while others will require management techniques and leadership training. Managers must ensure that staff are coached, facilitated to develop the necessary skills required to manage the change and that a mentorship programme is put into place to facilitate staff and enhance morale during the transition phase of the change and beyond. This will be supported by a management style that is facilitative, collaborative and co-operative during the change process, rather than hierarchical and controlling. In order to encourage dissemination, networking of best practice examples will encourage a culture of excellence.

The effects of change on patient care require monitoring. Clinicians should be involved in the process of change and reform from the start, and patients' rights must be protected throughout the process. In order to ensure professional and accountable practice, staff responsibilities should be promoted and defined. Multi-professional and multi-agency team working is necessary in order to ensure cohesion across the system, as team working will exploit the potential for networks of care. Regular communication and feedback with clinicians and non-clinicians will maintain momentum and enthusiasm for the change. Therefore, change agents or project managers play a vital part in managing communications throughout.[79]

---

[79]   Office for Health Management (2003), p. 20.

SUMMARY

- Health care managers may not always accept change, but they must learn to manage it.

- In order to manage change effectively and positively, both leadership and management skills are required, particularly in a volatile environment. The change process is deductive, about managing complexity and is often undertaken in order to prevent a more chaotic reality than that presently in force.

- When a model is used to guide change, consistency in approach can be achieved as the model serves to direct, guide and make sense of the change process.

- The communication process during transition consists of several key variables including consultation, education, participation, assertiveness, negotiation, understanding of change dynamics, and democratic decision-making.

- The transition period is one of low stability and high stress where undirected energy may lead to the derailing of the change process.

- Often, resistance to change arises because individuals prefer the old way of doing things and fear the consequences of change.

- If strategists do not manage existing cultural artefacts, such as key values and norms, the management of change will be unsuccessful, because the existing strategy is fostered and nourished by current cultural artefacts.

- It is not possible to change strong value-laden organisations where clinicians and non-clinicians often see excellence in care delivery and cost-effectiveness as two ends of a care delivery continuum, and thus, culturally incompatible.

- Change caused by redundancy has had injurious effects to those who have lost their jobs and to the survivors of the redundancy programme, and consequently, those reduction-in-staff programmes have not delivered the expected results.

- Health service change should involve a whole system approach and should focus on staff working in health care organisations, on patients, and on the general public who are the consumers of health care resources.

- Leadership programmes that emphasise action-oriented approaches to learning that encourage working in inter-professional and multi-disciplinary teams are required during change.

CHAPTER 8
LEADERSHIP FOR THE FUTURE

INTRODUCTION

Chapter 4 showed that the effects of restructuring on health service organisations and on health professionals has resulted in changes in the manner in which health care is delivered and on the collaborative process. These changes challenge the professionals' *modus operandi* and have resulted in managers working in professional organisations requiring management skills in addition to leadership skills. **Chapter 7** demonstrated that, in order to manage change effectively and positively, both leadership and management skills are required, particularly in a volatile environment, and, as the change process is deductive and about managing complexity, health service managers must possess the leadership skills required to bring followers into the new reality. This chapter explores leadership dynamics.

LEADERSHIP STATUS IN HEALTH CARE

Health care is being delivered through frequent change.[1] Patients are increasingly seeking information and choice regarding their health and exhibit higher expectations of health status than ever before; they demonstrate this choice by not tolerating old ways of providing care.[2] The economic challenges facing all health care organisations require them to be creative in designing strategies to select and develop managers who will become successful leaders by collaborating and co-ordinating with others to meet the needs of the wider organisation and community.[3] Professional organisations, likewise, are seeking professionals who have the knowledge and skills to lead their members into the future. Thus, managers require leadership skills that provide direction for health care organisations for the future.

It appears from the literature that there is a shortage of leadership skills in health care.[4,5] Carney[6] identifies the dearth of leadership skills

---

[1] Porter-O'Grady (1992).
[2] Leahy & Wiley (1998).
[3] Edwards (1996).
[4] Carney (1999).

existing among Irish nurses and Clarke[7] notes the shortage of leaders, and of leadership, in Canadian health care. Mahoney[8] suggests that, in order to have a voice in health care policy formulation, nurses in the US need to develop leadership skills and to assume leadership positions. The contemporary crisis in health professional leadership is due to a number of factors, including a litigious public, a more informed consumer, and the focus on cost-effectiveness.[9] This more knowledgeable and demanding public has led to the almost extinction of the "grateful society of patients", wherein the recipients of public service, including health care, were expected to be grateful for any help that they received. In discussing health care delivery in the US, McDaniel & Wolfe[10] suggest that there is a need for leaders who are multi-dimensional in orientation and who promote shared leadership and decision-making within their organisations and their professions. Managers also need to tap into the creative potential of their staff in order to survive in a competitive environment because creativity and innovation will ensure the survival of the organisation.[11]

DEFINING LEADERSHIP

Given the amount of attention devoted to leadership, one might expect that there would be common agreement amongst scholars regarding its definition. However, this is not the case; as noted by Stogdill,[12] there appears to be almost as many definitions as there are researchers in the field. In addition, there are as many definitions of leadership as there are theories of leadership, although the following definition appears to be appropriate:

> Anytime a person is a recognised authority and has followers who count on this person's expertise to carry out their objectives, the person is a leader.[13]

Or, alternatively, a leader is anyone who is responsible for giving assistance to others.[14] Effective leadership is defined as empowering

---

5   Mahoney (2001).
6   Carney (1999).
7   Clarke (2000).
8   Mahoney (2001).
9   Carney (1999).
10   McDaniel & Wolf (1992).
11   Carney (2002a).
12   Stogdill (1974).
13   Mahoney (2001), p.269.
14   La Monica (1994).

employees to produce extraordinary things in the face of challenge, turbulence and change.[15] Leadership has been defined in terms of group and social influence processes, trait and personality characteristics, the result of certain types of behaviour, and as the means to achieve organisational goals. As a result of this proliferation of the definition of the concept of leadership, Pfeffer[16] noted that our understanding is somewhat confused and ambiguous.

Leadership Theories

During the past century, the more dominant approaches have focused on three areas:

♦ Traits or personality of the leader.

♦ Behaviour or style of the leader

♦ The situational or contingency approach of the leader.

Researchers cast doubts on these theories,[17;18] as the measurement of traits used in these studies may have been suspect and, since then, other researchers have demonstrated that leader traits, such as flexibility, emotional competence and social sensitivity, may indeed be indicators of emerging leader behaviour.[19;20;21]

Researchers in the 1960s focused on observable behaviour or style and leader effectiveness. The research conducted by Lewin and his colleagues identified three styles of leadership, namely autocratic, democratic and *laissez faire*.[22;23] Dimensions of leadership were then explored in Ohio State University, where two different forms of behaviour were identified:

♦ Initiating behaviour, whereby the leader structured the work to be undertaken.

---

[15] Malloch & Porter-O'Grady (2006).

[16] Pfeffer (1977).

[17] Stogdill (1974).

[18] Bass & Avolio (1990).

[19] Zaccaro, Foti & Kenny (1991).

[20] Porter-O'Grady & Malloch (2002).

[21] Zaccaro *et al*. (1991), in a study of the relationship between interpersonal sensitivity and perceived leader status, found that 59% of the variance in leader emergence was trait-based.

[22] Lewin, Lippitt & White (1939).

[23] Lewin, Lippitt & White (1939) carried out their study through observation, under the auspices of the Iowa Childhood Studies. The researchers were interested in examining the effects of two different styles of leadership behaviour, autocratic and democratic, on young boys who were club members.

♦ Consideration behaviour, whereby friendliness and concern was demonstrated by the leader towards those undertaking the work.[24]

At this time, similar research was also being undertaken in the University of Michigan,[25] focusing on employee-centred leadership *versus* production-centred leadership. These early leadership studies, whilst not living up to their potential in terms of leader traits and leader behaviour, did set the scene for new forms, such as transactional and transformational leadership, that incorporate behaviours, such as empowerment and charisma, and which have proved to be more enduring than the early leader research.[26]

Between the mid-1960s and the late 1970s, leadership research focused on the situational or contingency approaches to leader behaviour,[27] whereby a leader's effectiveness was deemed to depend on the appropriateness of the fit between the task to be undertaken by the leader or the relationship existing between the leader and employees and the favourableness of the situation for the leader. Task-oriented leaders tend to be more effective when the situation they face is structured and good leader-employee relationships exists. The other studies centred on House's approach to leadership,[28] termed the path-goal approach, which focused on the interaction of leadership behaviours and situational factors. This theory assumes that effective leaders motivate by clarifying the paths to be taken so that goals are achieved and by ensuring that employees are rewarded for achieving these goals. These studies received mixed support from researchers.[29]

Following on from this, Kerr & Jermier[30] investigated whether leadership substitutes or potential moderators of leader behaviour, such as employees' abilities, knowledge and experience, task routine or expertise and organisational structures were capable of counteracting the leader's behaviour, thereby making it impossible for the leader behaviour to have any effect on employee performance. Although appearing to show promising early results, further research into the area of leader substitutes did not prove promising and few of the substitutes variables presented by Kerr & Jermier were found to moderate the relationship between the leader behaviours and these employee characteristics.[31,32]

---

24   Stogdill (1974).
25   Kahn & Katz (1978).
26   House & Podsakoff (1994).
27   Fiedler (1967).
28   House & Mitchell (1974).
29   House & Podsakoff (1994).
30   Kerr & Jermier (1978).
31   Howell, Dorfman & Kerr (1986).
32   Podsakoff, Toder & Schuler (1983).

However, none of these theories address the effects of leaders on employees' values, preferences, or intrinsic motivation. How leaders affect the total organisation or the organisational environment is unknown.[33] Disenchantment with leadership research occurred in the 1970s as a result of disappointing results from empirical studies undertaken in these areas.

Leadership: A New Focus

However, in the 1980s, leadership research took on a new focus, centring on how leaders can have an effect on the aspirations, motives and commitment of employees or followers. This research included leader charisma,[34,35] transactional leadership,[36] transformational leadership[37] and visionary leadership theory.[38] All of this research explores the emotional attachment of the follower to the leader, emphasising the inspirational, visionary and charismatic qualities of the leader, which appeal to the value-based system of the follower, in a positive manner, and infuse the follower with ideology, loyalty to the leader, values and moral purpose that the follower recognises, aspires to and, therefore, buys into. As a result, this leadership approach induces strong levels of commitment by the follower to the leader. House & Podsakoff[39] refer to this form of leadership as outstanding leadership that produces positive effects on the follower. Followers of outstanding leaders become committed to the vision of the leader through shared values and, as a result of this commitment, both leader and follower experience a sense of urgency to achieve goals. Work becomes more fulfilling and meaningful and the follower experiences a sense of self-worth and a perception of being appreciated for effort.

There is a motivational dimension to the charismatic leader. Charismatic leaders raise followers' awareness of the important values that both aspire to, thus allowing them to identify with the vision, mission and philosophy put forward by the leader, and thereby becoming committed to the collective objectives and goals of the organisation, rather than to their own interests.[40] Deeply-held views of individuals are shared with the leader and, in the process, followers become committed to the vision and mission specified by the leader.[41]

---

[33] House & Podsakoff (1994).
[34] House (1977).
[35] Conger & Kanungo (1987).
[36] Bass (1985).
[37] Burns (1978).
[38] Sashkin & Fulmer (1988).
[39] House & Podsakoff (1994).
[40] Carney (2006b).
[41] House & Shamir (1993), pp. 84.

Equally, the leader, through role modelling, allows the followers to pursue the vision articulated by the leader for the organisation, as leaders articulate a vision that describes a better future for the follower, but, in doing so, they demand a high degree of commitment, trust and confidence from their followers. Additionally, leaders display a high degree of confidence in their own abilities and have high self-esteem but they also recognise that their followers must perceive them to be credible, competent and trustworthy.[42] Therefore, future health care leaders will require vision and the capability to empower and support followers.

TRANSFORMATIONAL, CHARISMATIC & VISIONARY LEADERSHIP

Transformational and transactional leadership styles historically were defined as relations-oriented *versus* task-oriented[43] and participative *versus* directive, and as being located at the opposite ends of a continuum.[44] However, transformational and transactional styles were also viewed as distinct entities, allowing a leader to be both simultaneously or neither.[45] There has been some convergence and agreement during the past two decades, related to a new genre of leadership theories collectively called transformational leadership, charismatic leadership and visionary leadership.[46] Charismatic, inspirational and visionary leader behaviour demonstrates many of the qualities of transactional leadership, such as providing intellectual stimulation and inspiring confidence in followers.[47]

The leadership model developed by Bass & Avolio[48] differentiates between transactional and transformational models of leadership behaviour. Transactional leaders exert influence on employees by goal-setting, clarifying outcomes and providing relevant feedback[49] that, in the process, offers rewards such as job promotion in exchange for work accomplished or for demonstrating loyalty to the organisation. In contrast, transformational leaders exert additional influence by instilling a sense of confidence in employees that permits a higher achievement level than expected.

---

[42] Chen, Beck & Amos (2005).
[43] Fiedler (1967).
[44] Burns (1978).
[45] Bass (1998).
[46] House & Shamir (1993), p.84.
[47] Westley & Mintzberg (1989).
[48] Bass & Avolio (1990).
[49] House & Mitchell (1974).

Transformational leaders treat employees with consideration and, through charismatic behaviours, arouse inspirational motivation and provide intellectual stimulation in the process.[50] Transformational leaders develop followers through providing them with further responsibilities, and by having the confidence in them to fulfil those duties with self-assurance and inspiration.[51] In contrast, transactional leaders do not expect employees to undertake additional responsibilities or to develop themselves or followers further, but to agree to pre-set goals and objectives, and to undertake work to an acceptable, but not outstanding, level.[52]

Follower behaviour is defined in terms of the best style of follower. The best followers are those who think for themselves, give constructive criticism and are innovative and charismatic in their approach to work.[53] Followers are actively engaged in the task and, when undertaking the task, go above and beyond that which the job requires. Transformational leadership enhances empowerment among the leader's direct followers, whilst having the ability to empower followers.[54]

Exercising Empowerment & Power

To empower is to enable, to invest with power, to licence, to impart power. To enable means to empower, to authorise to make possible. Power, in contrast, is having the capacity to influence other people or the course of events, or a right, authority or control over another person.[55] It is necessary to analyse the concept of power and empowerment in order to clarify the meaning of empowerment, because, as Chandler[56] asserts, the two terms have different meanings. Previous sentences appear to indicate that the terms are synonymous but this is not necessarily so. Empowerment is the transfer of power, from the self to another person, in a manner that allows for the development of positive self-esteem and value in the other, and where authority is delegated and power is shared.[57] The qualities of the empowered nurse have been identified; these include moral principles that are based on respect and personal integrity, acknowledged as mastery over one's life, demonstrating courage, tenacity, self-esteem and expertise. Expertise is associated with the esteem given to one's

---

50   Bass & Avolio (1990).
51   Avolio & Gibbons (1988).
52   Bass (1985).
53   Kelley (1992).
54   Dvir, Eden, Avolio & Shamir (2002).
55   Soanes (2003).
56   Chandler (1991).
57   Rodwell (1996).

work. Other qualities involve innovation, creativity and sociability as demonstrated by social skills and flexibility in the workplace.[58;59]

Power, in contrast, as defined above, is perceived as control over another person. The real source of manager power dwells within the individual, in his or her knowledge and skills and the strength of his or her personality, and not from the authority that the organisation confers on the position of manager. Managers should exercise their power and authority in a manner that is appropriate to the situation. Senior and middle managers could possess a high need for power, but this power is used effectively through influencing others, and such managers should, in the exercise of power, be disciplined and controlled in ensuring that power is directed towards the benefit of the organisation and not for their own personal gain.[60] The real essence of power is based on a bottom-up rather than top-down approach, as power and the exercising of power merge together within empowerment. When empowerment is present, productivity and effectiveness increases within the organisation.[61] Transformational leadership emphasises the development of followers and promotes autonomy and empowerment.[62]

LEADERSHIP SKILLS FOR THE 21ST CENTURY?

Health service managers require new forms of leadership for the 21st century, including collaborative shared and co-operative forms that are multi-dimensional in orientation and innovative and creative in change, and that are capable of displaying team empowerment and organisational leadership. An examination of the leadership theories presented above highlights the fact that leadership concerns discovering the route ahead and involves encouraging and inspiring others to follow. Hence, leadership is most needed in changing times when the way ahead is not clear. Lorentzon & Bryant[63] contend that nursing leadership in the early part of the 20th century was characterised by autocratic, vocational, religious and military-style ideas and ideals. This led to medical dominance over nursing and nursing education that survived into the late 20th century.[64;65] A new

---

[58] Kuokkanen & Leino-Kilpi (2001).
[59] This study by Kuokkanen & Leino-Kilpo (2001) was undertaken in Finland and involved 30 nurses who participated in semi-structured interviews.
[60] McClelland & Burnham (2003), p.118.
[61] Kuokkanen & Leino-Kilpi (2001).
[62] Bass & Avolio (1990).
[63] Lorentzon & Bryant (1977).
[64] Henneman, Lee & Cohen (1995).
[65] Carney (2005).

style of leadership management, based on collaboration, wherein the relationships between those involved is non-hierarchical and power is shared,[66] is now emerging within nursing and other health care professions.

Identifying Leaders for the Future

It is recognised that choosing the "right" leader is not an easy task for the organisation, because, for example, superior problem-solving or decision-making capabilities can mask a deficiency in strategic thinking or in long-range conceptual thinking, and may indicate over-reliance on policies and procedures. Also, the "halo" effect, whereby certain skills or attributes perceived to be present in the prospective leader/manager are overvalued and others are undervalued. Senior managers might, for example, be drawn to the prospective manager's operational efficiency and overlook the deficiency in strategic management skills, or the ability to function in ill-defined, ambiguous situations, all of which may be a vital component of the leader/manager role. Additionally, a perceived lack of ambition can be misjudged by senior managers, as many leaders are modest and display little ambition and may, in fact, display a high degree of humility that is "far more evident among exceptional leaders than is raw ambition".[67]

To assess leadership potential requires skill and confidence; thus, in order to assess leader capability, senior managers should consider a range of leadership criteria including evidence of knowledge and skills, including so-called "soft" skills, such as trust and integrity. Also, senior managers should not be fearful in choosing a leader who may be different, if the role requires, and should not feel threatened by a new leader who is more skilled and has more experience than themselves. Close mentoring of the new leader is not always the best approach for the senior manager to take, as many excellent leaders prefer to select strong people and then to delegate fully to them. This approach allows the new leader to grow through their experiences in the new role.[68]

The leader should have vision and be able to function in a team and reach consensus decisions. But equally, the leader must be capable of acting and standing alone, and of making unilateral decisions when required, thereby possessing risk-taking ability.

---

[66] Henneman, Lee & Cohen (1995).
[67] Henneman, Lee & Cohen (1995), p.82.
[68] Henneman, Lee & Cohen (1995).

Developing Leadership Ability: A Question-based Tool

Organisations often rely on developing leadership ability in new managers, rather than on accurately identifying the potential leader in the first place. There is no doubt that leadership programmes are capable of producing better managers. However, Sorcher & Brant[69;70] question the ability of these programmes to produce leaders and suggest a question-based tool for evaluating potential leadership ability within existing employees or managers, although they caution that this is an imperfect process.

In order to assess a person's capacity to lead using this tool, a group-based evaluation takes place. The group involves the individual's manager and several other persons who have worked directly with the candidate. The leader of the discussion then probes the candidate's characteristics and behaviour by asking the group a set of questions that covers such areas as describing the candidate's integrity with, for example, a question that probes whether the candidate stands firm in his or her opinions or moves with the wind of politics. A second area probes how the candidate communicates information and expectations. Further sets of questions explore how the candidate reasons and analyses issues and how he/she runs his/her immediate work team. Other questions elicit information, for example, regarding the candidate's logical ability, how sound judgement is demonstrated and how the candidate works with individuals who have different styles and skills to the leader.

Organisational Climate

Organisational climate, as opposed to organisational culture that measures employees' beliefs and values, is viewed as a set of measurable properties of the work environment, that are perceived by staff who work in this environment to influence their motivation and behaviour.[71] A study by Mok & Au-Yeung,[72;73] found that certain factors existing in the organisation's climate were perceived as increasing feelings of empowerment. These factors are good communications and harmonious working relations, allied to challenges that incorporate the setting of high standards and goals and

---

69   Henneman, Lee & Cohen (1995).
70   Sorcher & Brant (2002) interviewed a large number of chief executive officers and
     other managers working with large organisations in the US since the 1980s.
71   Litwin & Stringer (1974).
72   Mok & Au-Yeung (2002).
73   This survey, undertaken in Hong Kong, amongst 331 nurses, examined the
     relationship of organisational climate and perceptions of empowerment, using
     factor analysis and multiple regression analysis.

defined performance standards. Further factors relate to management recognition for work output and, as a consequence, pride in being part of the organisation.

Organisational structure influences perceptions of empowerment by the presence of formal organisational charts and participative decision-making. In particular, manager-supportive leadership that values teamwork increases perceptions of empowerment. Feelings of empowerment are most likely to occur in work groups where the leader of the group is perceived as being supportive.[74] In a climate of health care delivery re-structuring, nurse managers are required to understand the social processes at play and to promote a climate that is conducive to strong leadership.[75] Thus, in order to do this, managers should examine the type of organisational climate that serves to promote or to inhibit empowerment.[76]

Contemporary Leadership Perspectives

In the future, different types of leaders will emerge to lead health care.[77,78] New leaders will require the ability to use more influence and less power and authority than before, in order to ensure a smooth flow of co-operative effective activity.[79] Key future leadership skills include having the capacity to motivate, coach, facilitate and negotiate.

A future leadership type is strategic leadership, which varies from leadership, in that leadership may refer to leaders at any level in the organisation, whilst strategic leadership refers to leaders at the top of the organisation.[80] Strategic leadership has also been found in leaders at middle level.[81]

Strategic leaders are crucial to the organisation's success, due to the decisions they are empowered to make,[82] and, therefore, they guide organisational learning[83] through the process of change in thought and action that involves incorporating new and old learning[84] and, in the process, leaders adopt both transformational and transactional leadership.[85]

---

[74] Kennedy (2005).
[75] Mok & Au-Yeung (2002).
[76] Laschinger, Wong, McMahon & Kaufmann (1999).
[77] Jooste (2004).
[78] This author used a conceptual framework, with departure as the key concept.
[79] Chapman (2001).
[80] Hambrick & Pettigrew (2001).
[81] Carney (2002a).
[82] Hambrick (1989).
[83] Lahteenmaki, Toivonen & Mattila (2001).
[84] Crossan, Lane & White (1999).
[85] Vera & Crossan (2004).

Acquisition of Leader Effectiveness Leadership Skills

Effective leadership is associated with more ethical behaviour, job satisfaction and, in a climate of organisational change, effective leaders produce desirable outcomes for employees.[86] Effective leadership also leads to patient satisfaction and is a requirement for effective care delivery.[87;88] Leadership effectiveness requires cohesiveness in thinking and lack of divisiveness in strategy development,[89;90] behaviours found to be lacking amongst clinicians and non-clinicians during health care strategy development.[91]

Leadership behaviour that focuses on the five behaviours identified by Kouzes & Posner[92] is appropriate for effective health care management. The first two leader behaviours are *challenging the process*, meaning that leaders are willing to seek out new opportunities to improve the manner in which the organisation is run, and *enabling others to act*, through skills development and acquisition and further education. The next leader behaviour is *inspiring a shared vision of the mission, goals and objectives of the organisation* and thereby influencing job satisfaction and organisational commitment in staff. *Modelling the way*, a further leader behaviour, means that health care leaders promote and deliver best practice care delivery and, therefore, set example by action, again leading to job satisfaction, effective care delivery and organisational commitment. Finally, the leader behaviour of *encouraging the heart*, through providing due recognition for work achieved, and instilling a sense of organisational commitment in employees is also necessary in modern health care delivery.[93]

Facilitators & Barriers

Facilitators and barriers influence leader effectiveness. Facilitators that enhance leadership effectiveness include changes to the economic environment whereby additional funding is provided for health care,[94] changes to health care strategy that is driven by health and social gain,[95] and academic institutions that promote health education.[96;97]

---

[86] McNeese-Smith (1995).
[87] Chiok Foong Loke (2001).
[88] This study by Chiok Foong Loke (2001) explored leadership behaviour and outcomes for nurses in a study undertaken with 18 nurses in Singapore.
[89] Chan & Cheng (1999).
[90] Masterson & Maslin-Prothero (1999).
[91] Carney (2004a).
[92] Kouzes & Posner (1995).
[93] Chiok Foong Loke (2001).
[94] Chan (2002).
[95] Department of Health (UK) (2002a).
[96] Chan (2002).

Barriers that hinder leadership effectiveness include dominance by a group of clinicians seeking to exercise control over perceived weaker clinician groups[98] and control over scarce resources by powerful groups over weaker groups.[99] Academic institutions are a major facilitating power in the development of leadership skills and knowledge but, conversely, lack of such educational opportunities are barriers to leadership effectiveness in the clinician groups affected.[100] Therefore, clinicians should identify the barriers and facilitators existing in the environment that influence or hinder effective leadership, and take steps to modify or overcome these barriers, thus exploiting further the facilitators that enhance leadership effectiveness.

Acquisition of Leadership Skills through Education

Leadership skills are acquired through education. This acquisition may be obtained through attendance at dedicated leadership and management programmes, continuing education seminars and particularly, through bachelor's and master's degree programmes, where leadership, management and administration are major components of the curriculum.

Grant, Boyle & Massey,[101] in setting out the functions of the leader, highlight certain leadership skills. These skills include acting as role models for other professionals, providing expert care based on theory and research and influencing organisational policy. Leadership means providing health care through a collaborative and ethical process that uses advocacy to effect change for the benefit of patients and the organisation. However, leadership skills need to be learned and developed over time through practice. Education for leadership also includes the wider aspects of management and administration that are currently part of master's degree programmes for health care professionals. These skills include clinical budgeting, health care economics and financial management, in addition to the management of human resources, organisations and strategy. Skills required are teamwork, managing change and communications, as well as research for evidence-based clinical outcomes. Carney[102] found that clinicians often felt intimidated by "management jargon" introduced by non-clinicians and, as a result, avoided discussion on important issues or

---

[97]   Chan's (2002) study, undertaken in Hong Kong, investigates the factors that influence the effectiveness of nursing leadership and was undertaken through a single case study method.

[98]   Davies (1995).

[99]   Manojlovich (2005).

[100] Chan (2002).

[101] Grant, Boyle & Massey (1999).

[102] Carney (2002a).

practised non-attendance at management meetings. Therefore, the acquisition of such skills allow clinicians and non-clinicians to understand "management speak" and, thereby, become patient advocates.

Additionally, from an organisational perspective, leaders require the ability to form network groups and strategic alliances with other health care groupings within the organisation and externally, with professional organisations, in order to maintain evidence-based research practices and to enhance organisational learning. Professional nursing and medicine standards and accreditation processes allow for self–regulation whilst, on the other hand, allowing for control over practice. This often results in professional tensions.[103] Professionals should be educated to develop creative, independent and interdependent skills that permit them to use their professional academic knowledge to work with other health care professionals and thus to influence health care decisions and strategy.[104]

Team Empowerment

Team empowerment also occurs and the make-up of various teams, such as project, management and work teams, demonstrate different performance drivers. For example, autonomy has been linked to performance in permanent work teams, although this has not been found to be the case in project teams where group work is important.[105]

Team empowerment is defined as the increased task motivation due to the team members' collective, positive assessments of their organisational tasks.[106] Empowerment in teams arises because team members perceive that the team is effective, that the work being undertaken is meaningful, that they have the power to make decisions and because their work makes a positive contribution to the organisation. In addition, the more often teams meet, the more highly empowered team members are, and the more likely the members are to make complex decisions without waiting for managerial approval, whereas teams that meet infrequently become passive and are more likely to refer to their managers for direction. Therefore, face-to-face interaction and regular meetings are important factors in influencing empowerment in teams.[107;108]

---

103 Falk & Adeline (1999).
104 Calpin-Davies (2003).
105 Cohen & Bailey (1997), p.245.
106 Kirkman & Rosen (2000).
107 Kirkman, Rosen, Tesluk & Gibson (2004).
108 This field study, undertaken by Kirkman, Rosen, Tesluk & Gibson (2004), to test the direct effect of team empowerment on virtual teams (those that met

Following on from **Chapter 7**, it is evident that change provides the opportunity for managers to exercise leadership in health service organisations. Change allows increased sensitivity to customer needs. Change leaders will become the most sought-after people in the new world of health care.[109] The change leader intuitively must spot early trends in health care management and assist staff in understanding these changing trends. In addition, the change leader must provide the vision and reassurance that positive change can be achieved and, in the process, must enable others to feel excited, empowered and enriched by the change. Accordingly, it follows from this that change leaders must be inquisitive thinkers capable of challenging the *status quo* and must possess the mental agility to visualise new possibilities, to conceptualise these possibilities and to think across boundaries. Mahoney[110] suggests that nursing administrators, educators and clinicians have the responsibility of keeping abreast of the rapidly-changing health care environment and making changes proactively. This responsibility implies that the climate existing in the organisation has an impact on empowerment practices. Therefore, health service managers have a responsibility to identify these factors and to act accordingly.

SUMMARY

♦ Managers require leadership skills that provide direction for health care organisations for the future.

♦ A litigious public, a more informed consumer, and the focus on cost-effectiveness in health care delivery have resulted in a crisis in health professional leadership.

♦ Any time a person is a recognised authority and has followers who count on this person's expertise to carry out their objectives, that person is a leader.

♦ Forms of leadership behaviour, such as transactional and transformational leadership, that incorporate behaviours, such as empowerment and charisma, have proved to be more enduring than early leader research.

♦ Leaders articulate a vision that describes a better future for the follower but, in doing so, they demand a high degree of commitment, trust and confidence from their followers.

---

infrequently), involved 280 team members, representing 35 teams, who responded to a survey.

[109] Kerfoot (1996).

[110] Mahoney (2001).

Charismatic, inspirational and visionary leader behaviour demonstrates many of the qualities of transactional leadership, such as providing intellectual stimulation and inspiring confidence in followers.

♦ Empowerment is the transfer of power from the self to another person in a manner that allows for the development of positive self-esteem and value in the other. Empowerment is present where good communications and harmonious working relations are allied to challenges that incorporate the setting of high standards and goals and defined performance standards.

♦ The leader is required to have vision, to be able to function in a team and reach consensus decisions. But equally, the leader must be capable of acting, standing alone, and of making unilateral decisions when required, thereby possessing risk-taking ability. Leadership effectiveness requires cohesiveness in thinking and a lack of divisiveness in strategy development.

♦ Barriers found to hinder leadership effectiveness include dominance by a group who seek to exercise control over perceived weaker groups, as well as control over scarce resources by powerful groups over weaker groups.

CHAPTER 9
MOTIVATION FOR HEALTH PROFESSIONAL MANAGERS

INTRODUCTION

It was evident in **Chapters 6 & 7** that relationship collaboration requires managers to change communication patterns constantly, as circumstances and processes undergo change and evolution. The path-goal theory outlined in **Chapter 8** assumes that effective leaders motivate by clarifying the paths to be taken so that goals are achieved; that there is a motivational dimension to the charismatic leader; and that new directions centre on the manner in which leaders are capable of affecting the motives of followers. Therefore, key future leadership skills for managers include having the capacity to motivate, coach, facilitate and negotiate. Chapter 9 presents motivational theories and techniques, the pathways to achieving job satisfaction and motivation, and an exploration of how managers inspire ordinary employees to do extraordinary things.

SOURCES OF EMPLOYEE MOTIVATION

Management success has been linked to motivation. However, as Frederick Herzberg[1] acknowledges, what has been unravelled about the psychology of motivation is small. In the 1950s and 1960s, Herzberg examined the sources of employee motivation amongst professional mangers. Herzberg's research, which has been replicated and corroborated by other investigators, involved 12 different investigations and 1,685 employees, from which 1,753 events experienced by professionals on the job were characterised. The findings of this research indicated that the work factors that make employees satisfied at work are not necessarily the factors that make them dissatisfied.

Herzberg found that factors intrinsic to the job, such as achievement, recognition, the work itself, responsibility, advancement and growth, if managed appropriately, lead to job satisfaction and

---

[1]   Herzberg (2003).

motivation. Conversely, Herzberg[2] found, in exploring 1,753 events on the job with the same group, that, if certain factors are managed inappropriately, this will lead to dissatisfaction and de-motivation. These factors are organisational policy and management, supervision, relationship with supervisor, work conditions, salary, relationship with peers, personal life, relationship with subordinates, status and security. Herzberg termed these "hygiene factors". Thus, motivating factors are the primary cause of satisfaction and motivation in the job, and hygiene factors are the primary causes of unhappiness and dissatisfaction in the job. This motivation-hygiene theory suggests that work may be enriched in order to bring about job satisfaction and subsequent effective utilisation of personnel in the work place. Drucker[3] adds to this thesis by maintaining that positive motivators are high standards of performance, the provision of information that is adequate for self-control, in addition to, participation as a responsible employee.

If employees perceive that their work is challenging and interesting, and if they are provided with a high level of responsibility by their organisation, they will be motivated to work. This motivation level will be achieved through employees translating the meaning of work into consistent thought patterns or habits of mind. Through this process, health care managers become experts in directing the way they think about, react to and respond to the complex situations encountered in today's challenging environment. This is termed "habits of mind" by Seligman in his work on learned optimism. Mackoff & Wenet, whose research was undertaken with 65 US leaders and drew on Seligman's work related to resilience,[4] term this process "inner work".

Achieving Job Satisfaction & Motivation

There has been much discussion on methods to achieve job satisfaction and motivation, which include job enrichment, job rotation and job loading. Job *enrichment* provides opportunities for the employees' psychological growth, such as providing more responsibility and accountability and less supervision and checking of the employees' work. Job *rotation* simply replaces one boring work role with another, in the mistaken belief that rotating provides job satisfaction. The original form of job *loading*, termed horizontal job loading, involved increasing the number of times an employee undertakes the same task. This form merely increased the meaninglessness of the work roles, as

---

[2]   Herzberg (2003).

[3]   Drucker (1989).

[4]   Mackoff & Wenet (2005), p.xi.

indeed, also occurred with job rotation. Herzberg[5] proposes a new form of motivator termed vertical job loading. Vertical job loading involves certain work principles, such as increasing the accountability of individuals for their own work or providing a complete unit, module or area of work that, in turn, provides the employee with the motivating factors of responsibility, recognition and achievement. A further vertical job loading motivator involves introducing new and more difficult tasks, not previously undertaken, or specialised expert tasks, thereby providing the employee with the motivators of growth, learning, responsibility and advancement.

Motivating the Manager

But what motivates a good manager? McClelland & Burnham[6,7] argue that a good manager is motivated by the need for achievement and the desire to do something better than what has been done before. The term "achievement motivation" is thought to influence leadership through the skilful use of power.

McClelland & Burnham identified three motivational manager groups:

♦ Affiliative managers have a need for affiliation, a strong desire to be liked, stronger than their desire to get things done, so that their decisions are aimed more at increasing their own popularity rather than on getting the work done more efficiently or promoting the goals of the organisation.

♦ The second group of managers are motivated by the need to achieve; they focus on setting and achieving goals, although they also put their own need for power and achievement before those goals.

♦ Institutional managers are interested, above all, in achieving power; they recognise that things are done and goals are achieved inside organisations only by influencing the people around them, therefore, they are interested in building power through influence, rather than through their own individual capabilities, knowledge and achievements.

McClelland & Burnham further argue that institutional managers, those that build power through influence, are the most effective leaders and managers, due to the fact that they exhibit more team

---

[5] Herzberg (2003), p.93.

[6] McClelland & Burnham (2003), p.118.

[7] This research was carried out in 25 large US business corporations amongst 500 managers participating in workshops that were designed to improve their managerial effectiveness in order to measure the motivation of those managers.

spirit than other motivational groups and because they envision organisational goals with greater clarity than other managers. As a consequence, their direct reports have a strong sense of responsibility and accountability. If the institutional manager leaves the organisation, he or she can be replaced more easily than the other types of managers, who often leave a sense of chaos behind them. This difference is because the institutional manager assists employees in achieving a sense of loyalty to their organisation and, as a result, employees are therefore capable of continuing to work effectively with a new manager. Therefore, it appears that concern for power is a necessary prerequisite of a good manager.

However, many senior managers discourage employees from speaking out and raising difficult issues that are essential to organisational performance, as the *status quo* must be maintained at all costs, even when the trust of employees and the integrity of the organisation are under threat by internal or environmental factors. Employees who challenge may be perceived as "troublemakers" or rebellious and may not be considered for promotion as a result. This scenario is a symptom of a closed communication culture that may be overcome if managers respect and trust their employees' abilities and encourage a spirit of openness in the organisation.

The articulation of clearly-defined organisational goals, that align the performance expected from individuals with its strategy, will start the process of changing the organisation's negative culture.[8,9] Furthermore, when individual purpose and mission are intertwined with the organisation's purpose and mission, synergies will result that will lead to increased motivation to implement the organisation's purpose and mission. This unleashing of energy and talent will result in creative and innovative strategies being implemented in the organisation. Also, effective systems, structures and processes should be aligned with the manager's mission and vision for further synergistic benefits to be realised.[10] In order to motivate employees, and to maximise the potential that is present in each individual, managers should provide clear objectives that are constantly reinforced and linked to the organisation's vision, purpose and strategies.[11] The main management challenge for managers of the future will be to lead and manage relationships between the organisation's mission and purpose effectively and, as a consequence,

---

[8]   Leskin (2003).
[9]   Leskin (2003, p. 37), an independent consultant in the US, writing in the *Harvard Business Review*.
[10] Covey (1996), p. 153.
[11] Price Waterhouse Integration Team (1996), p.90.

to be sufficiently motivated to shape the organisation's future and to achieve this goal.[12]

Inspiring Employees

But how do managers inspire ordinary employees to do extraordinary things? Several US leaders attempt to answer this question and in the process demonstrate how difficult this task is.[13] These leaders in their specialist fields agree that motivating others requires a clear understanding of each situation being faced by the employee, in addition to the establishment and communication of clear goals to employees and the construction for employees of a balanced set of tangible and intangible motivators. Such tangible motivators are salary and working conditions, while intangible motivators include factors such as recognition, achievement and growth.

Drucker[14] adds a new dimension to this debate in discussing how to motivate employees to reach peak performance. He disagrees with Herzberg that satisfaction is the key to future performance achievements and argues that responsibility is the only thing that will serve us well into the future. Drucker contends that it is possible to be satisfied with what another individual does, but that each individual, in taking responsibility for their own actions, will remain motivated to succeed. In addition, he argues that job satisfaction can only be achieved when the individual has assumed responsibility for his own actions.[15]

Several US business leaders present a wide armoury of strategies used by them to motivate others who work for them. Fiorina[16] advises starting with the truth, stating that the truth is established through customer comments, both positive and negative. Such comments are then communicated to employees who are then assisted to confront the reality of the work, or organisational situation, and to set high aspirations. According to Fiorina, this permits employees to "march pragmatically from reality to aspiration".[17] Bangle[18] suggests that

---

[12] Beckhard (1996), p.129.
[13] In a series of articles, published in the *Harvard Business Review* (2003), recognised leaders in business including the CEOs, Presidents, Chairman or Chief Development Officer of Hewlett-Packard, Mattel, BP America, Pfizer, Wachovia, Legend Group (Beijing), BMW, the 2002 National Teacher of the Year (California) and the Director of the University of Rhode Island's Institute for Underwater Archaeology at its Graduate School of Oceanography.
[14] Drucker (1999).
[15] Drucker (1989).
[16] Fiorina (2003)
[17] Fiorina (2003), p.42.
[18] Bangle (2003).

employees respond to the opportunity to be part of a new initiative and believes that the desire to contribute to something lasting is huge. A new initiative may be a programme designed to develop cultural aspirations or it may take the form of the development of new patient services that are designed to enhance patient care and the organisation's reputation for excellence. A further motivational technique is to make employees proud by celebrating their expertise through recognition.[19]

Baker[20] suggests that motivation occurs by non-compromising standards and personal values and by adherence to simple values, such as honesty, fairness, generosity and endeavour. Carney[21] advises that, for clinicians and non-clinicians to maintain self-motivational levels, they should not compromise the values they hold and that those values are excellence in patient care and a caring, quality, research-based approach to care delivery that is governed by integrity, confidentiality and trust. This means communicating the vision of the organisation to all clinicians and non-clinicians. Acknowledgement of their contribution to care delivery permits feelings of respect, trust and expertise to flourish.[22] Eckert[23] suggests that employees should repeatedly be informed of what is happening in the organisation, and of what is expected of them. In order for employees to be motivated to take responsibility for their own actions, they must be capable of visualising how their work achievements fit into the overall scheme of things in the organisation, and how it relates to the work of the whole organisation. This knowledge allows the employee to determine how much has been contributed to the organisation as a result of their effort and, therefore, to sustain motivation levels to succeed.[24]

Pillari[25] advocates risk-taking, by assisting employees to step into the uncomfortable zone where people and organisations are capable of achieving extraordinary results. Results are achieved by providing visible and confident support, at all times, through open discussion and by ensuring that roles and responsibilities are made clear to all involved, thereby, spreading risk across the team. Or, in working quickly through situations that involve painful decisions. In such cases, employees need to be informed of the action being taken and of the time frame involved. This involves managing the transition phase

---

[19] 2002 National Teacher of the Year, Coachella Valley High School.

[20] Baker (2003).

[21] Carney (2002a).

[22] Carney (2004a).

[23] Eckert (2003).

[24] Drucker (1989).

[25] Pillari (2003).

of change in a decisive and fair manner.[26] Emphasis on speed reduces resentment and the development of turf issues and paralysis by over analysis of the situation.[27] Additionally, setting challenge levels appropriate to individuals' differing abilities and competencies is necessary. Managers respond to high work challenges if they have first been involved in strategy development surrounding the challenge,[28] and Chuanzhi[29] advises that allowing employees to design personal work processes and making and executing personal decisions will motivate. Finally, Ballard[30] suggests leaping first and asking questions later. This motivating situation is particularly pertinent in emergency situations common in health service delivery, but assumes prior knowledge and experience in the area of practice. Motivating is not about coaxing or persuading employees to adopt the manager's point of view because, in an emergency situation, persuasion is not possible as there is limited time available, and consequently, there are circumstances when the leader or manager must make decisions and inform others what must be done. If there is trust in the manager's ability and expertise, this decision will be accepted.

MOTIVATION OF CLINICIANS & NON-CLINICIANS IN MANAGEMENT

Clinicians have a crucial role to play in the development and delivery of the health services. To a large extent, the quality of the health care delivered is dependent on the expertise, clinical judgement, skills and motivation levels of clinicians.[31,32] Health service managers acknowledge that clinicians should be involved in the development of strategic planning and implementation of these plans;[33] aims supported by the Irish health strategy document proposals.[34] Comparisons are made in this document to findings from similar studies undertaken in Britain and the US.

---

[26] Carney (2002b).

[27] McKinnell (2003).

[28] Carney (2002a).

[29] Chuanzhi (2003).

[30] Ballard (2003).

[31] Royal College of Surgeons in Ireland / Institute of Public Administration (2003).

[32] 'Clinicians in management: A review of clinical leadership', Discussion Paper No.4, prepared by Royal College of Surgeons in Ireland and Institute of Public Administration for the Office for Health Management. The OfHM is dedicated to leading management and organisation development for the health services.

[33] Carney (2002a).

[34] Department of Health & Children (2001).

The perception that exists is that involvement in strategic planning is governed by motivation to take part in the planning process and, as a result, motivation levels are governed by perceptions of non-involvement in strategic decision-making or by the view of clinicians that they were not invited to participate in strategic planning. Therefore, the motivation-to-be-involved level was lowered as a result; a view supported by the clinicians in the management training programme developed by the Royal College of Surgeons in Ireland. This programme aimed to provide a balanced involvement in decision-making amongst all health professionals. The researchers identified that clinicians should be involved in decision-making at strategic level and not just at operational level, in order to promote motivation amongst clinicians. [35]

Doctors generally accept that they have a role to play in management and non-clinicians perceive that health service management is their domain and responsibility. Other clinician groups perceive that they should be involved in management, as they act as advocates for patients. Yet these clinicians perceive that they are often excluded from the strategic process and they question how motivation levels to manage can be sustained in such circumstances. [36] Doctors perceived that managerial work was becoming an integral part of their work and that they were motivated to undertake management roles by their professional values and their vision for excellence in patient care. However, doctors did perceive that motivation levels to become involved in leadership and management roles did place demands on their clinical time and resulted in a loss of income "through time forgone in private practice".

Factors that hindered doctors' motivation to become involved in management in their organisations included existing working relationships with managers, poor administration structures and processes, and the absence of communication channels between management and doctors. Some doctors also feared a loss of control when moving into uncharted waters and away from their familiar clinical roles.

Doctors perceived that involvement by clinicians in management was hindered by existing organisational structures and by their perception that involvement in strategy development needs to have meaning. [37] This view was supported by Carney's study, [38] where it was found that clinicians perceived that:

---

[35] *Quality & Fairness: A Health System for You* (2001). Document No. 4, CIM series, investigates the attitudes of doctors towards taking on new or greater roles in planning and leadership roles within their organisations.

[36] Carney (2002a), pp.122-124.

[37] Carney (2002a), p.11.

♦ They were invited too late to the table by management.

♦ Only lip-service was being paid by management's invitation to become involved in strategy development.

Doctors require real decision-making power and need to be kept informed, "otherwise they lose faith in the process".[39] A further cause of concern for doctors is the fear that they would lose the respect and interest of their colleagues if it were perceived that the doctors' involvement in management was lip-service by management to doctors only.[40] Doctors and clinicians perceived this to be the case.[41]

The University of Leeds introduced a similar management development programme for clinical nurse managers and midwives in Ireland in order to explore ways, through management and development training, that nurses and midwives could be further empowered and motivated to become more involved in the management and delivery of their services.[42] Competency development formed the core of this training and was expected to reflect the competencies identified in the *Report on Nursing Management Competencies* previously undertaken.[43,44] It was found that this programme assisted nurse managers in using the material delivered in order to augment their management skills and in empowering others. Competencies identified were building and maintaining relationships and having resilience and composure, which were found by participants to lead to new enthusiasm, motivation and capability for

---

[38] Carney (2002a), pp.122-124.

[39] Royal College of Surgeons in Ireland / Institute of Public Administration (2003).

[40] Royal College of Surgeons in Ireland / Institute of Public Administration (2003), p.11.

[41] The clinicians in management initiative, launched in 1998 by the Office for Health Management in conjunction with the Royal College of Surgeons in Ireland and Institute of Public Administration, has the aim of further developing the management and leadership skills of clinicians so that they will have a greater say in the planning and development of the health services in Ireland. Discussion Paper No. 4, 'A review of clinical leadership' was prepared by RCSI and IPA for the OfHM.

[42] The *Leading & Empowered Organisation Programme (LEO) Report* is based on an evaluation of the LEO programme for clinical nurse managers, conducted by the Centre for the Development of Nursing Policy & Practice, University of Leeds. The LEO programme is recognised in the UK and US for its quality and relevance in the development of nurse managers.

[43] Office for Health Management (2002), pp.2-8.

[44] LEO Evaluation published in *Guidance on the Commissioning of Nursing Management Development Programmes: Front-Line & Middle-Line Nurse Managers* (Office of Health Management, 2002).

work. Building and leading a team and communicating and influencing skills were also deemed to be important for the role.

Further tools and skills viewed as necessary for service delivery are in the areas of evidence-based learning, resource allocation and planning and organisation of work. These skills were perceived as leading to clinical excellence and enhanced service quality. Nurse executives have a central role in patient safety, and are motivated through their professionalism to design systems of care to manage care delivery and to create an environment that promotes excellence in-patient care delivery.[45] The nurse executive is responsible for 24-hour per day clinical care of patients and is continually fostering the vigilance in care that is so necessary for patient safety. Maintaining this vigilance and presence means that nurse executives must be motivated to locate errors and identify vulnerability in systems, processes and equipment and the environment.[46]

The best motivators for health care clinicians are the development of expertise and competency development.[47] Core competencies for 21st century leaders include mastery in conceptual competencies, such as systems thinking, pattern recognition, synthesis and continuous learning. Managers must be motivated to encourage employees "to engage in a drastic re-conceptualisation of their worldviews and to scrutinise the core values, beliefs, and ideas that have shaped their management practices".[48] Managers must recognise the dynamics that are moving within their organisation, at system level, that are creating effects elsewhere, and be able to see the interactions that this system change causes in networks and relationships. This collaborative process is the context that motivates employees to change, as they now want their work to be more effective and thereby to contribute to better organisational outcomes.[49]

---

[45]   Association of Nurse Executives (2000).

[46]   Association of Nurse Executives (2000), p. 4.

[47]   Carney (2006a).

[48]   Krueger Wilson & Porter O'Grady (1999), p.50.

[49]   Wheatley (2001).

SUMMARY

- Management success is linked to motivation. If employees perceive that their work is challenging and interesting, and if they are provided with a high level of responsibility by their organisation, they will be motivated to work. Positive motivators are high standards of performance, information adequate for self-control, and participation as a responsible employee.

- When individual purpose and mission are intertwined with the organisations' purpose and mission, synergies result that lead to increased motivation to implement the organisation's purpose and mission.

- To motivate employees and maximise their potential, managers should provide clear objectives, constantly reinforced, and linked to the organisation's vision, purpose and strategies.

- For clinicians and non-clinicians to maintain self-motivational levels, they should not compromise the values they hold. These values are excellence in patient care and a caring, quality, research-based approach to care delivery. Values are governed by integrity, confidentiality and trust.

- Doctors perceive that managerial work is becoming an integral part of their work and are motivated to undertake management roles.

- The best motivators are the development of expertise and competency. Core competencies for the future include mastery in conceptual competencies, such as systems thinking, pattern recognition, synthesis and continuous learning. Employees must "engage in a drastic re-conceptualisation of their worldviews and scrutinise the core values that have shaped their management practices" to date.

CHAPTER 10
INVOLVEMENT IN STRATEGY DEVELOPMENT IN THE HEALTH SERVICE

INTRODUCTION

Previous chapters demonstrated that, during health care delivery, communication processes consist of several key success factors, including consultation, participation and negotiation. They also showed that, if employees perceive that their work is challenging and interesting, if they are involved in decision-making, and if they are provided with a high level of responsibility by their organisation, motivation to work will result. This chapter presents involvement strategies and techniques and the factors supporting and hindering involvement in strategy development.

MIDDLE MANAGERS' INVOLVEMENT IN STRATEGY DEVELOPMENT

Although middle manager involvement in strategy development does take place,[1,2] the level, nature and extent of this involvement in not-for-profit organisations, such as the health service, are not known. The role is ill-defined and often viewed as one of limited involvement, leading to misinterpretation by both senior and middle managers themselves in relation to the role, purpose and desired outcomes.[3] What is required for successful involvement in strategic planning is the understanding and support of senior management,[4] as a higher level of involvement is present when consultation takes place.[5]

---

1 Burgelman (1983).
2 Carney (2002a).
3 Floyd & Wooldridge (1992a).
4 Carney (2004b).
5 Chadderton (1995).

There are no theories or measurable constructs that rigorously describe the strategic roles of middle managers.[6,7] It is known that middle managers stimulate strategic thinking and, through this role, have the power to change the organisation's strategic direction. Even so, they are often viewed strictly in operational terms, and their potential for enhancing organisational strategy is frequently ignored by senior managers.[8,9,10] Middle managers play a key role in information processing by abandoning old ideas and by generating new information that frequently results in the development of new strategic initiatives, benefiting health care delivery as a result.[11,12]

The crucial role is depicted as one that provides information to senior management, the consequences of which are to change their perception of the issue in question.[13] Currie, in examining the influence of middle managers in the planning process in a 2,000-bed acute general hospital in the UK, found that managers, through involvement in the strategic process, enjoy an enhanced role within the work environment, leading to added value for the organisation in terms of patient care delivery.[14]

Factors Influencing Strategic Involvement

There are a number of key questions that should be asked in relation to strategic involvement. The first relates to what influences the middle manager's role in strategic involvement? It is recognised that a number of demographic factors appear to influence strategic involvement including age, gender, education, and length of time or tenure in management and in the management role. These factors are now considered.

Age

Age has been associated with middle manager strategic involvement[15] and, even though age does not have a significant effect on strategic

---

6   Floyd & Wooldridge (1992a).
7   Thomas & Dunkerley (1999).
8   Floyd & Wooldridge (1992a).
9   Floyd & Wooldridge (1994).
10   The middle manager's strategic role in management was first explored by Floyd & Wooldridge, in a study of 259 managers, working in 25 mainly for-profit organisations.
11   Nonaka (1988).
12   Thakur (1998).
13   Papadakis, Kaloghirou & Iatrelli (1999).
14   Currie (1999).
15   Angle & Perry (1981).

involvement,[16] older managers are more committed to the goals and objectives of the organisation.[17;18] Studies undertaken in the US found the median age of middle managers to be 43 years of age,[19;20] 44 years, and 45 years, respectively.[21;22] In a study undertaken in the Irish health service, the median age was found to be 38 years, with the majority in the 31-45 years age grouping.[23;24]

Gender

The second question relates to gender and whether the gender of the middle manager leads to greater levels of strategic involvement. Although the association with gender, particularly the male gender, has been identified as influencing middle manager involvement,[25] the effect of female gender on involvement has not been clearly defined.

In a study based on the UK 1981 Government Census, it was found that 80% of managers working in large organisations were male, with female managers concentrated at lower levels in the organisation.[26] In a follow-up study of the 1990 Government Census, it was discovered that these figures had changed slightly; almost one in three managers were now female, of which just 10% were in senior to middle management positions. In contrast, 70% of males were in management, with 40% of males in middle to senior management positions.[27]

A study of 150 British Institute of Management corporate members revealed that more women were involved in service and government sectors, than in industry, and that more women were being promoted to middle management positions.[28] Dempsey-Polan suggests that, in the past, women moved up into a strategic management position by virtue of being members of religious orders, through inherited wealth and influence, or as nurse directors or supervisors. These women were the few in decision-making roles. Even so, the number of women directing hospitals or health service organisations has decreased over

---

16 Carney (2002a).
17 Angle & Perry (1981).
18 Mintzberg (1989).
19 Thakur (1998).
20 This study by Thakur was undertaken in a small US manufacturing corporation.
21 Dutton, Ashford, O'Neill, Hayes & Wierba (1997).
22 Dutton *et al.*'s study was undertaken through two studies in the US telecommunications industry.
23 Carney (2002a).
24 Carney, in a study undertaken in the Irish health service with clinicians and non-clinicians in acute care hospitals, found that 55% were in the 31-45 age group.
25 Lincoln & Kalleberg (1990).
26 Dopson, Risk & Stewart (1992).
27 Dopson & Stewart (1993).
28 Wheatley (2001).

the past 100 years. In the health services, women have not kept pace with men in competing for senior management-leadership positions and female executives are mainly in professional roles at the middle management level.[29] This position appears to be now reversing in the health sector. In an Irish health service study, undertaken in acute care hospitals, it was found that both male and female managers were strategically involved, that male middle managers did not have greater strategic involvement than females, and that females were equally represented in the middle manager positions.[30] This emerging situation is a positive force for the future, considering that about half of all health care users are female.

Education

Does education level lead to greater levels of strategic involvement? In a study undertaken in large corporations in the US, almost 20% of middle managers were educated to diploma level, while just over 30% had post-graduate education up to the Master's in Business Administration level or equivalent.[31] In contrast, almost 20% of senior managers were educated to the level of Master's in Business Administration and the same number held Law degrees. However, this does not appear to be the situation in the health sector, where higher numbers of managers are educated to degree or higher levels.

In a study of 365 health service heads of department, it was found that the academic qualifications of the participants ranged from certificate to higher-level degrees, with over 80% educated to degree level and beyond. Of those, almost 40% of managers were educated to primary degree level, and nearly one quarter to master's degree level, reflecting the higher educational levels of individuals entering the health service in Ireland during the past 10 years in comparison to 20 years previously.[32] Higher educational qualifications influence the level of strategic involvement occurring,[33;34;35] and, subsequently, leads to higher standards in health care delivery. Carney[36;37] found that almost 80% of heads of department held a professional qualification, as well as a degree or higher level qualification, and that this education level influenced the level of strategic involvement occurring, thereby

---

[29]   Dempsey-Polan (1988).
[30]   Carney (2002a).
[31]   Thakur (1998).
[32]   Carney (2002a).
[33]   Robins (1997).
[34]   Norman & Cowley (1999).
[35]   Carney (2002a).
[36]   Carney (2002a), p.102-17.
[37]   Carney's (2002) study was undertaken with 365 middle managers.

leading to greater satisfaction with the role and higher health care standards.

Perceptions of Clinicians in Strategic Involvement

However, another dimension may be added to health service management. Even though strategic involvement occurs, there is a perception amongst middle manager clinicians who are heads of department that it is not the level of education that influences strategic involvement, but specific strategic management education. Even though 80% of managers are educated to degree level or higher, and even though they hold responsible management positions as head of department, just 10% of managers hold a recognised management qualification. These managers perceive that their level of knowledge and education relating to strategic management is deficient and, therefore, that they are ill-prepared for the strategic management role they are now expected to undertake. Furthermore, 80% of managers hold the qualification of their professional body, reflecting the investment in time by professionals in obtaining professional qualifications, to the probable exclusion of management education. Nonetheless, both education level and professional qualifications are perceived by managers as contributing to strategic involvement, even when specific management education is not undertaken.

Middle managers become the logical fusion of the deductive and inductive styles of management, responsible for integrating the viewpoints emanating from senior and lower level management.[38] The importance of on-going education in the preparation of middle mangers for their next move within organisations is acknowledged. Currently, due to the de-layering and restructuring that is taking place within the health sector, many managers, particularly in Britain and Ireland, are not prepared for the changing role that they will be expected to take on in the future,[39] and are educationally ill-prepared for new roles.[40] Senior managers must provide education and development for middle managers in order to allow them to develop modern management skills, so that these managers are in a position to revitalise and develop strong bonds with all levels in the organisation.[41;42]

---

[38]   Nonaka (1988).
[39]   Dopson, Risk & Stewart (1992).
[40]   Wheatley (2001).
[41]   Lebor & Stofman (1988).
[42]   Dopson & Stewart (1990).

Tenure

Does tenure or length of time in the organisation affect the middle manager's level of strategic involvement that takes place? There are mixed views in this area.

Tenure in the organisation affects the relationship between the most senior manager and the middle manager in many ways, including the level of strategic involvement that occurs,[43] but particularly in terms of the downward influence exerted on the middle manager by senior management.[44;45] Managers are constrained by the network of relationships within which they are enmeshed. Middle managers who have had good relations with senior managers for a longer period of time have developed a positive rapport with them and, therefore, have an added advantage over those who have not.[46] The average tenure length in American for-profit organisations is 20 years. Not-for-profit health service organisations differ in this respect, and appear to have a wide variation in the tenure length of professional clinicians and non-clinicians. An Irish study found a parallel between the experienced and inexperienced in terms of organisational experience, with 40% having tenure for less than eight years and almost 60% for between nine and 30 years. However, length of tenure in the organisation did not significantly influence the level of strategic involvement existing.[47] These findings are at variance with those of others, who indicate that tenure in the organisation affects the level of strategic involvement occurring, with longer tenure perceived as conferring greater strategic involvement than shorter tenure.[48] Why this is so is explained by the view that professional clinicians perceive that their professional status and the process of socialisation into the role that they underwent during training and development conferred upon them the right to be strategically involved, regardless of tenure length. Non-clinicians perceived that, due to their unique service management experience and knowledge, and in order for the organisation to successfully function, they must be strategically involved.

Reporting Tenure

The length of time reporting to the senior manager appears to have an impact on the level of middle manager involvement in strategy

---

43 Hrebiniak & Snow (1982).
44 Floyd & Wooldridge (1997).
45 Thakur (1998).
46 Dutton, Ashford, O'Neill, Hayes & Wierba (1997).
47 Carney (2002a).
48 Dutton, Ashford, O'Neill, Hayes & Wierba (1997).

development.[49;50] This is due to the relational context that exists between the chief executive officer and the middle manager, which allows the middle manager to obtain a hearing for his or her issues, therefore leading to a higher level of involvement and consultation.[51;52] In a study of 150 British Institute of Management managers, almost 90% were in their present position for less than six years.[53] In a different context, in the health service, Carney found that just over one-quarter were in their present position for less than one year, which should indicate a low level of strategic involvement; however, this did not appear to be the case, as the respondents were strategically involved, regardless of reporting tenure.[54][55] However, having access opportunities and the length of time reporting to the next-level-above-manager, also appear to influence access to top management.[56] Also, managers who worked for a particular superior for a longer period of time tended to be more successful than managers who worked for a shorter time,[57] and the number of years working for the same superior increases the potential of the middle manager to influence strategic involvement.[58]

THE INFLUENCE OF HIERARCHY ON STRATEGIC INVOLVEMENT

There is considerable evidence to suggest that hierarchy and bureaucratic organisations affect the level of strategic involvement that occurs. There may be several layers of middle management arranged in a hierarchical fashion in bureaucratic organisations,[59;60] resulting in ambiguity concerning the role and nature of middle managers.[61] This ambiguity poses difficulties in relation to the level of manager involvement occurring.

---

[49]   Dutton, Ashford, O'Neill, Hayes & Wierba (1997).
[50]   Currie (1999).
[51]   Chadderton (1995).
[52]   Dutton, Ashford, O'Neill, Hayes & Wierba (1997).
[53]   Wheatley (2001).
[54]   Carney (2002a).
[55]   Carney's (2002) study was undertaken with 365 middle managers.
[56]   Dutton & Duncan (1987).
[57]   Schilit (1987b).
[58]   Schilit (1987a).
[59]   Wells (1999).
[60]   Carney (2002a).
[61]   Mintzberg (1998).

Middle managers are variously positioned one step below the vice-president and two steps above the first-line supervisor[62] or 2.2 levels away from the chief executive officer.[63] Wooldridge & Floyd,[64] in a study of 25 mainly for-profit American organisations, found that 80% of managers were two levels, and almost 20% three levels, below the chief executive officer. However, wide variations in reporting levels and layers of hierarchy also occur. Carney[65] found that middle managers, in not-for-profit health service organisations, were between two and nine levels below the chief executive officer.

There are various reasons for this level of discrepancy. In the contemporary flattened organisation, management layers have been eliminated and middle managers now assume a greater strategic role, often without line management responsibility, which means they must now cope with the difficulties of their position, while justifying why their positions exist at all.[66] This structure has implications for organisational effectiveness, hierarchical reporting,[67] and for excellence in the provision of patient services.[68] Furthermore, there is a tendency toward decentralisation, which would relieve the burden of senior management and enlarge the tasks and responsibilities of middle management.[69] However, middle managers still looked to hierarchical career progression even though their organisations were facing downsizing.[70]

Organisation Age & Size

The age and the size of the organisation also influence strategic involvement, through the complexity of the hierarchical structures and the planning difficulties arising as a result.[71,72] Smaller organisations, those with less than 200 staff, are more conducive to innovation and upward influence[73,74] and, as a result, to a higher level of middle manager strategic involvement.[75,76] In addition, the older the

---

[62] Thakur (1998).
[63] Torrington & Weightman (1987).
[64] Wooldridge & Floyd (1990).
[65] Carney (2002a).
[66] Moss Kanter (1986).
[67] Stevens, Beyer & Trice (1978).
[68] Lebor & Stofman (1988).
[69] Staehle & Schirmer (1992).
[70] Thomas & Dunkerley (1999).
[71] Mintzberg (1989).
[72] Yasai-Ardekani & Haug (1997).
[73] Mintzberg (1979).
[74] Moss Kanter (1983).
[75] Yasai-Ardekani & Haug (1997).
[76] Floyd & Wooldridge (1997).

organisation, the more formalised the behaviour of the staff, due to familiarity and predictability in work practices and outcomes.[77] Health service organisations fall into this category in many countries. Yasai-Ardekani & Haug,[78;79] in their study relating to organisational complexity, used organisation size, as indicated by employee numbers, as a measure of organisation complexity.

Organisation size influences strategic involvement.[80] For example, in large organisations, with more than 2,000 staff, planning difficulties arise due to the complexity of the hierarchical structure.[81;82] It is reasonable to assume that some dimensions of structural hierarchy may influence strategic involvement, including the type of organisation middle managers work in. In Carney's study,[83] it was found that almost 40% of middle managers reported having three to five grades below them. However, this had positive outcomes in terms of the level of strategic involvement occurring as those who reported having three to five grades below had a significantly higher level of strategic involvement than those reporting no grades below. There also appears to be wide spans of control in some organisations, with 40% of managers reported as having 11 to 60 staff reports and 10% having 111 to 300 staff reporting to them. This span of control reflects a complex and strongly hierarchical structure that may provide the rationale as to why the number of grades below may influence strategic involvement.

MIDDLE MANAGERS' INFLUENCE LEVELS

It is evident, therefore, that layers of management create complexity in reporting structures.[84;85] Hierarchy appears to affect the level of upward influence that occurs, with the level of upward strategic influence demonstrated varying from little influence[86] to strong influence.[87;88] Middle managers should be involved in exercising

---

[77] Mintzberg (1979).
[78] Yasai-Ardekani & Haug (1997).
[79] This study by Yasai-Ardekani & Haug (1997) of 179 respondents from 50 different manufacturing and services organisations has been shown to be methodologically robust in many subsequent studies.
[80] Mintzberg (1989).
[81] Yip (1985).
[82] Mintzberg (1979).
[83] Carney (2002a).
[84] Yasai-Ardekani & Haug (1997).
[85] Mintzberg (1998).
[86] Hutt, Reingen & Ronchetto (1988).
[87] Schilit (1987b).

upward influence and in the formulation of corporate strategy,[89] as managers weigh the benefits that may accrue to them before attempting to influence strategically their next-level-above-manager.

Strategic awareness increases with organisational level and, conversely, there is a decline in strategic awareness at descending levels of the managerial hierarchy. This decline in awareness has implications for the strategic management required to build requisite organisation values into everyday management practices, and to provide excellence in the provision of service delivery.[90] Shorter hierarchies ensure that middle managers are closer to senior management and to the strategic policy arena.[91] The need for timely information generation, whereby senior management create the vision for the organisation and middle managers create and implement concrete concepts by which to realise the vision, is achieved through upward influence.[92] The level of access to strategic involvement processes is a factor in the actual level that takes place.

LEVEL OF CLINICIANS & NON-CLINICIANS' ACCESS TO STRATEGIC INVOLVEMENT

As clinicians and non-clinicians make up the majority of hospital middle management, their level of access to strategy development is important. Carney[93;94] found that this level varied between the groups, and the results obtained highlight that the access in both groups differ, as do the effects on patient care.

Clinicians, all heads of department in acute care hospitals, perceived that strategic involvement occurred to a limited extent, but that a requirement existed for the setting up of fora that would allow access to strategic meetings. This type of democratic focus is perceived as the most important facilitating factor in seeking strategic involvement. The need to understand the language of strategy and management, and to adopt an assertive approach to seeking strategy involvement is also required; however, due to a perceived lack of language-of-strategy-appreciation, a less than assertive approach to seeking involvement in strategy development existed. There is a need

---

[88] Floyd & Wooldridge (1992a).
[89] Dutton, Ashford, O'Neill, Hayes & Wierba (1997).
[90] Lebor & Stofman (1988).
[91] Dopson & Stewart (1990).
[92] Nonaka (1988).
[93] Carney (2002a), pp.122-25.
[94] Carney (2002a) in identifying a number of key themes emanating from interviews with both groups.

for the process of involvement to commence, at the earliest possible stage in the strategy development process, and not in the later stages of the process, when clinicians perceived this as paying "lip service" or as a "token gesture" to their involvement in the strategic process.[95]

There is a requirement for clinicians to identify their areas of expertise, and to have an appreciation that this expertise provides them with a critical asset in seeking strategy involvement from senior managers and from non-clinician managers. This expertise and professional approach to service delivery needs to be appreciated, understood and accepted by senior managers and by non-clinicians. However, there is also a requirement to avoid making excuses for non-involvement in the strategic process, and to cease the "learned helplessness mode" that some clinicians adopt. Respect for clinicians' ideas and acknowledgement of their professional expertise by senior managers is required.

A need for political awareness and astuteness in policy matters is necessary, so that the professional role and the socialisation process into the profession that clinicians undergo prepares them for their roles in health service management, from a political and strategic perspective. Due to the rapidly-changing, and cost-focused, nature of health service delivery, clinicians must become more politically aware, in order to become involved more meaningfully in the strategic process, and to seek out a higher profile both within the organisation and external to it. The development of strategic networks is important in order to secure resources for improving the organisational services delivered to clients. Clinicians view their professional roles as time-consuming and, therefore, not allowing time for strategic involvement. The professional role is rooted in patient advocacy but, due to the lack of strategic involvement, this advocacy role requires, in addition to professional and clinical responsibilities, strategic management commitment for best practice care delivery.[96]

There is a requirement for clinicians to develop a "big picture" approach to organisational planning and to subscribe to the strategic planning function. Therefore, the need to understand the mission of the organisation, and to be able to incorporate the mission, aims and objectives into the planning of services, is a priority requiring the merging of the professional and the management roles. Clinicians are required to justify service delivery outcomes, although the mechanism for achieving these outcomes often remains unclear. Setting up multi-disciplinary teams is one approach; thus, trust in each other and in the capabilities of the organisation is necessary in such a structure.

---

[95]   Carney (2004a).
[96]   Carney (2006b).

Non-clinicians perceive a need to adopt a democratic approach to strategy development, although this is not always the approach taken in organisations. Hierarchical structure hinders strategy development and, therefore, structures should be put in place in order to allow a greater level of strategic involvement to take place that allows non-clinicians to adopt a democratic inclusive approach to strategic decision-making. The need to build up trust in each other's capabilities through fairness, equity in inclusion and democracy is necessary to achieve consensus of strategy. Clinicians should seek genuine democratic involvement in the strategic process, not just lip service, as is frequently the case.

Non-clinicians need to understand and to value the clinician's role. A higher level of involvement is possible, if non-clinicians are invited by senior managers and by non-clinician middle manager colleagues to become part of the multi-disciplinary teams responsible for setting the strategic agenda. Consultative strategy groups are required and, ideally, these should be multi-disciplinary teams. Clinicians and non-clinicians need to know and understand the mission of the organisation and have a clear and focused strategic direction. Development and educational programmes in the areas of strategy development, budgeting and leadership would provide a more confident and assertive approach to the strategic issues affecting the delivery of services. Clinicians should be invited to contribute early enough in the strategic process to make a meaningful contribution to strategy development.

Non-clinicians need to understand and value the clinician's role in the delivery of services and, in addition, the clinicians' expertise should be understood and valued by non-clinicians and senior managers. There is a perception that cultural experiences influence the behaviour of both groups in relation to the management of services. Clinicians, particularly medical staff, should consult with non-clinicians in the delivery of services and, in the process, reach a greater level of understanding of the financial and budgetary implications for cost effective service delivery. A summary of the factors facilitating strategic involvement is presented in **Table 10.1**.

Table 10.1: Factors Facilitating Strategic Involvement

Clinician	Non-Clinician
Seek involvement in strategy by adopting an assertive approach	Adopt democratic approach to strategy development
Set up forum for access and strategic involvement	Ensure transparency and fairness in dealings with clinicians
Develop education for understanding the language of strategy	Seek genuine involvement in the strategic process
Appreciate own expertise	Understand and value clinician's role in the organisation
Adopt patient advocacy role and follow through on strategy	Ensure early/direct strategic communications
Develop time management skills	Set up multi-disciplinary groups to plan and deliver strategy
Become politically aware in relation to strategy	Have awareness of impact of new policies on clinician's and clients
Adopt high profile in the organisation	Examine and improve structures to allow for strategic involvement
Adopt leadership role	Set up consultative groups to develop strategy
Develop network of support	Plan rather than re-act
Cease learned helplessness mode	Invest in development needs of staff
Avoid excuses for non-involvement	Have clarity in goals, mission and strategic planning
Develop vision and "big picture" of organisation strategy	Provide departmental budgetary controls
Plan services and justify quality outcomes to non-clinicians	
Merge clinical and management roles in a strategic approach	
Set up multi-disciplinary teams	
Continue professional development of self	

PATIENT & CLIENT INVOLVEMENT

Patient and client involvement is growing in significance for all health care professionals who deliver care, particularly in the NHS in the UK, and in Ireland, where involvement has become a plank in reforms being introduced.[97,98] The NHS Plan[99] states that too many patients feel "talked at" rather than "listened to". Patients require more say in their treatment and future care. A Department of Health[100] document advises that such involvement must include positive and effective relationships between patients and the clinicians providing their care. And, with patients receiving social care, care managers are responsible for care management and for the funding of such care. Care management models ensure that health professionals work together with service users, and with carers, if relevant, in order to set out the appropriate care that is required.[101]

A study undertaken by Abbott, Johnson & Lewis[102] involving four groups of service users living in the community found considerable dissatisfaction with the care management provided. Whilst two groups were prepared to take an active role in their care and were satisfied with the service provided to them, the remaining two groups were dissatisfied and unclear with the care provided, with some having to take pro-active action in order to obtain the required services. Thus, what is required is regular contact with clients, which should be provided in a cost-effective manner. When social care is required, perhaps the care manager may be a social worker working in a co-ordinating role, thereby minimising the number of professionals visiting the home. The most cost-effective skills mix of qualified and less qualified staff may provide regular contact, not substituting for, but rather complementing, the professional nursing role.[103]

In contrast to the care management study, a study undertaken with patients over 70 years of age, regarding participation in their discharge planning from the hospital, found that the majority of patients felt that they had been involved in the discharge plan, welcomed the advice offered to them by the professionals undertaking the discharge planning, with some preferring that the professionals make decisions on their behalf.[104]

---

[97] Department of Health (UK) (2002b).
[98] Department of Health & Children (2001).
[99] Department of Health (UK) (2000a).
[100] Department of Health (UK) (1999).
[101] Abbott, Johnson & Lewis (2001).
[102] Abbott, Johnson & Lewis (2001).
[103] Abbott, Johnson & Lewis (2001).
[104] Roberts (2002).

However, confusion remains surrounding the term "user participation" in health and social care delivery. Many changes have begun, and now Trusts have a legal duty to involve and to consult with the public whenever major health changes are being considered. Patient & Public Involvement Forums, external to the NHS, and composed of members of the public who are service users, carers and members of voluntary organisations, will assist this process.[105] All health care professionals have a duty of care to their patients and have a vital role in involving patients in the discussions concerning their care.

Health service organisations also have a major part to play in involving health professionals in patient care initiatives. Organisations are required to acknowledge the expertise and professionalism of health service staff and to involve them, early on in the process and, not as is often perceived, too late to have any real meaning.[106;107] Additionally, effective partnership building, between professionals,[108] users of services and organisations, is necessary for successful and sustainable relationship building.[109] Moss Kanter[110] suggests that this relationship building is more effectively developed through individual excellence and on-going professional education and training of all professionals, and further advises that mutual investment in services offered, sharing of information and integration of service provision is important for relationship-building. This partnership approach will result in professionals having equal rights to make decisions on behalf of their clients and will contribute toward integrity in professional behaviour toward each other.

The concept of the nurse-patient partnership is unclear and the elements making up this relationship remain obscure due to the myriad of definitions of partnership that exist. A Canadian study, which explored the process of partnership, concluded that the nurse-patient partnership embodies power-sharing and negotiation and leads to patient empowerment, because empowerment allows the patient to act on his or her own behalf.[111;112]

---

[105] Robinson (2004).

[106] Carney (2002a), pp.122-25.

[107] Calpin-Davies (2003).

[108] Carney (2002a), pp.122-25.

[109] Calpin-Davies (2003).

[110] Moss Kanter (1994).

[111] Gallant, Beaulieu & Carnvale (2002).

[112] This study examined the concept of empowerment through Rodgers' (2001) evolutionary approach to concept analysis, and describes the antecedents, attributes and consequences to partnership.

SUMMARY

- A number of demographic factors influence strategic involvement. These are age, gender, education, and length of time or tenure in management and in the management role.

- Both male and female managers are strategically involved.

- Layers of management create complexity in reporting structures. Hierarchy affects the level of upward influence that occurs.

- Non-clinicians have a higher level of strategic involvement than clinicians, resulting from a higher level of strategic awareness and confidence than clinicians in the process.

- Clinicians and non-clinicians have a different approach to the factors affecting strategic involvement. This difference in perception appears to lead to a lack of trust in each other's role in the delivery of services in the organisation.

- There is a need to understand the language of strategy and management, and to adopt an assertive approach to seeking strategy involvement. Clinicians need to develop a "big picture" approach to organisational planning and to subscribe to the strategic planning function, while non-clinicians need to understand and value the clinician's role. A higher level of involvement is possible if non-clinicians are invited by senior managers, and by non-clinician middle manager colleagues, to become part of the multi-disciplinary teams responsible for setting the strategic agenda.

- Patient and client involvement is growing in significance for all health care professionals who deliver care, particularly in the NHS, and in Ireland, where involvement has become a major component in reforms being introduced.

- Health service organisations have a major part to play in involving health professionals in patient care initiatives. Organisations are required to acknowledge the expertise and professionalism of health services staff and to involve them, early on in the process and not, as is often perceived, too late to have any real meaning.

CHAPTER 11
ORGANISATIONAL &
PROFESSIONAL COMMITMENT
& ITS INFLUENCE ON HEALTH
SERVICE MANAGEMENT

INTRODUCTION

Chapter 9 demonstrated that, if employees perceive that their work is challenging and interesting, if they are involved in decision-making, and if they are provided with a high level of responsibility by their organisation, individuals will be motivated to work to the highest levels of their ability and, therefore, will benefit patient care delivery. **Chapter 10** showed that organisations are required to acknowledge the expertise and professionalism of health service staff, so that effective partnership-building between professionals and management and between professionals and users of services is developed. As a result of this collaboration and partnership, and due to the higher health care demands from patients for greater choice in the services offered and excellence in the services delivered, health professionals are required to demonstrate a higher level of involvement and commitment to their work than was previously expected of them. Chapter 11 will demonstrate that organisational climate and culture, job satisfaction and commitment are interlinked. It will also show that professional and organisational commitment to patient care delivery is guided by cultural and ethical values. Thus, the values system inherent in health care professionals will determine patient outcomes and predict employer commitment to delivering the highest standard of care.

THE CONCEPT OF ORGANISATIONAL COMMITMENT

Commitment to the organisation influences individual levels of commitment in various ways,[1,2] although the concept of organisational commitment is complex and involves many dimensions. Commitment is defined as employees encompassing a complex sense of loyalty that involves a strong belief in the goals of the organisation, congruence with the value system of the organisation and a willingness to serve the organisation through continued membership.[3] Commitment to the organisation influences commitment to key organisational strategies, thus ensuring that the mission, goals and strategic objectives are clearly understood and acted upon.

The psychological approach to organisational commitment ensures that employees have a psychological identification with the goals and beliefs of the organisation, and a willingness to concentrate efforts toward helping the organisation to achieve its goals.[4,5] This process results in identification with the organisation's objectives to the extent that individual and organisational goals are closely aligned.[6] Porter, Steers, Mowday & Boulian,[7] in a study involving 2,563 employees in nine divergent organisations, found that commitment was portrayed as the internalisation of the values of the organisation – that is, a willingness to concentrate efforts towards helping the organisation to achieve its goals and a desire to remain as a member of the organisation. In addition, these authors found that this loyalty develops over a period of time, and remains stable over time, and therefore, represents more than passive loyalty to the organisation.[8] Thus, identification with the organisation is reflected in the individual's sense of oneness with an organisation and is therefore an important aspect of organisational commitment.[9]

---

1   Randall & Cote (1991).
2   Cohen (1993).
3   Corser (1998).
4   Porter, Steers, Mowday & Boulian (1974).
5   Mowday, Steers & Porter (1979).
6   Guth & Macmillan (1986).
7   Porter, Steers, Mowday & Boulian (1974).
8   Mowday, Steers & Porter (1979).
9   Van Dick, Wagner, Stellmacher & Christ (2004).

Organisational Factors Affecting Behaviour

Organisational factors play a major role in affecting the behaviour and attitudes of employees.[10] This is due to the fact that employees bring a set of expectations to their role, and how they perceive these expectations to have been met or exceeded will determine their commitment to the organisation. Contemporary views on commitment related to goals are widespread in the literature.[11;12] Organisational systems and structures that align organisation goals with those of the manager will build commitment into strategy.[13] Therefore, for this to occur, managers must commit to and understand strategy.[14]

Additionally, employees display feelings of loyalty, affection, belongingness,[15] and emotional attachment to the organisation,[16] or bond with the organisation;[17] this personal commitment appears to lead to work commitment,[18;19] and increased levels of co-operative behaviour amongst employees.[20] A number of authors classify commitment as an attitudinal or behavioural concept[21;22] that results in positive behavioural benefits to the organisation in terms of commitment. This is an all-encompassing attitude that results from a sense of support, and acknowledgement of one's efforts on behalf of the organisation.[23] Poor implementation of strategy results from poor middle management understanding of, and commitment to, organisational strategy.[24] Managers are motivated more by perceived self-interest than by organisational interest, and thus, it is important that organisational and manager objectives are aligned in order to achieve commitment to strategy implementation.[25] Thus strategic policy will positively influence organisational commitment.[26]

[10]   Taylor, Audia & Gupta (1996).
[11]   Hollenbeck &. Klein (1987).
[12]   Klein (1987).
[13]   Floyd & Wooldridge (1992a).
[14]   Wooldridge & Floyd (1990).
[15]   Jaros, Jermier, Koehler & Sincich (1993).
[16]   Gruen, Summers & Acito (2000).
[17]   Carney (2002a).
[18]   Mottaz (1988).
[19]   Putti, Aryee & Phua (1990).
[20]   Gruen, Summers & Acito (2000).
[21]   Porter, Steers, Mowday & Boulian (1974).
[22]   Putti, Aryee & Phua (1990).
[23]   Ogilvie (1986).
[24]   Floyd & Wooldridge (1992a).
[25]   Guth & Macmillan (1986).
[26]   Putti, Aryee & Phua (1990).

The Commitment Model

The commitment model incorporates high commitment, high involvement and high performance,[27] and is central to discourse in organisational theory.[28;29] Close involvement levels are attributed to the occupation and will result in high occupational commitment, creative innovation and spontaneous problem-solving behaviour.[30;31] Having a high level of involvement in work-based activities results in a sense of support and acknowledgement of one's efforts on behalf of the organisation;[32] managers are committed to their organisations and this form of commitment strongly influences the level of strategic involvement occurring.

Commitment is due to a sense of willingness and goodwill that results from the perception that support for clinician and non-clinician ideas and well-being exists.[33] This form of acknowledgement produces a reciprocal sense of obligation to support the organisation's goals and leads to organisational commitment.[34;35] A further indication of commitment to the organisation is when managers are willing to put in a great deal of effort, beyond that normally expected, in order to help the organisation be successful, and are prepared to tell their friends that the organisation is a great place to work and that they really care about its progress and development, thereby demonstrating a positive attitude toward the organisation. There is a significant correlation between strategic involvement and commitment to the organisation.[36;37] However, often professional and organisational commitment may be at variance, particularly amongst professional clinicians, where commitment to the profession and to the organisation may be in conflict.[38;39] Nonetheless, commitment to the organisation is a critical success factor in nurturing, promoting and growing the senior manager-middle managers' strategic involvement relationship and affiliation with the organisation and is a vital component in the development and maintenance of strategic involvement.

---

[27] Wood & Menezes (1998).
[28] Lawler, Mohrman & Ledford (1995).
[29] Porter O'Grady & Malloch (2002).
[30] Corser (1998).
[31] Cohen (2000).
[32] Ogilvie (1986).
[33] Carney (2002a).
[34] Eisenberger, Fasolo & Davis-LaMastro (1990).
[35] Shore & Tetrick (1991).
[36] Carney (2002a).
[37] Carney (2002a), in a survey of 365 health service professional managers, clinicians and non-clinicians, found that commitment predicted strategic involvement.
[38] Willcocks (1994).
[39] Corser (1998).

ORGANISATIONAL CLIMATE, JOB SATISFACTION & COMMITMENT

Conversely, the commitment displayed by the organisation, as an entity, to employees is also important. This commitment is the interaction between the employee and the organisational managers and is determined, to a large extent, by the organisation's climate.

It appears that organisational climate predicts job satisfaction. In two samples of general and psychiatric nurses working in Hong Kong,[40;41] it was found that the level of involvement and commitment displayed by managers toward employees was important in predicting absenteeism.[42] Therefore, managers are advised to pay particular attention to the psychosocial environment of the workplace in order to create an organisational climate that encourages communication and involvement and, thereby, limits absenteeism.[43;44] Leaders should also strive to create an organisational climate where excellence is fostered and in which job satisfaction and organisational commitment are seen as important factors in delivering patient care.[45]

A study undertaken amongst nurses and managers working in intensive care units in Singapore[46;47] found that leadership behaviour explained why job satisfaction, organisational commitment and productivity occurred. Additionally, a British study exploring nurses' commitment to nursing and control over their environment when working "shifts" found that nurses working on permanent night shifts had lower levels of commitment to nursing than those not working night shifts; however, nurses with positive perceptions of their future career development opportunities were more strongly committed to nursing than those not having this perception.[48;49] These authors recommend that managers have a role in setting out career

---

[40] Oi-ling (2002).

[41] Oi-ling (2002) undertook a quantitative study with 144 general and psychiatric nurses.

[42] Kahn & Byosiere (1992), p.592.

[43] Weinberg & Creed (2000).

[44] Hemingway & Smith (1999).

[45] Knox (2004).

[46] Chiok Foong Loke (2001).

[47] This survey explored the relationship between the five leadership behaviours identified by Kouzes & Posner and the employee outcomes of 100 nurses and 20 managers working in general, intensive care and coronary care units in an acute care hospital in Singapore.

[48] Brooks & Swailes (2002).

[49] Brooks & Swailes (2002) undertook a survey with 2,987 nurses in Britain working in hospitals, care homes and hospices, in the context of nursing shortages and the demands from employers for greater work flexibility.

opportunities, so that nurses have a clear perception of their career development potential in order to minimise the negative effect of "shift" working. In an earlier study, Brooks[50] identified that permanent night nurses considered themselves to be marginalized and unappreciated by the managers, whilst also coping with the perception of some of their day colleagues who questioned their commitment to nursing, and found that greater choice and control over the hours worked would reduce these perceptions.

It is clear that organisations have an ethical obligation to create a healthy working environment where communication and involvement is fostered. The ultimate responsibility for the organisation's environment lies with management. One way to achieve a professional environment is to establish centres for nursing excellence that provide a structure for organising professional disciplines within an organisation. A purpose of this centre, amongst others, is to recognise and value the contribution made by clinicians in the organisation and to provide a mechanism for non-clinician professionals to understand the work of clinicians,[51] thereby, fostering a multidisciplinary collegial approach to health service delivery.

NEW COMMITMENT PERSPECTIVES

Several recent perspectives have emerged in the field of organisational commitment that would benefit health service delivery. Organisational citizenship behaviour (OCB) is a relatively new concept,[52] first introduced into the organisational behaviour and commitment literature by Organ,[53] and developed further by others.[54,55] Organisational citizenship behaviour is defined as:

> "behaviour that is discretionary, not directly or explicitly recognised by the formal reward system, and that in aggregate promotes the effective functioning of the organisation ... the behaviour is not an enforceable requirement of the role or the job description ... the behaviour is a matter of personal choice".[56]

50   Brooks (2002).
51   Knox (2004).
52   Coyle-Shapiro, Kessler & Purcell (2004).
53   Organ (1988).
54   Organ & Ryan (1995).
55   Podaskoff, MacKenzie, Paine & Bachrach (2000).
56   Organ (1988), p.4.

This form of citizenship behaviour could mean staying late to finish work or assisting a colleague when not asked to do so. An Australian study, exploring the concept of organisational citizenship behaviours in a group of teachers found that contract teachers reported more job insecurity and more organisational citizenship behaviours than permanent teachers.[57;58] As many health service professionals work in part-time positions, the results from this study have resonance for them. Citizenship behaviours for the contract teachers were related to feelings of insecurity and perceptions that they had limited influence in the workplace over their role-related duties with fewer opportunities to use their skills. In contrast, permanent teachers perceived that they had more responsibility, more work variety, greater decision-making roles and greater use of their relevant skills. However, permanent teachers did not demonstrate higher levels of affective commitment or stronger identification with their organisation than contract teachers. Therefore, managers should not assume that non-permanent staff or staff working night shifts are less committed to their work roles or to the organisation than the permanent staff.

Organisational Citizenship Behaviour

Coyle-Shapiro, Kessler & Purcell[59;60] add a further dimension to organisational citizenship behaviour. In a study undertaken amongst almost 400 clinicians and non-clinicians in British hospitals, these authors found that employees undertook organisational citizenship behaviours for two reasons. The first reason related to employees viewing OCB from a sense of reciprocation for fair and positive treatment received by them from the organisation, and the second reason was related to employees' defining OCB as part of their job – therefore, they were willing to undertake this form of behaviour.

OCB is viewed as being positively associated with organisational commitment and this commitment, in turn, results in role enlargement or the individual taking on greater decision-making and responsibility in the work situation. A further framework used to describe OCB relates to perceived organisational support received by the individual, and how well the employee perceives that he or she has been treated by the organisation. Therefore, the relationship that the employee has with the organisation is important in gaining an understanding of

---

[57] Feather & Rauter (2004).

[58] This study, comprising 101 teachers in permanent employment and 53 on fixed-term contracts, was distributed through the Australian Education Union *via* a survey.

[59] Coyle-Shapiro, Kessler & Purcell (2004).

[60] This survey was undertaken with 387 hospital clinicians and non-clinicians in a NHS hospital in Britain, on the subject of organisational citizenship behaviour.

OCB. If OCB is viewed as a form of mutual commitment, the individuals will enlarge their job responsibilities and, in turn, incorporate this behaviour into their role commitment. A further concept, organisational identification, has been positively linked to OCB.[61] This concept leads to employee behaviour that is congruent with the organisation's values and identity,[62] again an important factor in health service management.

VALUES AS A PREDICTOR OF COMMITMENT

Different countries exhibit different cultural values that, in turn, predict commitment to the organisation. Two types of commitment are predicted by values: affective and continuance. *Affective* commitment is defined as emotional attachment to, identification with, and involvement in one's organisation,[63;64] leading to a match between human and organisational values,[65] while *continuance* commitment applies to the employee's need to stay with the organisation, usually because few alternative jobs exist and leaving the organisation would incur sacrifice.[66] Making this decision implies that the employee exercises rational choice regarding where one wants to be and what one wants.[67]

Research on organisational commitment has been undertaken in several countries and the predictors of commitment differ in each country. A large study undertaken by Glazer, Daniel & Short,[68] amongst 900 hospital nurses mostly working in in-patient units in Hungary, Italy, UK, and USA, and who were native to each country, found a positive relationship between higher order human values, such as trust and loyalty, and organisational commitment. In a study of Malaysian nurses, Pearson & Chong[69] found that the key Malaysian values were "harmony, non-aggressiveness, and a strong preference for a relationship-based orientation", and that these values predicted affective commitment. Amongst Korean workers, key values include a warm, supportive climate,[70] which again predicted affective commitment. These values were subsequently found, in Korean

---

61   Shamir & Kark (2004).
62   Kiluchi (2005).
63   Allen & Meyer (1990).
64   Porter, Steers, Mowday & Boulian (1974).
65   Schim, Zoorenbos & Borse (2005).
66   Meyer, Irving & Allen (1998).
67   Bar-Hayim & Berman (1992).
68   Glazer, Daniel & Short (2004).
69   Pearson & Chong (1997).
70   Sommer, Bae & Luthans (1996).

workers, to mean loyalty and devotion to the organisation.[71] In a comparative study of Japanese and American workers, Near[72] found that, in Japan, seniority was a predictor of commitment, whilst in the US, freedom predicted commitment. In Knoop's study of Canadian nurses, pride in their work was found to be the strongest predictor of affective commitment, followed by valuing consideration for their supervisor, receiving recognition for their work and having influence in the organisation.[73] Perhaps allocentric values, such as tradition, respect and seniority, may be predictors of commitment in countries where the culture encourages employees to trust their organisation, to fit into the group,[74] and to develop a sense of obligation to the organisation and, thereby, the organisation becomes the family unit.[75] In comparison, in countries where idiocentric values, such as freedom and achievement, are promoted, these values become the important predictors of commitment.[76;77] Additionally, in countries, such as Italy and Hungary, where a balance among individuals is promoted and endorsed, conservation values, such as an emphasis on belongingness which promotes affective commitment,[78] will be stronger than in cultures, such as Britain, Ireland and the US where personal achievement, freedom, influence and recognition are embedded in the countries' culture.[79]

However, in countries where contractual agreements are entered into with employees, such as Britain, Ireland and the US, mastery over others and over one's work, as well as autonomy to undertake one's work in a creative and innovative manner, is important.[80;81] Consequently, trust may not be built up over time and job security may not be assured. Therefore, achievement, power, mastery over one's work and over others is not fulfilled, and such employees will move to another organisation that is perceived to offer greater job satisfaction and prospects for promotion.[82] Development and

---

[71]   Bae & Chung (1997).
[72]   Near (1989).
[73]   Knoop (1994).
[74]   Abrams, Ando & Hinkle (1998).
[75]   Glazer, Daniel & Short (2004).
[76]   Glazer, Daniel & Short (2004).
[77]   This quantitative study was undertaken amongst 900 hospital nurses from mostly in-patient units in Hungary, Italy, UK & USA. Two measurement scales were used to measure commitment and values, and translated into the language of each country.
[78]   Schwartz (1999).
[79]   Glazer, Daniel & Short (2004).
[80]   Abrams, Ando & Hinkle (1998).
[81]   Schwartz (1999).
[82]   Glazer, Daniel & Short (2004).

recognition of expertise, and professional career enhancement, are important motivators to commit to the organisation.

In the present climate of multi-cultural recruitment of health care professionals, where values are an indication of culture, it is important for health service managers to have an understanding of the cultural values an individual employee might hold. This knowledge of cultural values will guide and assist managers in developing motivational strategies and change management strategies that will, in turn, influence the employees' commitment to their new organisations.[83;84;85]

Carney proposes that ethical values are part of the essence of health care management and delivery and that, even though studies in this area have identified what some of those values are, few studies have been undertaken to identify whether the values and beliefs held are ethical, and what the outcomes, positive and negative, to holding such values are. She identified 11 ethical values, including excellence in care delivery and employees holding a positive value system that results in demonstrable trust, integrity, confidentiality and justice for patients. Other values include some not previously classified as ethical values, including managerial receptiveness/managerial non-receptiveness, depending on whether the employee perceives that their work and contribution is appreciated or not. Another value relates to organisational dependability/lack of organisational dependability – whether employees perceive that they can depend upon their organisation to support them when necessary. A further ethical value identified relates to peer cohesion/lack of peer cohesion, perceived as colleagues demonstrating a bond (or lack of bonding) with each other and with the goals and mission of the organisation. Finally, personal contribution to the organisation and a sense of personal importance is perceived as being an important ethical value in promoting a positive ethical environment.[86] Therefore, professional and organisational commitment to patient care delivery is guided by ethical values because the values system inherent in health care professionals will determine patient outcomes. A summary is presented in **Tables 11.1 and 11.2.**

---

[83]   Carney (2004b).
[84]   Yousef (2000).
[85]   Carney (2006a).
[86]   Carney (2006b).

Table 11.1: Negative Values & Beliefs[87]

♦ Negative managerial receptiveness
♦ Lack of organisation dependability
♦ Negative job challenge
♦ Negative goal clarity
♦ Negative role clarity
♦ Lack of peer cohesion

Table 11.2: Positive Values & Beliefs[88]

♦ Excellence in care delivery
♦ Positive value system
♦ Trust
♦ Integrity
♦ Confidentiality
♦ Justice
♦ Managerial receptiveness
♦ Organisational dependability
♦ Positive job challenge
♦ Personal importance/contribution to the organisation
♦ Peer cohesion

---

[87] Carney (2002a).
[88] Carney (2002a).

SUMMARY

♦ Commitment refers to employees encompassing a complex sense of loyalty that involves a strong belief in the goals of the organisation, congruence with the value system of the organisation and a willingness to serve the organisation through continued membership.

♦ Commitment to the organisation influences commitment to key organisational strategies, thus ensuring that the mission, goals and strategic objectives are clearly understood and acted upon.

♦ Employees display feelings of loyalty, affection, belongingness, and emotional attachment to the organisation or bond with the organisation.

♦ A further indication of commitment to the organisation is when managers are willing to put in a great deal of effort beyond that normally expected, in order to help the organisation to be successful; they are prepared to tell their friends that the organisation is a great place to work and that they really care about its progress and development, thereby demonstrating a positive attitude toward the organisation.

♦ It is clear that organisations have an ethical obligation to create a healthy working environment where communication and involvement is fostered; the ultimate responsibility for the organisation's environment lies with management.

♦ Organisational citizenship behaviour is defined as behaviour that is discretionary, not directly or explicitly recognised by the formal reward system, is a matter of personal choice and that, in aggregate, promotes the effective functioning of the organisation.

♦ Different countries exhibit different cultural values that, in turn, predict commitment to the organisation.

♦ Development and recognition of expertise, and professional career enhancement, are important motivators "to commit to the organisation".

CHAPTER 12
ORGANISATIONAL CULTURE & ITS EFFECT ON HEALTH SERVICE MANAGEMENT

INTRODUCTION

Previous chapters demonstrated that health care is delivered through frequent change and, because of this, that professional organisations seek key individuals who have the knowledge and skills to lead their members into the future. The leader influences organisational culture by acting as a role model for other professionals, by influencing organisational policy and by providing health care through a collaborative and ethical process. Socio-cultural dimensions represent the demographic characteristics, norms, customs and values of the population within which the organisation operates and strategy evolves through the cultural and social processes that exist within the organisation. It has also been demonstrated that involvement and commitment by professionals in the development of strategy is influenced by the organisation's structure, the prevailing culture in the organisation and the motivation level of employees to deliver a high quality of patient care.

HISTORICAL DIMENSIONS OF CULTURE

In the 1940s and 1950s, research into culture was first conducted and centred primarily in the field of anthropology.[1] Research into organisational culture did not develop until the 1970s and the early 1980s,[2,3] while the notion of culture, as a concept, was developed in the 1980s.[4,5] Carney views culture as complex organisational dynamics and interaction patterns and hidden agendas[6] that are formed as a

---

[1]   Whyte (1951).
[2]   Trice, Belasco & Alutto (1969).
[3]   Pettigrew (1977).
[4]   Deal & Kennedy (1982).
[5]   Kilmann, Saxton, Serpa & Associates (1985).
[6]   Carney (2002a).

continuous sequence.[7] Culture is defined as observed behavioural regularities that occur during interactions between individuals – for example, the language used, the rituals that are employed and the customs and traditions that evolve.[8] Culture is further described in terms of standards, values and group norms,[9] as the espoused values and credo of an organisation,[10] as the climate of the organisation,[11] and as the embedded skills and competencies of organisational members.[12] Socialisation and the view that an organisation may have more than one culture are further dimensions that have been added to the definition of organisational culture. Therefore, it is evident "that culture is a multidimensional, multifaceted phenomenon, not easily reduced to a few major dimensions."[13] Thus there is a need for managers to understand culture, and to acknowledge that organisational learning and employee development will not be understood fully without a clear understanding of the cultural dynamics operating within the organisation.

CULTURAL BELIEFS

An organisation's culture can be studied at three levels: artefacts, values and assumptions. *Artefacts* are the organisational structures that are visible to the members of the organisation. *Values* are the strategies, goals and philosophies of the organisation's members. The basic, underlying *assumptions* of group members include taken-for-granted beliefs, perceptions, thoughts and feelings. Even though certain basic assumptions are evident, taken for granted and are not normally confronted or debated, the culture of the organisation will become evident at the level of observable artefacts and in the shared values, norms and rules of behaviour of the organisation's members.

Group norms are sets of shared values that have been validated through a consensus process. The social validation of group norms arises when certain values are confirmed by the shared experiences of the group and these norms are passed onto new members as being the correct way to do things. This mechanism of embedding and meshing culture is undertaken at an unconscious level in most organisations. Although culture resides in the minds of the members of the

---

7   Daymon (2000).
8   Pepper (1995).
9   Kilmann, Saxton, Serpa & Associates (1985).
10   Schein (1992).
11   Schneider, Brief & Guzzo (1996).
12   Henderson &. Clark (1990).
13   Schein (1992), p.68.

organisation, it is transmitted through visible expressions, such as formal and informal routines and every day rituals of existence undertaken by members of the organisation.[14] Over time, shared experiences develop into a set of core values that become embedded in individual and organisational philosophy and ideology that ultimately serves to guide action and behaviour. This process is an important mechanism in the transmission of shared professional assumptions, values, artefacts and symbols from the master to the student and in the development of the socialisation process that professional clinicians undergo.[15] Therefore, the internal orientation of employees is based primarily on the culture, values, beliefs, ethics and assumptions of the organisation's staff; this is particularly evident amongst health service employees, although the orientation may differ between clinicians and non-clinicians.

STRONG ORGANISATIONAL CULTURE

Culture can very rarely be imposed and, in most organisations, culture is a learned behaviour that is absorbed rather than being overtly taught,[16] and is seen as a mechanism of social control that explicitly manipulates group members into perceiving, thinking, feeling and behaving in certain ways.[17,18] The organisation's culture is viewed as a critical driver of values and norms, in other words, "the way we do things around here";[19] it plays a powerful and pervasive role in shaping the life of the organisation[20] and in forming a strong organisational culture. Strong shared culture is a driving force in the organisation[21] and is capable of driving individual behaviour.[22] Strong culture is continuously reinforced through employees behaving in a similar manner to their colleagues.[23] Strong shared values are associated with commitment, self-confidence and ethical behaviour.[24]

Culture is described in various ways: as cohesive and tightly knit,[25] thick and widely shared,[26] stable and more intense than in other

---

[14] Linstead & Grafton-Small (1992).
[15] Hatch (1993).
[16] Deal & Kennedy (1988).
[17] Van Maanen & Kunda (1989).
[18] Carney (2002a), p.122-26.
[19] Deal & Kennedy (1988).
[20] Saffold (1988).
[21] Posner, Kouzes & Schmidt (1985).
[22] Mead (1978).
[23] Wickens (1995).
[24] Posner, Kouzes & Schmidt (1985).
[25] Deal & Kennedy (1983).

organisations,[27] or characterised by rule-based expectations.[28] Strong culture indicates that the goals of the organisation are known, understood and acted upon by members of the organisation, thereby ensuring that the employees' goals are aligned with those of management. Thus, in this regard, strategy and culture are essentially synonymous.[29]

Strong culture is a system of informal rules that spells out how people are to behave most of the time which implies that, in order for strong culture to take effect, communication and involvement must occur, albeit at an informal level. Strong culture enables staff to feel better about what they do, and, as a result, they are more likely to work harder. Therefore, managers should think consciously about the role of the workplace in mediating the behaviour of employees, and of the positive effects that accrue from positive culture-building for both the employees and the organisation. Culture has the potential to be one of the most powerful influences on strategic development, and strategic management in general,[30] and the management of cultural norms in clinicians and non-clinicians is a challenge for health care managers.

CULTURE IN HEALTH SERVICE ORGANISATIONS

The concept of culture is difficult to interpret within not-for-profit organisations, as distinct from for-profit environments, as cultural differences are not present to the same extent in for-profit organisations as they are in not-for-profit organisations. Cultural differences in not-for-profit organisations include competing value systems, bureaucratic constraining forces that are at variance with the high-minded value system of the public service and a more rigorous ethical system of control.[31]

Not-for-profit health service organisations are made up of a large proportion of clinicians and non-clinicians. Professional organisations, such as hospitals, exist in turbulent, changing, complex environments, which are populated by ever-demanding clients.[32] Managing professional staff through the merging of professional and managerial

---

[26]   Sathe (1983).
[27]   Schein (1984).
[28]   Schall (1983).
[29]   Saffold (1988).
[30]   Rosen (1995).
[31]   Whorton & Worthley (1981).
[32]   Carney (2004b).

roles[33] is occurring in the health service and in most public sector professions.[34] The balancing of these two cultures reveals how new cultures emerge as a result of clinicians being faced with complex and competing pressures.[35] This adjustment requires a greater level of strategic involvement than in the past.[36;37] Cultural analysts have neglected the study of occupational subcultures and multi-cultural relationships,[38;39] and of organisations where entrenched cultural values are present.[40] It is evident that subcultures and multi-cultures now co-exist in health service organisations.[41]

Cultural analysis will serve to make sense of the professional-manager debate within health service organisations.[42] Research theories point to not just one culture in these organisations but to multiple cultures, and to several co-existing and competing sub-cultures.[43;44] Studies pertaining to doctors-as-managers[45] and the impact of "managerialism" on social workers[46;47] indicate that competing cultures exist. In contrast, research into non-clinician professional accountants[48] and non-clinician managers indicate that these groups balanced the professional-managerial culture divide in a positive manner.[49]

The term "cultural chameleons" has been used by Thorne to describe a group of clinical directors working within the British health service.[50] She found that this group of clinical directors was working in an environment where complex and multi-cultural relationships were more interdependent than hierarchical, and that people of divergent cultures worked alongside each other in a relationship of "asymmetric complementarity" that required commitment to the organisation's goals to be effective. In addition, Thorne found that a "cell culture", rather than a "subculture", emerged, which consisted of discrete

---

33   Ferlie & Pettigrew (1996).
34   Causer & Exworthy (1999).
35   Schein (1984).
36   Drucker (1988b).
37   Wells (1999).
38   Trice (1993).
39   Bloor & Dawson (1994).
40   Harris (1999).
41   Thorne (2000).
42   Exworthy & Halford (1999).
43   Williams, Dobson & Walters (1993).
44   Currie (1999).
45   Harrison, Hunter, Marnoch & Pollitt (1992).
46   Jones (1999).
47   Halford & Leonard (1999).
48   Thorne (2000).
49   Carney (2002a).
50   Thorne (2000).

groups of professionals working in similar roles and displaying different sets of norms. Carney[51] supports this view.

In modern health care delivery, the challenge for managers in managing the organisation's culture includes the ability to understand, to co-operate with and to manage cultural diversity. This process includes the management of not just the cultural differences that exist between clinicians and non-clinicians but also the cultural ethnic differences that now exist in health care management. Oh[52] questions whether health care organisations generally expect health care workers who come from different cultures to adapt completely to the host country or to the host country organisation. Success or failure in health care will depend upon the degree to which the manager is capable of integrating people with different ways of delivering patient care. A major challenge for all concerned is the integration of diverse cultural approaches and differences in motivational, communication and value systems so that members of the organisation will work together successfully to achieve the common aims of the organisation. Therefore, health care managers require orientation towards cognitive complexity and should have an intuitive sensitivity to different ethnic workers and their cultures, and to be oriented toward self-monitoring which demands personal flexibility and the ability to adjust to the social and cultural values and the ethical demands of various cultures.[53] In essence, organisational values are culture in action.

ORGANISATIONAL VALUES:
CULTURE IN ACTION

Organisational values are influenced by human values. Human values are determined by the personal principles by which an individual lives[54] and act as standards by which choices are made on how to behave in particular circumstances.[55] Some authors, such as Schwartz[56] and Schwartz & Sagiv,[57] theorise that human values are individual responses to cognitive requirement – for example, social interaction needs and group needs.

---

[51]   Carney (2002a).
[52]   Oh (2004).
[53]   Oh (2004).
[54]   Schwartz (1992).
[55]   Elizur, Borg, Hunt & Magyari Beck (1991).
[56]   Schwartz (1994).
[57]   Schwartz & Sagiv (1995).

These authors identify 10 human value need types that are consistent across cultures:

◆ Power.

◆ Achievement.

◆ Self-direction.

◆ Hedonism.

◆ Stimulation.

◆ Universalism.

◆ Tradition.

◆ Conformity.

◆ Benevolence

◆ Security.

Maslow,[58] in developing his "hierarchy of needs", placed safety and security needs as the first and second most important human requirement, just above the physiological need for water and food. A year earlier, McClelland[59] recognised the need for achievement as an important human need.

In order to determine how human values influence health service organisational culture, comparisons are made between the cultural norms identified by Carney[60];[61]and the definitions of higher order values proposed by Schwartz[62] and Schwartz & Sagiv.[63] In identifying the "dos", the "don'ts" and "the way things are done around here", Carney revealed differing perceptions related to the organisation's cultural norms, both positive and negative. Clinicians follow a set of procedures that are linked to the profession rather than to the area of work. Various clinician and non-clinician groups appear to have fundamentally different beliefs; however, diverse beliefs are not detrimental to services delivery nor result in a better service of care for patients, as all professionals are focussed on the same outcome. The health professionals' core values are excellence in care delivery, equity in service delivery, safety, confidentiality in dealing with patients, client advocacy, respect and dignity for patients and loyalty and staff integrity. [64]

---

58 Maslow (1954).
59 McGregor (1953).
60 Carney (2002a).
61 Her research involved 352 health care clinician and non-clinician managers, working in acute care hospitals in Ireland.
62 Schwartz (1994).
63 Schwartz & Sagiv (1995).
64 Carney (2006a).

Achievement: Competency, Professional Approach & Consensus

The human value of achievement is identified by Schwartz[65] as personal success through competence and is recognised by Carney[66] in the cultural value system of health care professionals in Ireland through their competent approach to work. She identifies "excellence in client care service delivery" as the delivery of high quality, equitable and focused standards of care. A professional approach is perceived by clinicians and non-clinicians as being of "personal importance" and is identifiable in their highly professional and committed approach to work through the development of protocols for standards of care. Carney also found that the presence of "positive interpersonal relationships" in health service organisations contributes to collaborative and participative communications between managers. This is evidenced by a consultative, broad-based consensus approach to decision-making, whereby discussion and challenge are welcomed.

Universalism: Respect for Patients & Staff & Clinical Efficiency

The human value of universalism identified by Schwartz and Schwartz & Sagiv[67,68] is represented as responsibility for society, fairness, understanding and tolerance. Carney found these values manifested in health service professionals through shared value systems, strong ethical beliefs and respect for patients and colleagues.[69] This value is also recognisable in staff's approach to patients: "operational efficiency" is perceived as delivering to the client what is required by them in a friendly, accessible, consistently fair and individualistic manner.[70]

Benevolence: The Client-centred Approach

The human value of benevolence is identified as preservation and enhancement of the welfare of in-group members,[71,72] and is also recognisable in the cultural value system of professionals through their client-centred approach. Benevolence is indicated by a positive and, in

---

65   Schwartz (1992).
66   Carney (2002a).
67   Schwartz (1994).
68   Schwartz & Sagiv (1995).
69   Carney (2002a).
70   Schwartz & Sagiv (1995).
71   Schwartz (1992).
72   Schwartz & Sagiv (1995).

many instances, a passionate approach to client-centred care, whereby the patient is always placed first.[73]

Tradition: Positive Responses to New Initiatives & to Changes in Work Practices

The human value of tradition is identified as respect, commitment and acceptance of customs and ideas,[74] and is recognisable in the cultural value system of professionals through their organisations' positive responses to new initiatives and to work practice changes, and in the professional's respect and acceptance of other's ideas. Initiation is sought, encouraged and practiced in a positive matter that benefits patient care.[75]

Self-direction: Creative & Best Practice Approaches to Care Delivery

The human value of self-direction is identified as independent thought, freedom and choice, creativity and exploration,[76] and is recognisable in the cultural value system of professionals through creative and best practice approaches to care delivery. Of importance to managers is the presence of "shared organisational goals", perceived as the presence of a clearly-defined and understood mission statement, and a united vision for the organisation's future direction and purpose, whilst continually striving to improve services and raising standards of quality and service to patients. Service is delivered through a safe, creative, innovative and *critical thinking approach to care delivery that encourages best practice.*[77]

Security: Equity, Safety in Care Provided, Respect, Partnership & Multi-disciplinary Teamwork

The human value of security is identified as maintenance of social balance by ensuring reciprocity, safety and harmony between staff and others,[78] and is recognisable in the cultural values system of professionals through equity, safety in care provided and respect. These cultural norms relate to professional status through expertise and competence, professional approach to service delivery and a

---

[73] Carney (2006b).
[74] Schwartz & Sagiv (1995).
[75] Carney (2006a).
[76] Schwartz (1992).
[77] Carney (2002a).
[78] Schwartz & Sagiv (1995).

professional organisation. Partnership in decision-making and a multi-disciplinary team approach is also represented, in addition to equity in service delivery through inclusiveness for all and objectivity in the approach to equity. The presence of good morale and motivation levels and the development of new initiatives for client services are also important to clinicians and non-clinicians in the delivery of services.[79]

A summary of positive organisational consequences to these positive organisational values is presented in **Table 12.1**.

Table 12.1: Positive Organisational Consequences[80]

◆ Excellence in patient care delivery
◆ Shared organisational goals/mission/vision
◆ Operational and clinical efficiency
◆ Positive value systems/shared values
◆ Sound interpersonal relationships
◆ Professional status/professional approach
◆ Partnership in decision-making/team approach
◆ Equity in care delivery
◆ Good morale/motivation levels
◆ New initiative development/innovative practice

ETHICAL VALUES & BELIEFS

A strong sense of ethical values and beliefs appear to be universal within health care organisations. It is evident that the value-for-money, profit-shareholder-value and return-on-investment cultural ethos of for-profit organisations are not evident, to any extent, in health care organisations. The organisational norms and depiction of "the way things are done around here" in health care organisations are consistent and focused on a wide range of values and beliefs. The various groups within health care organisations have fundamentally different beliefs that are recognised through diverse core beliefs and

---

[79] Carney (2002a).
[80] Carney (2002a).

the presence of multiple agendas. Clinicians and non-clinicians influence organisational culture through the provision of efficient, friendly services to patients. This critical norm must be maintained regardless of diverse beliefs or agendas. The most striking and enduring core value of health care organisations is "patient care" and the importance of excellence in care delivery. These values and beliefs were best summarised by one respondent as: human dignity, compassion, justice, equality of service, as well as quality and advocacy.[81]

NEGATIVE CULTURAL NORMS

Negative cultural norms are also present in health care organisations, in the form of "negative managerial receptiveness", and are identified as a lack of appreciation for work effort shown to employees by fellow clinicians, by non-clinicians and by senior management. Other negative cultural norms relate to hierarchical structure, whereby bullying, inappropriate use of power, tight control and conformity are present.[82]

Power: Hierarchical, Bureaucratic & Closed Organisational Structures that are not Dependable

The human value of power is identified by Schwartz & Sagiv as social control or dominance over people and resources.[83] Carney says that power is recognisable in the negative cultural value system of professionals through their perception of inappropriate use of power over each other by certain colleagues. The human value of power is also identifiable through loss of trust in the organisation and the inability to depend upon the organisation due to its dominance over staff and resources[84;85]or through a "lack of organisational dependability" in health service organisations.[86] This cultural norm results from hierarchical, bureaucratic and closed organisational structures that over-emphasise rules and regulations and result in a lack of dependability in the organisation.

---

[81] Carney (2006b).
[82] Carney (2006b).
[83] Schwartz & Sagiv (1995).
[84] Schwartz & Sagiv (1995).
[85] Tierney (2000).
[86] Carney (2004b).

Lack of Peer Cohesion & Negative Managerial Receptiveness

Additionally, "lack of peer cohesion" is seen as a sense of isolation and mistrust amongst established organisational groupings. This mistrust exists between clinicians, such as nurses; between professional clinician groupings, such as doctors and nurses or doctors and physiotherapists; and between clinicians and non-clinicians. This mistrust is manifested through "negative managerial receptiveness", whereby clinician managers perceive a lack of appreciation of the manager's role, expertise and value by non-clinician managers. In contrast, non-clinicians perceive "negative managerial receptiveness" as a lack of interest in the management side of their role by clinicians and by top managers.

Clinician values may also be at variance with the perceived values and ethics of senior management in the areas of efficiency and cost effectiveness. Negative managerial receptiveness often results in bullying, focus on power, the presence of power bases and a sense of tight control being exercised. The presence of professional protectionism amongst professional clinicians also exists.[87;88;89]

Lack of Organisational Dependability

"Lack of organisational dependability" occurs when existing structures are disorganised, hierarchical or bureaucratic, and where a closed approach to new ideas and innovations and an over-emphasis on rules exist. A sense of a lack of dependability is related to how the organisation might respond to operational difficulties. If clinicians perceive that an organisation is not being run in an efficient manner, there will also be a perception that deterioration in the quality of care delivered is occurring.[90;91]

It is evident that there are negative organisational consequences to the presence of perceived diverse beliefs in organisations. These negative consequences include lack of appreciation for the role and expertise of others that results in mistrust and poor communication. This mistrust ultimately leads to low morale and a low level of initiative in developing new services. If existing organisational structures are disorganised and hierarchical, the consequences will be an over-emphasis on rules, and a perception that the organisation is being run in an inefficient manner, and that, due to these inefficiencies,

---

[87]   Carney (2004a).
[88]   Carney (2006b).
[89]   Carney (2006a).
[90]   Carney (2002a).
[91]   Carney (2006a).

the quality of care delivery is deteriorating. Therefore, in order to achieve ethical care delivery in health service organisations, the organisation's culture should be quality focused and patient-centred,[92] incorporating trustworthy collaboration between professionals in service delivery,[93] thereby regaining the respect, confidence and trust of disheartened patients and employees.[94]

Additionally, the dynamic changes in health care currently being experienced will promote evolving cultures whereby health care leaders will create an environment in which team learning is promoted, empowerment is practised and where commitment in excellence to care delivery is valued over compliance with rules and regulations.[95] A summary of negative organisational consequences to these negative cultural norms is presented in **Table 12.2.**

Table 12.2: Negative Organisational Consequences[96]

♦ Negative managerial receptiveness
♦ Poor communications
♦ Lack of organisational dependability
♦ Negative goal clarity
♦ Negative job challenge
♦ Lack of peer cohesion
♦ Power groupings
♦ Lack of partnership and mistrust between professional groups
♦ Goal divergence/lack of "big picture"
♦ Lack of multidisciplinary team approach

---

[92] Pulce (2002).
[93] Meehan (2003).
[94] Magill & Prybil (2004).
[95] Koloroutis (2004). p.67.
[96] Carney (2002a).

SUMMARY

♦ Culture is defined as observed behavioural regularities that occur during interactions between individuals and is a multi-dimensional, multi-faceted phenomenon, not easily reduced to a few major dimensions.

♦ Group norms are sets of shared values that have been validated through a consensus process. The social validation of group norms arises when certain values are confirmed by the shared experiences of the group and these norms are passed onto new members as being the correct way to do things, or "the way we do things around here".

♦ Strong culture indicates that the goals of the organisation are known, understood and acted upon by members of the organisation.

♦ Cultural differences in not-for-profit organisations include competing value systems, bureaucratic constraining forces that are at variance with the high-minded value system of the public service and a more rigorous ethical system of control. In modern health care delivery, the challenge for managers in managing the organisation's culture includes the ability to understand, to co-operate with and to manage cultural diversity.

♦ Organisational values are influenced by human values. Human values are determined by the personal principles by which an individual lives and act as standards by which choices are made on how to behave in particular circumstances. These values may be positive or negative.

♦ Human values include universalism, benevolence and tradition.

CHAPTER 13
STRATEGIC CONSENSUS OF
HEALTH SERVICE STRATEGY

INTRODUCTION

Previous chapters demonstrated that clinicians and non-clinicians are central to health care delivery and that the on-going changes in the structure and delivery of health services has produced new ways of organising and managing work. Health care organisations require managers who will become successful leaders by collaborating and co-ordinating with others and by being capable of managing the changes occurring in a dynamic health service. Therefore, change leaders will become the most sought-after people in the new world of health care. It was also demonstrated that successful health care delivery is dependent, to a large extent, upon the types of interactions occurring amongst clinicians and non-clinicians. These interactions, if collaborative and strategic in nature, result in positive benefits for the clinician, the non-clinician and the patient. Health service managers and professionals are required to demonstrate higher levels of involvement and commitment to their work than that previously expected of them. Therefore, commitment to the organisation is a critical success factor in nurturing, promoting and developing the senior manager-middle manager strategic involvement relationship and affiliation with the organisation. Cultural and ethical values demonstrated by health care professionals are an indicator of professional and organisational commitment.

In this chapter, the importance of strategic consensus and the factors identified or alluded to in previous chapters that have an impact on, and that contribute to, strategic consensus are discussed and integrated. Factors, such as organisational commitment, strategic involvement, organisational structure, organisational culture and values systems inherent in culture are interwoven, so that the meaning and understanding of consensus in the context of health service management are explored and defined.

UNDERSTANDING CONSENSUS

General agreement on the concept of consensus does not exist, as authors have attempted to define the concept in various ways. The literature suggests that certain factors are important determinants of consensus, and that there are limited and conflicting interpretations of the concept of strategic consensus. Although the relevance of consensus to involvement in strategy formulation is not well understood, there is a requirement for the integration of strategic consensus when formulating strategy.

Strategic consensus is achieved through the sharing of strategic information and direct exposure to strategic priorities. Health care is delivered in a turbulent and constantly changing environment that is influenced by changing demographic, technological, environmental and financial factors that often result in less consensus on the organisations' strategic direction. Authors have highlighted the importance of consensus in strategic decision-making and of strategy development as a consensus-building process.[1,2] Despite the perceived importance of strategic consensus, little research had been conducted, due to the absence of a conceptual framework linking the concepts that might contribute to the consensus-performance relationship,[3,4] until Carney[5] researched strategic consensus and found that certain managerial, organisational and cultural factors lead to strategic consensus. It is clear that conflicting interpretations of the concept of strategic consensus exist and that the relevance of consensus to involvement in strategy formulation is not understood.[6,7] Research on consensus is related to strategy formulation,[8,9,10,11] to the environment[12]

---

[1]   Nielsen (1981).
[2]   Hrebiniak & Joyce (1984).
[3]   Dess & Origer (1987).
[4]   Dess & Origer's (1987) study related to the conceptual integration of organisation environment, organisation structure and strategic consensus in strategy formulation.
[5]   Carney (2002a).
[6]   Floyd & Wooldridge (1992b).
[7]   After conducting a series of semi-structured interviews with senior, middle and operating managers in manufacturing and financial environments and presenting the information in a case study form, Floyd & Wooldridge (1992b) developed a strategic map of the domains of cost differentiation and cost effectiveness, and defined four levels of "strategic consensus".
[8]   Hrebiniak & Snow (1982).
[9]   Bourgeois & Singh (1983).
[10] Hrebiniak & Snow (1982) undertook this study amongst 247 senior managers in 88 organisations in the US.
[11] Bourgeois & Singh (1983) undertook further analysis on the same data set as Bourgeois' (1980) study in 25 chief executive officers.

and to group or organisational performance.[13] In addition, consensus-mediating factors, such as organisational structure have been identified as influencing strategic consensus,[14;15;16] whereby collaborative and cultural patterns are used in consensus building among the organisation's hierarchical levels.[17;18]

Consensus Definitions

Little has been written about the concept of strategic understanding or agreement and, as a result, these concepts are unsatisfactorily portrayed collectively as agreement, understanding and consensus, often resulting in a lack of clarity and ambiguity; consensus-building that leads to agreement has been explored in terms of participative management,[19] and as the outcome of the decision-making process.[20;21] Consensus may be defined in terms of an individual or a group context, as a generic concept, or as related to strategic consensus. Consensus is also defined as the agreement of all parties to a group decision – that is, when all members have explored the issues involved, are in agreement, and each is satisfied about future action.[22] Consensus of strategy or strategic consensus is defined as agreement by managers on the strategic fundamentals of the organisation.[23] Consensus is strategic understanding and commitment related to strategic involvement, but not necessarily to organisational performance, and is defined "as the product of middle management commitment to, and understanding of, strategy."[24;25] This combination of consensus and commitment results in a collective heart and mind in

---

[12] Dess (1987).

[13] DeWoot, Heyvaert & Martou (1977/1978).

[14] Bourgeois (1985).

[15] Carney (2002a).

[16] Bourgeois (1985) undertook this study of 99 senior managers in 20 public for-profit organisations in 17 industries and examined the relationship between consensus and perceived environmental factors.

[17] Brodwin & Bourgeois (1984).

[18] Brodwin & Bourgeois (1984), in a study of management practices in 19 organisations, found that five patterns of strategy formulation-implementation approaches were used.

[19] Mintzberg (1978).

[20] Schweiger, Sandberg & Ragan (1986).

[21] Schweiger, Sandberg & Ragan (1986) explored consensus and group strategy formation in a study involving 120 students in simulated conditions.

[22] Holder (1976).

[23] Floyd & Wooldridge (1992a).

[24] Wooldridge & Floyd (1990).

[25] Wooldridge & Floyd (1990, p. 235), in a qualitative study related to strategic consensus definition, and undertaken in for-profit organisations in the US that included 11 banks and nine manufacturing organisations.

managers who act in consort with a common set of strategic priorities and hold a shared understanding and commitment. Agreement, among all categories of managers, on the fundamental priorities of the organisation, enhances strategic goal achievement and results in consensus regarding the goals of the organisation.[26] Consensus is also viewed as being related to the beliefs of the organisation, particularly when beliefs are unvaried and simple, and therefore, result in strategic consensus that is easier to achieve and is sustainable over time.[27]

Consensus in Organisations

One of the first authors to study the notion of consensus in organisations was Stagner,[28] whose analysis of 109 responses from *Fortune 500* organisations indicated a link between managerial cohesiveness and decision-making. Interestingly, the findings of the first empirical study related to consensus revealed that consensus on goals and consensus on means to achieve goals did not produce high organisational performance and that consensus on means was more important than consensus on ends.[29;30] Conversely, Grinyer & Norburn[31;32] investigated the level of consensus in the relationship between organisational objectives and planning systems and found a very high level of disagreement among managers. This disagreement related primarily to the perceived value of formal planning processes and to consensus on the goals and the means. The findings of these studies, all undertaken in for-profit public organisations, suggest that agreement on goals and objectives may not be a requisite for organisational effectiveness. In contrast, Dess[33;34] found a positive relationship between consensus on objectives and methods in for-profit organisations.

There are difficulties in managing strategic consensus in a turbulent environment, when priorities are constantly shifting, as a lack of

26   Floyd & Wooldridge (1992b).
27   Dutton & Duncan (1987).
28   Stagner (1969).
29   Bourgeois (1980).
30   Bourgeois (1980) carried out the first empirical study related to consensus, in which a sample of 67 managers in 12 organisations was examined.
31   Grinyer & Norburn (1977/1978).
32   Grinyer & Norburn (1977/1978) investigated the level of consensus in the relationship between the organisational objectives and the planning systems in a study of 91 senior managers in 21 British companies in 13 different organisations.
33   Dess (1987).
34   Dess (1987) found a positive relationship between consensus on objectives and methods in his study of 19 private, for-profit organisations, which explored the environment and consensus in strategy formulation in US hospitals amongst 86 strategic decision-making teams.

consensus exists in organisations competing in such an environment resulting in less consensus on the strategic direction of the organisation.[35] Therefore, the integration of organisation environment, organisation structure and strategic consensus is required in the formulation of strategy. In hospitals, often classified as turbulent environments,[36] strategic consensus is achieved through the sharing of strategic information and direct exposure to strategic priorities. This process is based upon the cultural patterns prevailing in the organisation. However, as culture forms through a continuous sequence of interaction between all relevant parties, there cannot be consensus when there are multiple perspectives,[37;38] or where the views and knowledge of particular groups within the organisation, such as clinicians and non-clinicians, are not appreciated or accepted by senior management.[39]

The Concept of Consensus

The concept of consensus is viewed as agreement on means for innovative activities amongst group decisions,[40] and as being related to the acceptance of strategic decisions. Competitive or co-operative conditions exist amongst groups within the organisation when mandatory consensus or majority decision-making is required. These conditions result in enhanced organisational performance.[41;42] Conversely, the formation of coalitions by groups or individuals influences strategic consensus in a negative manner by making goal attainment problematic.[43] It appears that lack of group cohesiveness exists where the consensus process is forced upon participants, resulting in dissent and lack of agreement on strategic decisions. However, well-structured procedures offering a narrow range of alternatives will promote consensus-building in decision-making. In contrast, the Japanese are notoriously consensus-orientated and companies tend to mediate among individuals rather than accentuating differences.[44;45]

---

[35] Floyd & Wooldridge (1992b).
[36] Wells (1999).
[37] Daymon (2000).
[38] Daymon's (2000) longitudinal case study was undertaken in a media organisation exploring the cultural aspects of the organisations studied.
[39] Carney (2006a).
[40] DeWoot, Heyvaert & Martou (1977/1978).
[41] Tjosvold & Field (1983).
[42] Tjosvold & Field (1983) undertook a simulated study on 114 students, arranged in four groups.
[43] Narayanan & Fahey (1982).
[44] Porter (1996).

THE ROLE OF THE MIDDLE MANAGER IN STRATEGIC CONSENSUS

Research on consensus has been related to senior management and to organisations and, up until 1990, did not focus on the middle manager. Researchers have supported the idea that strategy is formulated through consensus-building among senior management.[46] However, conversely, it is acknowledged that consensus should be part of the strategy formulation process,[47] and that consensus of the organisation's strategic direction and goals will not be achieved unless middle managers are directly involved in the strategic process.

So, what is the importance of strategic consensus by middle managers? It is recognised that middle managers will resist decisions made at the strategic level if they are not involved in the process at the earliest opportunity.[48;49] Few middle managers articulate the same goals as their superiors, and those who disagree with strategic initiatives block the implementation of strategy.[50;51;52] The strength of this disagreement varies and is dependent upon the perceived level of involvement.

Four levels of strategic consensus have been identified amongst managers. In the first level of strategic consensus, managers have a common understanding and a shared commitment to strategy; however, at the second level, termed "blind devotion", although managers are well intentioned, they are ill informed. At the third level, referred to as "informed scepticism", managers are informed about strategy but are unwilling to act. At the fourth level, termed "weak consensus", shared understanding and commitment to organisational strategy are low.[53] In different organisations, any or all of the levels may be appropriate. In addition, a high degree of consensus is achieved when shared strategic understanding and commitment are high. Conversely, low consensus occurs when this relationship of understanding and commitment is not present.[54;55]

---

45   Porter (1996) conducted interviews in Japanese companies and explored how consensus was achieved.
46   Dess (1987).
47   Bower & Doz (1979).
48   Floyd & Wooldridge (1992b).
49   Carney (2002a).
50   Floyd & Wooldridge (1992b).
51   Carney (2004a).
52   A strategic map constructed by Floyd & Wooldridge (1992b), relating to the domains of cost differentiation and cost effectiveness, defined four levels of "strategic consensus".
53   Floyd & Wooldridge (1992b).
54   Wooldridge & Floyd (1990).

The Strategic Decision Process

Studies undertaken in US and Irish hospitals found that consensus-building is an important factor in the strategic decision process, and that it is influenced by loyalty to the team and to the organisation.[56;57] The dominant culture existing in not-for-profit health service organisations has an influence on strategic consensus.[58] It is recognised that social validation of group norms arises when certain values are confirmed by the shared experiences of group members within an organisation. These norms are validated through a consensus process that is passed onto new members as being the correct way to do things.[59]

Methods used to generate consensus-building in organisations include problem-solving teams and analytical tools. In contrast, methods used to generate consensus building in the "cultural approach" tend to be built into the organisation's systems. This blending of cultural methods incorporates the manipulation of logos and symbols, leadership style and behaviour patterns and organisational groupings or "clans" concepts.[60] This form of the cultural-methods-approach is found in literature pertaining to organisational culture.

EVIDENCE FOR MIDDLE MANAGER STRATEGIC CONSENSUS IN HEALTH SERVICE ORGANISATIONS

There is a significant relationship between strategic involvement and strategic consensus. Strategic involvement and organisational commitment, when both are present, are better predictors of strategic consensus than when involvement or commitment is present as a single entity. Commitment has the greatest impact in predicting consensus amongst hospital managers. Additionally, involvement predicts consensus, as consensus of strategy amongst managers increases by almost 40% when involvement is present. Also, if a strong

---

[55] *Re* consensus and the middle manager, Wooldridge & Floyd (1989) published a theoretical paper, which attempted to encourage debate into the effect of the strategic process on consensus.

[56] Dooley & Fryxell (1999).

[57] *Re* consensus-building, Dooley & Fryxell's (1999) study was undertaken in US hospitals and involved 86 strategic decision-making teams.

[58] Carney (2002a).

[59] Schein (1992).

[60] Brodwin & Bourgeois (1985).

culture exists, a high level of commitment is also present; in fact, when commitment is present the strength of the organisation's culture is increased five-fold. Therefore, the organisation's culture makes a unique contribution to the prediction of consensus by demonstrating that strong culture increases consensus of strategy amongst middle managers six-fold. The organisation's culture ensures that middle managers are committed to their professions and to their organisations and, therefore, influence the level of consensus of strategy occurring amongst such managers (**Figure 13.1**).

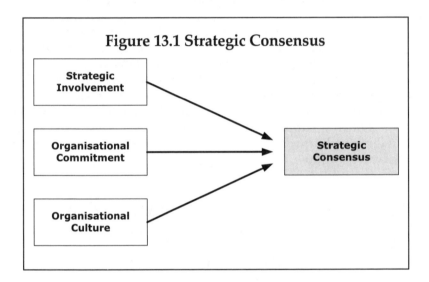

Consensus in Clinicians & Non-Clinicians

However, in relation to clinicians and non-clinicians, clinicians' level of strategic involvement and strategic consensus is greater than that of non-clinicians in organisations where a very strong culture exists. Non-clinicians working in organisations with a very strong culture have a higher level of strategic involvement than those working in organisations with weaker culture. There are higher levels of consensus of strategy in both clinicians and non-clinicians working in stronger organisational culture than those working in weaker organisational culture. Therefore, clinicians and non-clinicians who work in strong organisational cultures have a greater level of strategic consensus than those who work in weaker organisational culture.

The future goal of health service managers should be to provide a strong organisation culture that promotes involvement, collaboration and participation by clinician and non-clinician managers in the development of strategy.[61] The Consensus Model is presented in **Figure 13.2**.

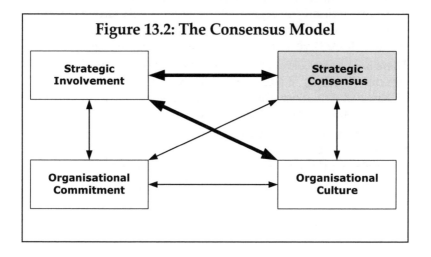

Figure 13.2: The Consensus Model

SUMMARY

♦ Strategic consensus is achieved through the sharing of strategic information and direct exposure to strategic priorities.

♦ Consensus may be defined in terms of an individual or group context, as a generic concept or as related to strategic consensus. Consensus is also defined as the agreement of all parties to a group decision, whereby all members have explored the issues involved, are in agreement, and each is satisfied about future action to be taken.

♦ Strategic consensus is the product of middle management commitment to, and understanding of, strategy.

♦ A lack of consensus exists in organisations competing in a turbulent environment, resulting in less consensus on the strategic direction of the organisation. Strategic consensus is achieved through the sharing of strategic information and through direct exposure to strategic priorities.

♦ Consensus-building is an important factor in the strategic decision process; it is influenced by loyalty to the team and to the organisation, indicating that the dominant culture existing in the organisation influences strategic consensus.

---

[61] Carney (2002a).

♦ Strategic involvement and organisational commitment, when both are present, will influence the level of consensus of strategy.

♦ Clinicians' strategic involvement and strategic consensus is greater than non-clinicians' in organisations where a very strong culture exists, and non-clinicians working in organisations with a very strong culture have a high level of strategic involvement.

♦ There are high levels of consensus in both clinicians and non-clinicians working in strong organisational cultures; therefore, the fostering of strong organisational culture is an important factor in the maintenance of organisational stability.

♦ Professional clinicians and non-clinicians working in strong organisational cultures have a greater level of strategic consensus than those working in weaker organisational cultures.

CHAPTER 14
AN INTEGRATIVE APPROACH TO STRATEGIC MANAGEMENT IN THE HEALTH SERVICES: THE CONSENSUS MODEL

INTRODUCTION

The integrative approach to strategic management, through the defining of the consensus model, is a new concept. The consensus model incorporates the management principles, organisational, behavioural and cultural patterns that form health services strategic management. Strategic management is the platform from which health services are delivered and forms its central core. Strategic planning is the critical component of strategic management, because effective health care delivery requires that management have sufficient information about themselves and their environment, and possess the managerial capabilities that allow effective strategic planning to occur. The critical components of the strategic planning process are the generation and formulation of strategic options, the evaluation of strategic alternatives, and the likely impact of the proposed decisions on others. Therefore, health service managers require sufficient knowledge of strategy and its management in order that the factors hindering or promoting effectiveness and efficiency in health care planning, implementation and evaluation may be determined. However, there is little agreement on the definition of strategic management and it is believed that this lack of consistency is due to its multi-dimensional and situational nature.

THE INTEGRATIVE APPROACH TO
STRATEGIC MANAGEMENT

The integrative approach to strategic management is demonstrated throughout this book. The process by which organisational strategies are developed is influenced by several factors, including the planning process undertaken, political, cultural or enforced choice.[1] Collaboration in the strategic process is a critical factor in the development of strategy, as collaboration ensures that strategy is understood and supported by the entire organisation.[2] In successful organisations, senior management use an integrative process that involves middle managers in the development of the strategic plan, thereby leading to the development of distinctive competencies in managers that then become part of the new vision of the organisation. This integrative process then becomes the driver for the development of new managerial and strategic competencies in middle and operational managers that further enhances and develops their roles within the organisation.[3] Conversely, unsuccessful organisations are those where formal planning does not occur and strategies emerge from informal decisions and entrenched values.[4]

Integrating Managerial Effectiveness

Health services organisations are mainly not-for-profit organisations; therefore, a further complication is added to the managerial process in the management of such organisations, as strategies developed for the private sector are not appropriate for the not-for-profit sector. Even so, many hospital managers have adopted the managerial techniques and systems of the for-profit organisations as a perceived means of improving their operations, thereby enhancing the level of service delivered to patients and clients[5,6]and, in the process, not-for-profit hospitals have become increasingly business-like in terms of organisation and management.[7] This is due, in part, to professional clinicians adopting, and becoming more involved in, new strategic management roles and responsibilities, in addition to their clinician practice roles.[8] This involvement, whilst contributing to a more holistic

---

[1]   Bailey, Johnson & Daniels (2000).
[2]   Bryant, Dobal & Johnson (1990).
[3]   Burgelman (1991).
[4]   Harris (1999).
[5]   Oster (1995).
[6]   Wells (1999).
[7]   Carney (2001a).
[8]   Jowett (1996).

approach to care delivery, has also contributed to strategic management difficulties in hospitals because, in the health service, the emphasis is on a caring approach to the delivery of health care rather than on the generation of profits for the organisation,[9] often a cause of conflict for health service professionals.

Additionally, competition for health services has resulted in the introduction of managed care, in order to produce efficiencies in health care delivery, through controlling costs and by improving quality. Therefore, individual hospitals are required to control costs and to increase operational efficiency, while continuing to provide high quality care, thus increasing the pressure that clinicians and non-clinicians are placed under when delivering patient care.[10] It is now recognised that a change in the traditional self-image, perceptions, values and roles of individual health professionals is taking place and that, through this process of change, the middle manager clinician and non-clinician become the strategists, the organisation builders and the directors of operations. Involvement by middle managers in strategy development, therefore, is a critical organisational success factor in successful strategic management because, if this group perceives that they are being excluded from the strategic process, they will be a recurring source of resistance to the development of new organisational strategy. Therefore, what is required for successful strategic management is the recognition that strategic management be viewed as a bottom-up and top-down integrative multi-layered process.

Integrating Professional Organisations

The success or otherwise of managerial effectiveness is dependent upon the collaborative process, yet difficulties in strategy development in hospitals arise, due to the increased complexity of their hierarchical systems,[11] the changing demographic shifts and the emerging populations within society that impinge on the health sector and on health service management. Therefore, a collective organisational mindset is necessary for the integration of the organisation's mission and objectives. This integration is based upon collaborative management, whereby employees view the organisation as an interacting network rather than a hierarchy. In this way, employees are encouraged to solve their own problems and to become involved in future organisational planning. The manager's role in collaborative management is to bring out the positive aspects of the employees'

---

[9]   Wells (1995).
[10] Douglas & Ryman (2003).
[11] Jaques (1990).

mindset. This is achieved in health care management through inspiring, engaging and leading employees through a process of involvement, collaboration and consensus,[12] which requires a finely-tuned interpersonal adeptness.[13]

One of the common criticisms of hierarchical health service organisations is that they are outmoded, too slow and unwieldy for the turbulent modern world, yet some have survived because they have remained flexible and responsive to their changing environments by incorporating new practices, management techniques and technologies, in effect, new mindsets.[14] Yet, it is evident that layers of management create complexity in reporting structures,[15;16] requiring a collaborative management. To counter-balance this effect, new ways of organising and doing work are now occurring through knowledge workers, project teams and cross-departmental groups. Knowledge workers with clearly-defined career pathways have made hierarchical managers almost redundant.[17] Also, a focus on people, processes and rewards enhances employee motivation and commitment levels, thereby increasing organisational productivity and efficiency.[18] Relationship-building, collaborative practices and interactions, and networking will determine the success of changed organisational structure. This type of interactive process is taking place in the US through the formation of "magnet" hospitals, renowned for their approach to excellence.

The creation of reliable and efficient hospitals through knowledge workers and knowledge economies are driven by collegial nurse-physician relationships. Few health care organisations remain in a stable state for long today, due to challenging environmental, financial and technological changes. Therefore, a socio-cultural health care system is required that offers its members the choice to change the structured mindset of the organisation. Such change is brought about by promoting participation, involvement and collaboration in the delivery of health care rather than by competition,[19] thereby permitting organisational members to develop the ability to adjust to, or recover from, change easily.[20]

---

12   Carney (2002a).
13   Krueger Wilson & Porter O'Grady (1999).
14   Leavitt (2003).
15   Yasai-Ardekani & Haug (1997).
16   Mintzberg (1998).
17   Oxman & Smith (2003).
18   Carney (2004b).
19   Weick & Sutcliffe (2001).
20   Merriam-Webster Online.

Integrating Change Processes

The effect of restructuring on health service organisations and on the structure and delivery of health services has resulted in new ways of organising and doing work. A consequence of these changes is that health service managers need to have change management skills. The management of change draws from psychological, behavioural, political, social and cultural dimensions, many of which may be conflicting. In order for the change process to be successful, the communications process during change should include several key factors, including:

◆ Consultation.

◆ Education.

◆ Participation.

◆ Assertiveness.

◆ Negotiation.

◆ Understanding of change dynamics.

◆ Democratic decision-making.[21]

Schyns[22] model of "preparedness for occupational change" revealed that the core concepts required for successful change are self-efficacy and leadership, and indicates that, for change to occur, the leader requires persistence in overcoming obstacles. Therefore, leadership is required. Support systems to aid problem-solving may be needed, as well as active facilitators to map out, for managers and staff, the desired, possible and eventual change patterns that are emerging.

Organisations should also be prepared to assist and to educate their employees to take on new tasks, roles and processes.[23] The role and importance of personal, professional and organisational values are important in health service management. Adherence and commitment to organisational values and ethics remains strong in health service organisations, particularly in hospitals, where the provision of excellence in service delivery is the key organisational value. It is important, for the successful management of change, that strategists manage existing cultural artefacts, such as key values, norms, rituals, ceremonies, language systems and myths about the organisation's successes or failures.[24] This is required because existing strategy is fostered and nourished by current cultural artefacts, and new organisational strategy will require a different cultural mindset from

---

[21]   Carney (2000).
[22]   Schyns (2004).
[23]   Bloom & Sheerer (1992).
[24]   Carney (2002a).

its members.[25] Thus, through communication, group participation, leadership and education, managers should introduce the new strategy that will complement existing cultural artefacts, whilst also promoting the need for efficient management and cost effective care delivery.[26]

Integrating Leadership & Motivation

Leadership forms a key component of the strategic integrative process, which is centred around how leaders can have an effect on the aspirations, motives and commitment of employees or followers. Emphasis on the inspirational, the visionary and the charismatic qualities of the leader appeals to the values-based system of the follower in a positive manner through infusing the follower with ideology, loyalty to the leader, values and moral purpose that the follower recognises, aspires to and, therefore, buys into.[27;28] As a result, followers of outstanding leaders become committed to the vision of the leader through shared values. Contemporary health service managers require leadership skills that include collaborative shared and co-operative forms that are multi-dimensional in orientation and innovative in change. Instilling a sense of organisational commitment in employees is also necessary in modern health care delivery.[29] This collaborative process is the context that motivates employees to change, as they now want their work to be more effective and, thereby to contribute to better organisational outcomes.[30]

Thus, motivation is a further factor in the integrative approach to strategic management. If employees perceive that their work is challenging and interesting, and if they are provided with a high level of responsibility by their organisation, they will be motivated to work and to produce higher levels of work output than previously, resulting in a responsible employee. Positive motivators, such as encouragement, involvement and participation in decision-making will produce high standards of performance, leading to the need to attain "achievement motivation", which, in itself, influences leadership through the skilful use of power.[31] This unleashing of the appropriate use of power, energy and talent results in positive benefits for the organisation, because, when individual purpose and mission are intertwined with the organisation's purpose and mission, synergies

[25] Higgins & McAllaster (2004).
[26] Carney (2006a).
[27] Bass (1985).
[28] Burns (1978).
[29] Chiok Foong Loke (2001).
[30] Wheatley (2001).
[31] McClelland & Burnham (2003).

result that lead to increased motivation to implement the organisation's purpose and mission. This process is self-motivational, because, in order for employees to become motivated to take responsibility for their actions, they must be able to visualise how their work achievements fit into the overall scheme of things in the organisation.

The patient also benefits from increased employee motivation levels; this occurs as a result of clinicians and non-clinicians maintaining self-motivational levels and, thereby not compromising the values that they hold. The development of expertise and competencies are the best motivators for health care clinicians, as professionals are motivated, through their professionalism, to design and manage systems of care delivery and to create an environment that promotes excellence in patient care delivery.[32]

Integration of Involvement & Commitment

Perceptions exist amongst clinicians and non-clinicians that involvement in strategic planning is governed by the motivation to take part in the planning process and, as a result, motivation levels are governed by the perceptions of involvement or non-involvement in strategic decision-making. Thus, managers, through involvement in the strategic process, enjoy an enhanced role within the work environment, leading to added value for the organisation in terms of patient care delivery.[33] The professional role is rooted in patient advocacy. Involvement in strategy development permits clinicians to identify their areas of expertise and to appreciate that this expertise provides them with a critical asset in acting as advocates for their patients, thereby enhancing self-motivation levels.[34]

Due to health care demands from patients, for greater choice in the services offered, and for higher levels of excellence in the services delivered, health professionals are required to demonstrate a higher level of involvement and commitment to their work than has been previously expected of them. Commitment is an intricate mechanism that encompasses a complex sense of loyalty involving a strong belief in the goals of the organisation and congruence with its value system.[35] A high level of involvement in work-based activities results in a sense of acknowledgement of one's efforts on behalf of the organisation resulting in commitment to the organisation.[36]

---

[32]   Carney (2002a).
[33]   Currie (1999).
[34]   Carney (2004a).
[35]   Corser (1988).
[36]   Carney (2004a).

Organisational managers have an ethical obligation to create a healthy working environment where communication and involvement are fostered. As the ultimate responsibility for the organisation's environment lies with management, leadership behaviour by managers is necessary in order to create an organisational climate where job satisfaction and organisational commitment are promoted.[37] A contemporary form of commitment, termed organisational citizenship behaviour (OCB), is positively associated with organisational commitment. OCB produces loyalty to the organisation and results in the individual taking on greater responsibility and decision-making in the work situation.[38] However, conflict may arise in health care management due to differing ideology amongst professionals. This conflict relates to the mechanism of care delivery and is due to the value-laden environment or context in which negotiations occur.[39] Therefore, managers require an understanding of the biases resulting from value conflict and the ability to lead, in order to create an organisational climate where involvement and commitment are promoted.[40]

Integrating Organisational Culture

Organisational culture influences health care management. The internal culture of the organisation is the set of key values, beliefs, understanding and norms that members of an organisation share. Due to changing demographic shifts and emerging populations within society, socio-cultural factors are impinging on health care delivery. Socio-cultural dimensions represent the demographic characteristics, norms, customs and values of the population within which the organisation operates. Managers must manage the cultural differences that exist between clinicians and non-clinicians and the cultural ethnic differences that now exist in health care management.[41] Different clinician and non-clinician groups appear to have fundamentally different beliefs. Professional clinicians follow a different set of procedures that appear to be linked to the profession rather than to the area of work. However, diverse beliefs are not deemed to be detrimental to service delivery, nor to result in a better service of care for patients, as all clinicians are focussed on the same outcome. Core values are excellence in care delivery, equity in service delivery, safety, confidentiality in dealings with clients, client advocacy, respect and

---

[37]   Chiok Foong Loke (2001).
[38]   Coyle-Shapiro, Kessler & Purcell (2004).
[39]   Wade-Benzoni, Hoffman, Thompson, Moore, Gillespie & Bazerman (2002).
[40]   Carney (2006b).
[41]   Oh (2004).

dignity for patients, loyalty and staff integrity.[42] A strong organisational culture results in the presence of positive interpersonal relationships. Strong organisational culture is perceived by managers as contributing to a collaborative and participative form of communications that is evident through the presence of a consultative, broad based consensus approach to decision-making.[43]

Integrating Consensus

There are difficulties in managing strategic consensus in a turbulent environment, when priorities are constantly shifting, resulting in less consensus on the strategic direction of the organisation.[44] Therefore, the achievement of consensus is a critical success factor in health care management. Consensus of strategy is achieved through a number of pathways and influences. The consensus platform includes managerial, organisational and behavioural structures, in addition to leadership, involvement, commitment and culture.

The dominant culture existing in organisations influences strategic consensus, through the social validation of group norms; these standards are endorsed through a process of agreement and are passed onto new members as being the correct way to do things.[45] In previous chapters, it was demonstrated that a significant relationship exists between involvement and consensus, and between involvement and commitment, that results in involvement and commitment predicting consensus. It was also demonstrated that, when a strong culture exists in the organisation, a high level of commitment is also present. Therefore, the organisation's culture influences the level of strategic consensus occurring amongst managers. In addition, non-clinician managers who work in strong organisational cultures, where cultural norms, values and beliefs are strong and cohesive, have a greater level of strategic consensus than those who work in weaker organisational cultures where a dilution of organisational culture exists, due to the presence of sub-cultures, multi-cultures and cell-cultures. A climate where discussion and challenging of views is accepted, results in a consensus approach to organisational strategy.[46]

The influence of organisational culture on consensus is manifested through shared value systems that incorporate shared beliefs, respect for clients and staff, and strong ethical beliefs amongst managers. A strong culture also results in a positive and passionate approach to client-centred care, where the client is placed first, where services

---

42 Carney (2002a), p.126.
43 Carney (2006a).
44 Floyd & Wooldridge (1992b).
45 Schein (1992).
46 Carney (2002a).

revolve around clients and where a holistic approach to patient care incorporates evidence-based practice. Additionally, commitment influences the organisation's culture through its norms, values, philosophy, goals and mission. Shared values and the presence of a sound value system is present when employees know what is required of them and what is important to patients. The core and abiding cultural values of middle managers, regardless of their functional role, is the provision of ethical-based services to patients. However, traditional loyalty to the organisation may be inappropriate for a mature employment relationship and, therefore, unquestioning loyalty to the organisation is cautioned so that exploitation of employees through the inappropriate use of power does not occur.[47;48] Where managerial behaviour contradicts professional values, conflict may arise in service delivery. This conflict occurs because a traditional component of the clinician role is the management of organisational culture, whereby the values of the professional team are critical to successful organisational outcomes,[49] rather than the cost of services provided. However, patient services will be enhanced, if both clinicians and non-clinicians are willing to take greater responsibility for cost efficiencies. Thus, it is important for managers to foster a strong organisational culture, thereby ensuring the maintenance of ethical cultural norms such as caring, professionalism and excellence in care delivery. As both groups are strategically involved, two different perspectives will be obtained through the participation of clinicians and non-clinicians in strategic matters, and in the recognition that both groups have different perspectives in care delivery. The strategic model discussed in **Chapter 13** will contribute towards improving the quality and effectiveness of health care, through the generation of knowledge-based innovation, evidence-based practice and new ways of thinking about quality. In Chapter 14, the integrative approach to strategic management is presented (see **Figure 14.1**).

---

[47] Heckscher (1995).
[48] Carney (2002a).
[49] Johnson (1990).

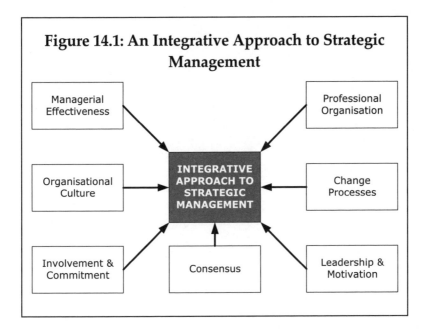

Figure 14.1: An Integrative Approach to Strategic Management

BIBLIOGRAPHY

Abbott, S., Johnson, L. & Lewis, H. (2001). `Participation in arranging continuing health care packages: Experiences & aspirations of service users', *Journal of Nursing Management*, Vol.9, pp.79-85.

Abrahamson, E. (1991). `Managerial fads & fashions: The diffusion & rejection of innovations', *Academy of Management Review*, Vol.16, pp.586-612.

Abrahamson, E. (2004). 'Avoiding repetitive change syndrome', *MIT Sloan Management Review*, Winter, p.93.

Abrams, D., Ando, K. & Hinkle, S. (1998). `Psychological attachment to the group: Cross-cultural differences in organisational identification & subjective norms as predictors of workers' turnover intentions', *Personality & Social Psychology Bulletin*, Vol.24, pp.1027-39.

Ackroyd, S. (1998). `Nursing', in Laffin, M. (ed.), *Beyond Bureaucracy: The Professions in the Contemporary Public Sector*, Aldershot: Ashgate Publishing.

Adams, A., Lugsden, E., Chase, J., Arber, S. & Bond, S. (2000). `Skill-mix changes and work intensification in nursing', *Work, Employment & Society*, Vol.14(3), pp.541-55.

Adamson, B.J & Kenny, D.T. (1995). `The impact of perceived medical dominance on the workplace satisfaction of Australian and British nurses', *Journal of Advanced Nursing*, Vol.21, pp.172-83.

Allen, N.J & Meyer, J.P. (1990). `The measurement & antecedents of affective, continuance & normative commitment to the organisation', *Journal of Occupational Psychology*, Vol.63(1), pp.1-18.

Amabile, T.M., Patterson, C., Mueller, J., Wojcik, T., Odomirok, P.W., Marsh, M. & Kramer, S.J. (2001). `Academic-practitioner collaboration in management research: A case of cross-profession collaboration', *Academy of Management Journal*, Vol.44, pp.418-31.

American Organisation of Nurse Executives (2000). *Strategies for Leadership: Nursing Leadership for Patient Safety*, Chicago: American Organisation of Nurse Executives.

Anderson, W.R.J., Cooper, C.L. & Willmott, M. (1996). `Sources of stress in the NHS: A comparison of seven occupational groups', *Work & Stress*, Vol.10(1), pp.88-95.

Angle, H.L. & Perry, J.L. (1981). `An empirical assessment of organisational commitment & organisational effectiveness', *Administrative Science Quarterly*, Vol.26, pp.1-14.

Argyris, C. (1990). *Overcoming Organisational Defences*, New York: Allyn & Bacon.

Armenakis, A.A., Harris, S.G. & Field, H.S (1999). 'Making change permanent: A model for institutionalising change interventions', *Research in Organisational Change & Development*, Vol.12, pp.97-128.

Ashford, B.E. & Saks, A.M. (2000). `Personal control in organisations: A longitudinal investigation with newcomers', *Human Relations*, Vol. 53, pp.311-39.

Ashford, S., Rothbard, N.P., Piderit, S.K. & Dutton, J.E. (1998). 'Out on a limb: The role of context & impression management in selling gender-equity issues', *Administrative Science Quarterly*, Vol.43, pp.23-57.

Ashmos, D.P., Duchon, D. & McDaniel, R.R. Jr. (1998). `Participation in strategic decision-making: The role of organisational predisposition & issue interpretation', *Decision Sciences*, Vol.29(1), pp.25-51.

Audia, P.G., Locke, E.A. & Smith, K.G. (2000). `The paradox of success: An archival & a laboratory study of strategic persistence following radical environmental change', *Journal of Management*, Vol.63, pp.837-53.

Audit Commission (2000). *The PCG Agenda: Early Progress of Primary Care Groups in the 'New NHS'*, London: Audit Commission.

Avolio, B.J & Gibbons, T.C. (1988). 'Developing transformational leaders: A life span approach', in Conger, J.A & Kanungo, R.N. (eds.), *Charismatic Leadership: The Elusive Factor in Organisational Effectiveness*, pp.276-308, San Francisco, CA: Jossey-Bass.

Bae, K. & Chung, C. (1997). `Cultural values & work attitudes of Korean industrial workers in comparison with those of the United States & Japan', *Work & Occupations*, Vol.24, pp.80-96.

Baggs, J.G, Schmitt, M.H. & Mushlin, A.L. (1999). `Association between nurse-physician collaboration & patient outcomes in three intensive care units', *Critical Care Medicine*, Vol.2(9), pp.1991-98.

Bailey, A., Johnson, G. & Daniels, K. (2000). `Validation of a multi-dimensional measure of strategy development processes', *British Journal of Management*, Vol.11(2), pp.151-62.

Baker, L.M. (2003). `Moving mountains, motivating people', *Harvard Business Review*, January, p.43.

Ballard, R.D. (2003). `Moving mountains, motivating people', *Harvard Business Review*, January, p.46.

Bandura, A. (1977). `Self-efficacy: towards a unifying theory of behavioural change', *Psychological Review*, Vol.84, pp.191-215.

Bandura, A. (1995). 'Exercise of personal and collective efficacy in changing societies' in Bandura, A. (ed.), *Self-efficacy in Changing Societies*, p.2, Cambridge: Cambridge University Press.

Bangle, C. (2003). `Moving mountains, motivating people', *Harvard Business Review*, January, p.42.

Bar-Hayim, A. & Berman, G.S. (1992). `The dimensions of organisational commitment', *Journal of Organisational Behaviour*, Vol.13, pp.379-87.

Barney, J. (1995). `Looking inside for competitive advantage', *Academy of Management Executive*, Vol.9, pp.49-61.

Barr, H. (1994). *Perspectives on Shared Learning*, London: CAIPE, The UK Centre for the Advancement of Inter-professional Education.

Barr, H. (1996). `Ends & means in inter-professional education: Towards a typology', *Education for Health*, Vol.9, pp.341-52.

Barr, H. (2000a). *Inter-professional Education 1997-2000: A Review*, London: UKCC.

Barr, H. (2000b). *Inter-professional Education Today, Yesterday & Tomorrow*, Occasional Paper No. 1, London: LTSN for Health Sciences and Practice.

Bass, B.M. & Avolio, B.J. (1990). `The implications of transactional & transformational leadership for individual, team & organisational development', in Woodman, R.W. & Pasmore, W.A. (eds.) (1990). *Research in Organisational Change & Development*, Vol.1, pp.231-72, Greenwich, CT: JAI Press.

Bass, B.M. (1985). *Leadership & Performance Beyond Expectations*, New York: Free Press.

Bass, B.M. (1988). *Transformational Leadership: Industry, Military & Educational Impact*, Mahwah, NJ: Lawrence Erlbaum Associates.

Bates, E. & Lapsley, H. (1985). *The Health Medicine*, Victoria: Penguin Books.

Beckhard, R. (1996). `On future leaders', in Hesselbein, F., Goldsmith, M. & Beckhard, R. (eds.), *The Leader of the Future*, The Drucker Foundation Future Series, San Francisco, CA: Jossey-Bass.

Beyer, J.M. & Trice, H.M. (1979). `A re-examination of the relations between size & various components of organisational complexity'. *Administrative Science Quarterly*, Vol.24, pp.48-64.

Bloom, P.J. & Sheerer, M. (1992). `Changing organisations by changing individuals: A model of leadership training', *Urban Review*, Vol.24, pp.263-86.

Bloor, G. & Dawson, P. (1974). `Understanding professional culture in the organisational context', *Organisation Studies*, Vol.15(2), pp.275-95.

Bolton, S. (2004). `A simple matter of control? NHS hospital nurses & new management', *Journal of Management Studies*, Vol.41(2), pp.319-33.

Bourgeois, L.J. III & Singh, J.V. (1983). `Organisational slack & political behaviour among top management teams', *Academy of Management Proceedings*, Vol.43, pp.43-47.

Bourgeois, L.J. III (1980). `Performance & consensus', *Strategic Management Journal*, Vol.1(3), pp.227-48.

Bourgeois, L.J. III (1985). `Strategic goals, perceived uncertainty & economic performance in volatile environments', *Academy of Management Journal*, Vol.28(3), pp.548-73.

Bowen, J. & Ford, R. (2002). `Managing service organisations: Does having a "thing" make a difference?', *Journal of Management*, Vol.28, pp.447-69.

Bower, J.L. & Doz, Y. (1979). `Strategy formulation: A social and political view', in Schendel, D.E. & Hofer, C.W. (eds.), *Strategic Management: A New View of Business Policy & Planning*, Boston, MA: Little Brown.

Bower, J.L. (1970). *Managing the Resource Allocation Process: A Study of Corporate Planning & Investment*. Boston, MA: Graduate School of Business Administration, Harvard University.

Bowman, C. & Asch, D. (1987). *Strategic Management*, London: Macmillan Education.

Boyle, D.K. & Kochinda, C. (2004). `Enhancing collaborative communication of nurse & physician leadership in two intensive care units', *Journal of Nursing Administration*, Vol.34(2), pp.60-70.

Bradshaw, P.L. (1995). `The recent health reforms in the United Kingdom: Some tentative observations on their impact on nurses & nursing in hospitals', *Journal of Advanced Nursing*, Vol.21, pp.975-79.

Bridges, W. (1995). *Managing Transitions: Making the Most of Change*, London, Nicholas Brearley Publishing.

Brodbeck, F.C. & Remdisch, S. (1993). `Implementing group work in the car manufacturing industry: The foreman as a focal factor', in Smith. M.J. & Salvendy, G. (eds.), *Human-computer Interaction: Applications & Case Studies*, Proceedings of the Fifth International Conference on Human-Computer Interaction, Orlando, FL, Vol.1, Amsterdam: Elsevier, pp. 32-37.

Brodwin, D.R. & Bourgeois, L.J. III (1984). `Five steps to strategic action', *California Management Review*, Vol.26(3), pp.176-90.

Brodwin, D.R. & Bourgeois, L.J. III (1985). `Strategic goals, perceived uncertainty, and economic performance in volatile environments', *Academy of Management Journal*, Vol.28(3), pp,548-73.

Brooks, I. & Swailes, S. (2002). `Analysis of the relationship between nurse influences over flexible working & commitment to nursing', *Journal of Advanced Nursing*, Vol.38(2), pp.117-26.

Brooks, I. (2002). `Nurse retention: Moderating the ill effects of shift work', *Human Resource Management Journal*, Vol.10, pp.16-30.

Brown, B., Crawford, P. & Darongkamas, J. (2000).`Blurred roles & permeable boundaries: The experience of multi-disciplinary working in community mental health', *Health & Social Care in the Community*, Vol.8, pp.425-35.

Brown, S. (1996). `Incorporating political socialisation theory into Baccalaureate nursing education', *Nursing Outlook*, Vol.44(3), pp.120-23.

Brown, S.L. & Eisenhardt, K.M. (1997). `The art of continuous change: Linking complexity theory & time-paced evolution in relentlessly shifting organisations', *Administrative Science Quarterly*, Vol.42, pp.1-34.

Bruch, H. & Ghoshal, S. (2002). `Beware the busy manager', *Harvard Business Review*, February, p.63.

Bryant, L., Dobal, M. & Johnson, E. (1990). `Strategic planning: Collaboration & empowerment', *Nursing Connections*, Vol.3(3), pp.31-36.

Buchanan, D., & Boddy, D. (1992). *The Expertise of the Change Agent*, New York: Prentice Hall.

Budhwar, P.S. (2000). `Strategic integration & devolvement of human resource management in the UK manufacturing sector', *British Journal of Management*, Vol.11(3), pp.285-302.

Burgelman, R.A. (1983a). `A model of the interaction of strategic behaviour, corporate context & the concept of strategy', *Academy of Management Review*, Vol.8(1), pp.61-70.

Burgelman, R.A. (1983b). `A process model of internal corporate venturing in the diversified major firm', *Administrative Science Quarterly*, Vol.28(2), pp.223-44.

Burgelman, R.A. (1991). `Intra-organisational ecology of strategy-making & organisational adaptation: Theory & field research', *Organisation Science*, Vol.2(3), pp.239-62.

Burns, J.M. (1978). *Leadership*, New York: Harper & Row

Burns, L., Gazzoli, G. Dynan, L. & Wholey, D. (2000). `Impact of HMO market structure on physician-hospital strategic alliances', *HSR: Health Service Research*, Vol.35, pp.101-32.

Calpin-Davies, P.J. (2003). `Management & leadership: A dual role in nursing education', *Nurse Education Today*, Vol.23, p.6.

Carnell, C. (1995). *'Managing Change in Organisations'*, London: Prentice Hall International.

Carney, M. (1999). `Leadership in nursing: Where do we go from here? The ward sisters' challenge for the future', *Nursing Review*, Vol.17(1/2), pp.13-18.

Carney, M. (2000). 'The development of a model to manage change: Reflection on a critical incident in a focus group setting. An innovative approach', *Journal of Nursing Management*, Vol.8, pp.265-72.

Carney, M. (2001a). `Middle manager involvement in strategy development in not-for-profit organisations: Development of conceptual model', *Conference Proceedings Publication*, Doctoral Colloquium, University College Cork, Cork, 31 April-1 May.

Carney, M. (2001b). `Middle manager involvement in strategy development in not-for-profit health service organisations: The relationship between involvement, organisational commitment & understanding/consensus'. *Conference Proceedings Publication*, Irish Academy of Management Conference, University of Ulster, Magee College, Derry, 6-7 September.

Carney, M. (2001c). `Strategy development in Irish hospitals – multi-professional involvement: Fact or fallacy?' *Conference Proceedings Publication*, Annual Research Conference, School of Nursing & Midwifery Studies, Trinity College, Dublin, 14-16 November.

Carney, M. (2002a). *A Strategic Consensus Model for Not-for-profit Organisations*, Unpublished PhD Thesis, Dublin: University College Dublin.

Carney, M. (2002b). `The management of change: Using a model to evaluate the change process', *Seminars for Nurse Managers, Strategies for Leadership & Management*, Vol.10(3), pp.206-11.

Carney, M. (2004a). `Perceptions of professional clinicians & non-clinicians on their involvement in strategic planning in health care management: Implications for inter-disciplinary involvement', *Nursing & Health Sciences*, Vol.6(4), pp.321-28.

Carney, M. (2004b). `Middle manager involvement in strategy development in not-for-profit organisations: The Director of Nursing perspective - How organisational structures impact on the role', *Journal of Nursing Management*, Vol.12(1), pp.13-21.

Carney, M. (2004c). 'The advanced nurse practitioner: Why educate nurses & midwives to advanced practice level?, *Irish Nurse, incorporating the All Ireland Journal of Nursing & Midwifery*, Vol.6(8), pp.18-20.

Carney, M. (2005). `Nurses as managers: A history of nursing management in Ireland & England', in Fealy, G.M. (ed.), *Care to Remember: Nursing & Midwifery in Ireland*, Dublin: Mercier Press, pp.185-97.

Carney, M. (2006a). `Understanding organisational culture: The key to successful middle manager strategic involvement in health care delivery?' *Journal of Nursing Management*, Vol.14 (1), pp.23-33.

Carney, M. (2006b). `Positive & negative outcomes from values & beliefs held by health care clinician & non-clinician managers', *Journal of Advanced Nursing*, Vol.54(1), pp.111-120.

Cascio, W.F. (2002a). `Downsizing: What do we know? What have we learned?' *Academy of Management Executive*, Vol.7, pp.95-104.

Cascio, W.F. (2002b). Strategies for responsible restructuring, *Academy of Management Executive*, Vol.16(3), p.80-91.

Caulkin, S. (1995). `Take your partners', *Management Today*, February, pp.26-30.

Causer, G. & Exworthy, M. (1999). `Professionals as managers across the public sector', in Exworthy, M. & Halford, S. (eds.) *Professionals & the New Managerialism in the Public Sector*, Buckingham: Open University Press, pp. 83-101.

Chadderton, H. (1995). `An analysis of the concept of participation within the context of health care planning', *Journal of Nursing Management*, Vol.3, pp.221-28.

Chadwick, C., Hunter, L.W. & Walston, S.L. (2004). `Effects of downsizing practices on the performance of hospitals', *Strategic Management Journal*, Vol.25(5), pp.405-28.

Chaffee, E.E. (1985). `Three models of strategy', *Academy of Management Review*, Vol.10(1), pp.89-98.

Champy, J.A. (1997). `Preparing for organisational change', in Hesselbein, F., Goldsmith, M. & Beckhard, R. (eds.), *The Organisation of the Future*, The Drucker Foundation Future Series, San Francisco, CA: Jossey-Bass.

Chan, S. & Cheng, B.S. (1999). 'Nurses' political participation in Hong Kong: A study', *Journal of Nursing Management*, Vol.7, pp.167-75.

Chan, S. (2002). `Factors influencing nursing leadership effectiveness in Hong Kong', *Journal of Advanced Nursing*, Vol.38(6), pp.615-23.

Chandler, A.D. Jr. (1962). *Strategy & Structure: Chapters in the History of the American Industrial Enterprise*, Cambridge, MA: MIT Press.

Chandler, G. (1991). `Creating an environment to empower nurses', *Nursing Management*, Vol.22(8), pp.20-23.

Chapman, J.A. (2001). `The work of leaders in new organisational contexts', *The Journal of Management Development*, Vol.20(1), p.57.

Chen, H-C., Beck, S.L. & Amos, L.K. (2005). `Leadership styles & nursing faculty job satisfaction in Taiwan', *Journal of Nursing Scholarship*, Vol.37(4), pp.374-380.

Chiok Foong Loke, J. (2001). `Leadership behaviours: Effects on job satisfaction, productivity and organisational commitment', *Journal of Nursing Management*, Vol.9, pp.191-204.

Christensen, C.M. & Raynor, M.E. (2003). `Why hard nosed executives should care about management theory', *Harvard Business Review*, September, pp.65-74.

Chuanzhi, L. (2003). `Moving mountains, motivating people', *Harvard Business Review*, January, p.47.

Clarke, P. (2000). *Organisations in Action: Competition between Contexts*, London: Routledge.

Clarke, T. (2004a). `The fashion of management fashion: A surge too far?' *Organisation*, Vol.11(2), pp.297-306.

Clarke, T. (2004b). `Controversies & continuities in management studies: Essays in honour of Karen Legge', *Journal of Management Studies*, Vol.41(3), Special issue, pp.367-76.

Cody, N. (2000). *Competencies that Increase the Effectiveness of the Nurse Managers' Role*, Unpublished Master's in Nursing Thesis, University College Dublin.

Cohen, S.G. & Bailey, D.E. (1997). `What makes teams work: Group effectiveness research from the shop floor to the executive suite?', *Journal of Management*, Vol.23(3), pp. 239-90.

Cohen, A. (1993). `Organisational commitment and turnover: A meta-analysis', *Academy of Management Journal*, Vol. 36(5), pp.1140-57.

Cohen, A. (2000). The relationship between commitment forms and work outcomes: A comparison of three models', *Human Relations*, Vol.53(3), pp.387-417.

Cohen, W., Florida, R., Randazzese, L. & Walsh, J. (1998). `Industry & the academy: Uneasy partners in the cause of technological advance', in Noll, R.G. (ed.), *Challenges to Research Universities*, Washington, DC: Brookings Institution Press.

Conger, J. (1997). `How generational shifts will transform organisational life', in Hesselbein, F., Goldsmith, M. & Beckhard, R. (eds.), *The Organisation of the Future*, The Drucker Foundation Future Series, San Francisco, CA: Jossey-Bass.

Conger, J.A. & Kanungo, R.N. (1987). `Toward a behavioural theory of charismatic leadership in organisational settings', *Academy of Management Review*, Vol.12,(4), pp.637-647.

Corser, W.D. (1998). `The changing nature of organisational commitment in the acute care environment: Implications for nursing leadership', *Journal of Nursing Administration*, Vol.28(6), pp.32-36.

Cotton, J.L. (1993). *Employee Involvement: Methods for Improving Performance & Work Attitudes*. London: Sage.

Covey, S. (1996). `Three roles of the leader in the new paradigm', in Hesselbein, F., Goldsmith, M. & Beckhard, R. (eds.), *The Leader of the Future*, The Drucker Foundation Future Series, San Francisco, CA: Jossey-Bass.

Coyle-Shapiro, J.A-M., Kessler, I. & Purcell, J. (2004). `Exploring organisationally-directed citizenship behaviour: Reciprocity or "It's my job"?', *Journal of Management Studies*, Vol.41(1), pp.85-103.

Cross, R. & Prusak, L. (2002). `The people that make organisations stop - or go', *Harvard Business Review*, Vol.80(6), pp.104-12.

Crossan, M., Lane, H. & White, R. (1999). `An organisational learning framework: From intuition to institution', *Academy of Management Review,* Vol.24, pp.522-38.

Cullen, L., Fraser, D. & Symonds, I. (2003). `Strategies for inter-professional education: The inter-professional team objective structured clinical examination for midwifery & medical students', *Nurse Education Today,* Vol.23, pp.427-33.

Currie, G. (1999). `The influence of middle managers in the business planning process: A case study in the UK NHS', *British Journal of Management,* Vol.10, pp.141-55.

Cyert, R.M. & March, J.G. (1963). *A Behavioural Theory of the Firm,* Englewood Cliffs, NJ: Prentice Hall.

Daft, R.L. & Weick, K.E. (1984). `Toward a model of organisations as interpretation systems', *Academy of Management Review,* Vol.9(2), pp.284-95.

Daft, R.L. (2004). *Management,* 7th edition, St. Paul, MN: Southwestern College.

Davies, C. (1995). *Gender & the Professional Predicament in Nursing,* Buckingham: Open University Press.

Daymon, C. (2000). `Culture formation in a new television station: A multi-perspective analysis', *British Journal of Management,* Vol.11(2), pp.121-35.

Deal, T.E & Kennedy, A.A. (1983). `Culture: A new look through old lenses', *Journal of Applied Behavioural Science,* Vol.19(4), pp.498-505.

Deal, T.E. & Kennedy, A.A. (1982). *Corporate Cultures: The Rites & Rituals of Corporate Life,* Reading, MA: Addison-Wesley.

Deal, T.E. & Kennedy, A.A. (1988). *Corporate Cultures: The Rites & Rituals of Corporate Life,* Harmondsworth, Middx.: Penguin.

Dempsey-Polan, L. (1988). `Women: Once & future leaders in health administration', *Hospital & Health Services Administration,* Vol.33(1), pp.89-98.

Department of Health & Children (2001). *Quality & Fairness: A Health System for You,* Dublin: Government Publications.

Department of Health & Children (2004). *Report on Health Strategy.* Dublin: Government Publications.

Department of Health (1989). *Report of the Commission on Health Funding,* Dublin: Government Publications.

Department of Health (1994). *Report on Shaping a Healthier Future: A Strategy for Effective Health Care in the 1990s,* Dublin: Government Publications.

Department of Health (1999). *The New National Institute for Clinical Excellence Opens for Business,* Press Release 1999/0193, London: Department of Health.

Department of Health (UK) (2000a). *The NHS Plan: A Plan for Investment, A Plan for Reform,* London: HM Stationery Office.

Department of Health (UK) (2000b). *A Health Service for All the Talents: Developing the NHS Workforce,* London: HM Stationery Office.

Department of Health (UK) (2001a). *Practice Placements* (Discussion Paper). London: HM Stationery Office.

Department of Health (UK) (2001b). *Working Together - Learning Together: A Framework of Lifelong Learning,* London: HM Stationery Office.

Department of Health (UK) (2002a). *HR in the NHS Plan: More Staff Working Differently,* London: HM Stationery Office.

Department of Health (UK) (2002b). *Learning from Bristol: The DH Response to the Report of the Public Enquiry into Children's Heart Surgery at the Bristol Royal Infirmary 1984-1995*, London: HM Stationery Office.

Dess, G.G. & Origer, N.K. (1987). `Environment, structure & consensus in strategy formulation: A conceptual integration', *Academy of Management Review*, Vol.12(2), pp.313-30.

Dess, G.G. (1987). `Consensus on strategy formulation & organisational performance: Competitors in a fragmented industry', *Strategic Management Journal*, Vol.8(3), pp.259-77.

DeWoot, P., Heyvaert, H. & Martou, F. (1977/78). `Strategic management: An empirical study of 168 Belgian firms', *International Studies of Management & Organisation*, Vol.7(3/4), pp.60-75.

Dombeck, M. (1997). `Professional personhood: Training, territoriality & tolerance', *Journal of Inter-professional Care*, Vol.11, pp.9-21.

Dooley, R.S. & Fryxell, G.E. (1999). `Attaining decision quality & commitment from dissent: The moderating effects of loyalty & competence in strategic decision-making teams', *Academy of Management Journal*, Vol.42(4), pp.389-402.

Dopson, S. & Stewart, R. (1990). `What is happening to middle management?', *British Journal of Management*, Vol.1(1), pp.3-16.

Dopson, S. & Stewart, R. (1993). `Information technology, organisational restructuring & the future of middle management', *New Technology, Work & Employment*, Vol.8(1), pp.10-20.

Dopson, S., Risk, A. & Stewart, R. (1992). `The changing role of the middle manager in the United Kingdom', *International Studies of Management & Organisation*, Vol.22(1), pp.40-53.

Douglas, T.J. & Ryman, J.A. (2003). `Understanding competitive advantage in the general hospital industry: Evaluating strategic competencies', *Strategic Management Journal*, Vol.24, pp.333-47.

Dranove, D., Simon, C. & White, W. (1998). `Determinants of managed care penetration', *Journal of Health Economics*, Vol.17, pp.729-45.

Drucker, P. (1988a). *Managing in a Time of Great Change*, New York: Truman Talley Books.

Drucker, P. (1988b). `The coming of the new organisation', *Harvard Business Review*, Vol.66(1), pp.45-53.

Drucker, P. (1989). `Motivating to peak performance', in Drucker, P. (ed.), *The Practice of Management*, Oxford: Heinemann Professional, pp. 296-305.

Drucker, P. (1997). `Toward the new organisation', in Hesselbein, F., Goldsmith, M. & Beckhard, R. (eds.), *The Organisation of the Future* The Drucker Foundation Future Series, San Francisco, CA: Jossey-Bass.

Drucker, P. (1999). *Management: Tasks, Responsibilities, Practices*, Oxford: Butterworth Heinemann.

Drucker, P. (2002). `They're not employees, they're people', *Harvard Business Review*, Vol.80(8), pp.95-102.

Duques, R. & Gaske, P. (1997). `The "Big" organisation of the future, in Hesselbein, F., Goldsmith, M. & Beckhard, R. (eds.), *The Organisation of the*

Future The Drucker Foundation Future Series, San Francisco, CA: Jossey-Bass.

Dutton, J.E & Ashford, S.J. (1993). `Selling issues to top management', *Academy of Management Review*, Vol.18(3), pp.397-428.

Dutton, J.E & Duncan, R.B. (1987). `The creation of momentum for change through the process of strategic issue diagnosis', *Strategic Management Journal*, Vol.8(3), pp.279-95.

Dutton, J.E., Ashford, S.J., O'Neill, R.M. & Lawrence, K.A. (2001). `Moves that matter: Issue-selling & organisational change, *Academy of Management Journal*, 2001, Vol.44(4), pp.716-736.

Dutton, J.E., Ashford, S.J., O'Neill, R.M., Hayes, E. & Wierba, E.E. (1997). `Reading the wind: How middle managers assess the context for selling issues to top managers', *Strategic Management Journal*, Vol.18(5), pp.407-25.

Dvir, T., Eden, D., Avolio, B.J. & Shamir, B. (2002). `Impact of transformational leadership on follower development & performance: A field experience', *Academy of Management Journal*, Vol.45(4), pp.735-44.

Dyer, J. & Singh, H. (1998). `The relational view: Co-operative strategy & sources of inter-organisational competitive advantage', *Academy of Management Review*, Vol.23, pp.660-79.

Dyson, R.G. (1990). *Strategic Planning: Models & Analytical Techniques*, Chichester: Wiley.

Ebadan, G. & Winstanley, D. (1997). `Downsizing, delayering & careers: The survivor's perspective', *Human Resource Management Journal*, Vol.7(1), pp.79-91.

Eckert, R.A. (2003). `Moving mountains, motivating people', *Harvard Business Review*, January, pp.44.

Edwards, I., Jones, M., Carr, J., Braunack-Mayer, A. & Jensen, G.M. (2004). `Clinical reasoning strategies in physical therapy', *Physical Therapy*, Vol.84(4), p.313.

Edwards, P.A. (1996). `Are nurses ready for the current challenges of health care?', *Journal of Nursing Administration*, Vol.26, Sept. 11-17, p.9.

Eisenberger, R., Fasolo, P. & Davis-LaMastro, V. (1990). `Perceived organisational support & employee diligence, commitment & innovation', *Journal of Applied Psychology*, Vol.75(1), pp.51-59.

Elizur, D., Borg, I., Hunt, R. & Magyari Beck, I. (1991). `The structure of work values: A cross-cultural comparison', *Journal of Organisational Behaviour*, Vol.12, pp.21-38.

Exworthy, M. & Halford, S. (eds.) (1999). *Professionals & the New Managerialism in the Public Sector*, Buckingham: Open University Press.

Falk, R. & Adeline, R. (1999). `Power & caring: A dialectic in nursing', *Advances in Nursing Science*, Vol.19(1), pp.3-17.

Faulk, D.R. & Ternus, M.P. (2004). `Strategies for teaching public policy in nursing: A creative approach', *Nurse Educator*, Vol.29(30), pp.99-102.

Fayol, H. (1949). *General & Industrial Management*, London: Pitman.

Feather, N.J. & Rauter, K.A. (2004). `Organisational citizenship behaviours in relation to job status, job insecurity, organisational commitment &

identification, job satisfaction & work value', *Journal of Occupational & Organisational Psychology*, Vol.77(1), pp.81-94.

Feldman, S.P. (1986). `Management in context: An essay on the relevance of culture to the understanding of organisational change', *Journal of Management Studies*, Vol.23, pp.587-607.

Fenton-O'Creevy, M. (1998). `Employee involvement & the middle manager: Evidence from a survey of organisations', *Journal of Organisational Behaviour*, Vol.19(1), pp.67-84.

Ferlie, E. & Pettigrew, A. (1996). `Managing through networks: Some issues & implications for the NHS', *British Journal of Management*, Vol.7 (Special Issue), S81-S99.

Fiedler, F. (1967). *A Theory of Leadership Effectiveness*, New York: McGraw-Hill.

Finch, J. (2000). `Inter-professional education & teamworking: A view from the education providers', *British Medical Journal*, Vol.321, pp.1138-40.

Fiorina, C. (2003). `Moving mountains, motivating people', *Harvard Business Review*, January, p.42.

Floyd, S.W & Wooldridge, B. (1996). *The Strategic Middle Manager: How to Create & Sustain Competitive Advantage*, San Francisco, CA: Jossey-Bass.

Floyd, S.W. & Wooldridge, B. (1992a). `Middle management involvement in strategy & its association with strategic type: A research note', *Strategic Management Journal*, Vol.13, Special issue, pp.153-67.

Floyd, S.W. & Wooldridge, B. (1992b). `Managing strategic consensus: The foundation of effective implementation', *Academy of Management Executive*, Vol.6(4), pp.27-39.

Floyd, S.W. & Wooldridge, B. (1994). `Dinosaurs or dynamos? Recognising middle management's strategic role', *Academy of Management Executive*, Vol.8(4), pp.47-57.

Floyd, S.W. & Wooldridge, B. (1997). `Middle management's strategic influence & organisational performance', *Journal of Management Studies*, Vol.34(3), pp.465-85.

Fraser, D., Symonds, M., Cullen L. & Symonds, I. (2000). `A university department merger of midwifery and obstetrics: A step on the journey to enhancing inter-professional learning', *Medical Teacher*, Vol.22(2), pp.179-83.

Freeth, D., Hammick, M., Koppel, I., Reeves, S. & Barr, H. (2002). *A Critical Review of Evaluations of Inter-professional Education*, London: LTSN.

Freidson, E. (1970). *Profession of Medicine*, New York: Harper & Row.

Freidson, E. (1976). *Professionalism Reborn: Theory, Prophecy & Policy*, Cambridge: University of Chicago Press.

Freidson, E. (1984). `The changing nature of professional control', *Annual Review of Sociology*, Vol.10, pp.1-20.

Funnell, P. (1995). `Exploring the value of inter-professional shared learning', in Soothill, K., Mackay, L. & Webb, C. (eds.), *Inter-professional Relations in Health Care*, London: Edward Arnold.

Gair, G. & Hartery, T. (2001). `Medical dominance in multi-disciplinary teamwork: A case study of discharge decision-making in a geriatric assessment unit', *Journal of Nursing Management*, Vol.9(1), pp.3-11.

Galbraith, J.K. (1997). `The reconfigurable organisation', in Hesselbein, F., Goldsmith, M. & Beckhard, R. (eds.), *The Organisation of the Future*, The Drucker Foundation Future Series, San Francisco, CA: Jossey-Bass.

Gallant, M.H., Beaulieu, M.C. & Carnvale, F.A. (2002). `Partnership: An analysis of the concept within the nurse-client relationship', *Journal of Advanced Nursing*, Vol.40(2), pp.149-57.

Gavin, J.N. (1995). `The politics of nursing: A case study - clinical grading', *Journal of Advanced Nursing*, 1995, Vol.22(2), pp.379-85.

General Medical Council (1997). *The New Doctor*. London: General Medical Council.

Gill, J. & Whittle, S. (1993). Management by panacea, *Journal of Management Studies*, Vol.30(2), pp.281-95.

Glaister, K.W. & Falshaw, J.R. (1999). `Strategic planning: Still going strong?', *Long Range Planning*, Vol.32(1), pp.107-16.

Glazer, S., Daniel, S.C. & Short, K.M. (2004). `A study of the relationship between organisational commitment & human values in four countries', *Human Relations*, Vol.57(3), pp.323-45.

Glen, S. & Reeves, S. (2004). `Developing inter-professional education in the pre-registration curricula: Mission impossible?', *Nurse Education in Practice*, Vol.4, pp.45-52.

Goffee, R. & Scase, R. (1986). `Are the rewards worth the effort? Changing managerial values in the 1980s', *Personnel Review*, Vol.15, pp.3-6.

Gosling, J. & Mintzberg, H. (2003). `The five minds of the manager', *Harvard Business Review*, November, p.54.

Grant, M., Boyle, A. & Massey, V. H. (1999). *Nursing Leadership, Management & Research*, Springhouse Notes, The A+ Review Series, Springhouse, PA: Springhouse Corporation.

Green, R., Cavell, G. & Jackson, S. (1996). `Inter-professional clinical education of medical & pharmacy students', *Medical Education*, Vol.30, pp.129-33.

Greenglass, E. & Burke, R. (2000). 'The relationship between hospital restructuring, anger, hostility & psychosomatics in nursing', *Journal of Community & Applied Social Psychology*, Vol.10, pp.155-61.

Grimshaw, D. (1999). `Changes in skills-mix and pay determination among the nursing workforce in the UK', *Work, Employment & Society*, Vol.13(2), pp.295-328.

Grinyer, P.H. & Norburn, D. (1977/1978). `Planning for existing markets: An empirical study', *International Studies of Management & Organisation*, Vol.7(3/4), pp.99-122.

Gruen, T.W., Summers, J.O. & Acito, F. (2000) `Relationship marketing activities, commitment & membership behaviours in professional associations', *Journal of Marketing*, Vol.64(3), pp.34-39.

Guth, W.D. & Macmillan, I.C. (1986). `Strategy implementation *versus* middle management self-interest', *Strategic Management Journal*, Vol.7(4), pp.313-27.

Halford, S. & Leonard, P. (1999). `New identities? Professionalism, managerialism & the construction of self', in Exworthy, M. & Halford, S. (eds.) *Professionals & the New Managerialism in the Public Sector*, Buckingham: Open University Press.

Hall, P. & Weaver, L. (2001). `Inter-disciplinary education & teamwork: A long and winding road', *Medical Education*, Vol.35, pp.867-75.

Hambrick, D. & Pettigrew, A. (2001). `Upper echelons: Donald Hambrick on executive & strategy', *Academy of Management Executive*, Vol.15(3), pp.36-44.

Hambrick, D. (1989). `Guest editor's introduction: Putting top managers back in the strategy picture', *Strategic Management Journal*, Vol.10, p.5.

Hambrick, D.C. & D'Aveni, R.A. (1988). `Large corporate failures as downward spirals', *Administrative Science Quarterly*, Vol.33(1), pp.1-23.

Hambrick, D.C. (1983).`Some tests of the effectiveness & functional attributes of Miles & Snow's strategic types', *Academy of Management Journal*, Vol.26(1), pp.5-26.

Hambrick, D.C. (1994).`1993 presidential address: What if the academy actually mattered', *Academy of Management Review*, Vol.19, p.13.

Hamel, M.T. & Prahalad, C.K. (1994). *Competing for the Future: Breakthrough Strategies for Seizing Control of your Industry & Creating the Markets of Tomorrow*, Boston, MA: Harvard Business School Press.

Hammer, M. (2001). *The Agenda: What Every Business Must Do to Dominate the Decade*, New York: Crown Business Publishers.

Harden, R.M. (1998). `Effective multi-professional education: A three-dimensional perspective,' *Medical Teacher*, Vol.20(5), pp.402-08.

Harris, L.C. (1999). `Initiating planning: The problem of entrenched cultural values', *Long Range Planning*, Vol.32(1), pp.117-26.

Harrison, S. & Pollitt, C. (1994). *Controlling Health Professionals: The Future of Work & Organisation in the National Health Service*, Buckingham: Open University Press.

Harrison, S., Hunter, D.J., Marnoch, G. & Pollitt, C. (1992). *Just Managing: Power & Culture in the National Health Service*, London: Macmillan.

Hatch, M.J. (1993). `The dynamics of organisational culture', *Academy of Management Review*, Vol.18(4), pp.657-93.

Heckscher, C. (1995). *White-collar Blues: Management Loyalties in an Age of Corporate Restructuring*, New York: Basic Books.

Hemingway, M.A. & Smith, C.S. (1999). `Organisational climate & occupational stressors as predictors of withdrawal behaviours & injuries in nurses', *Journal of Occupational & Organisational Psychology*, Vol.72, pp.285-99.

Henderson, R.M. & Clark, K.B. (1990). `Architectural innovation: The reconfiguration of existing product technologies & the failure of established firms', *Administrative Science Quarterly*, Vol.35(1), pp.9-22.

Henneman, E.A., Lee, J.L. & Cohen, J.I. (1995). `Collaboration: a concept analysis', *Journal of Advanced Nursing*, Vol.21, pp.103-109.

Hertting, A., Nilsson, K., Theorell, T. & Satterlund Larsson, U. (2004). `Downsizing & re-organisation: Demands, challenges and ambiguity', *Journal of Advanced Nursing*, Vol.45(2), pp.145-54.

Hertting, A., Nilsson, K., Theorell, T. & Satterlund Larsson, U. (2003). `Personnel reductions & structural changes in health care-work life experience of medical secretaries', *Journal of Psychosomatic Research*, Vol.54, pp.161-70.

Herzberg, F. (2003). `One more time: How do you motivate employees? Motivating people', *Harvard Business Review*, January, pp.87-96.

Hesselbein, F., Goldsmith, M. & Beckhard, R. (eds.) (1997). *The Organisation of the Future*, The Drucker Foundation Future Series, San Francisco, CA: Jossey-Bass.

Hewison, A. (1999). 'The new public management & the new nursing: Related by rhetoric', *Journal of Advanced Nursing*, Vol. 29(6), pp.1377-84.

Higgins, J.M. & McAllaster, C. (2004). 'If you want strategic change, don't forget to change your cultural artefacts', *Journal of Change Management*, Vol.4(1), pp.63-73.

Hoggett, P. (1996). 'New modes of control in the public service', *Public Administration*, Vol.74(1), p.9.

Hojat, M., Nasca, T., Cohen, J., Fields, S., Rattner, S., Griffiths, M., Ilbarra, D., Alcorta de Gonzales, A., Torres-Ruiz, A., Ilbarra, G. & Garcia, A. (2001). 'Attitudes towards physician-nurse collaboration: A cross-cultural study of male & female physicians & nurses in the US & Mexico', *Nursing Research*, Vol.50, pp.123-28.

Holder, J.J. Jr. (1976). 'Decision-making by consensus', in Ivancevich, J.M & Donnelly, J.H Jr. (eds.), *Readings in Organisations: Behaviour, Structure, Processes*, revised edition, Plano, TX: Business Publications.

Hollenbeck, J.R. & Klein, H.J. (1987). 'Goal commitment & the goal-setting process: Problems, prospects & proposals for future research', *Journal of Applied Psychology*, Vol.72(2), pp.212-20.

Horsburgh, M., Lamdin, R. & Williamson, E. (2001). 'Multi-professional learning: The attitudes of medical, nursing & pharmacy students to shared learning', *Medical Education*, Vol.35, pp.876-83.

Hoskisson, R., Hitt, M., Wan, W. & Yiu, D. (1999).'Theory & research in strategic management: Swings of a pendulum', *Journal of Management*, Vol.25, pp.417-56.

House, R.J & Mitchell, T.R. (1974). 'Path-goal theory of leadership', *Journal of Contemporary Business*, Vol.3, pp.81-97.

House, R.J & Shamir, B. 'Towards the integration of transformational, charismatic & visionary theories', in Chemers, M.M. & Ayman, R. (eds.), *Leadership Theory & Research: Perspectives & Directions*, San Diego, CA: Academic Press.

House, R.J. & Podsakoff, P.M. (1994). 'Leader effectiveness: Past perspectives & future directions for research', in Greenberg, J. (ed.). *The State of the Science in Organisational Behaviour*, Lawrence, NJ: Erlbaum Associates.

House, R.J. (1977). 'A 1976 theory of charismatic leadership', in Hunt, J.G. & Larson, L.L. (eds.), *Leadership: The Cutting Edge*, Carbondale, IL: Southern Illinois University Press.

Howell, J.P., Dorfman, P.W. & Kerr, S.K. (1986). 'Moderator variables in leadership research', *Academy of Management Review*, Vol.11(1), pp.88-102.

Hrebiniak, L.G. & Joyce, W.F. (1984). *Implementing Strategy*, New York: Macmillan.

Hrebiniak, L.G. & Snow, C.C. (1982). 'Top-management agreement & organisational performance', *Human Relations*, Vol.35, pp.1139-58.

Hutt, M.D., Reingen, P.H. & Ronchetto, J.R. (1988). 'Tracing emergent processes in marketing strategy formation', *Journal of Marketing*, Vol.52(1), pp.4-19.

Hyde, A., Lohan, M. & McDonnell, O. (2004). *Sociology for Health Professionals in Ireland*, Dublin: Institute of Public Administration.

Izreali, D.N. (1975). 'The middle-manager & the tactics of power expansion: A case study'. *Sloan Management Review*, Vol.16(2), pp.57-70.

Jaques, E. (1989). *Requisite Organisations: The CEO's Guide to Creative Structure & Leadership*, Kingston, NY: Cason Hall.

Jaques, E. (1990). 'In praise of hierarchy', *Harvard Business Review*, Vol.68(1), pp.127-33.

Jaros, S.J., Jermier, J.M., Koehler, J.W. & Sincich, T. (1993). 'Effects of continuance, affective & moral commitment on the withdrawal process: An evaluation of eight structural equation models', *Academy of Management Journal*, Vol.36(5), pp.951-95.

Jauch, L.R. & Glueck, W.F. (2003). *Business Policy & Strategic Management*. New York: McGraw-Hill International Editions.

Johnson, G. & Scholes, K. (2002). *Exploring Corporate Strategy: Text & Cases*, 6th edition, New York: Financial Times Prentice Hall.

Johnson, L.J. (1990). 'Strategic management: A new dimension of the nurse executive's role', *Journal of Nursing Administration*, Vol.20(9), pp.7-10.

Jones, J. (1999). 'Social work: Regulations & managerialism', in Exworthy, M. & Halford, S. (eds.) *Professionals & the New Managerialism in the Public Sector*, pp.37-49, Buckingham: Open University Press.

Jooste, K. (2004). 'Leadership: A new perspective', *Journal of Nursing Management*, Vol.12, pp.217-23.

Jowett, S. (1996). *Every Nurses' Business: The Role of Marketing on Service*. London: Kings Fund.

Judge, T.A., Thoresen, C.J., Pucik, V. & Welbourne, T.M. (1999). 'Managerial coping with organisational change: A dispositional perspective', *Journal of Applied Psychology*, Vol.84, pp.107-22.

Kahn, D. & Katz, R.L. (1978). *The Social Psychology of Organisations*, 2nd edition, New York: Wiley.

Kahn, R.L. & Byosiere, P.B. (1992). 'Stress in organisations', in Dunnette, M.D. & Hough, L.M. (eds.), *Handbook of Industrial/Organisational Psychology*, Palo Alto, CA: Consulting Psychologist Press.

Katavich, L. (1996). 'Physiotherapy in the new health system in New Zealand', *New Zealand Journal of Physiotherapy*, Vol.24, pp.11-13.

Keenan, J. (1999). 'A concept analysis of autonomy', *Journal of Advanced Nursing*, Vol.29(3), pp.556-62.

Kelley, G. (1976). 'Seducing the elites: The politics of decision-making and innovation in organisational networks', *Academy of Management Review*, Vol.1(3), pp.66-74.

Kelley, R.E. (1992). *The Power of Followership*, New York: Currency & Doubleday.

Kennedy, B.R. (2005). 'Stress & burnout of nursing staff working with geriatric clients in long-term care', *Journal of Nursing Scholarship*, Vol.37(4), pp.381-82.

Kenny, D.T. & Adamson, B.J. (1992). 'Medicine & the health professions: Issues of dominance, autonomy & authority', *Australian Health Review*, Vol.15, pp.319-35.

Kerfoot, K. (1996). `On leadership: The new nursing leader for the new world order of health care', *Orthopaedic Nursing*, Vol.15(4), pp.43-45.

Kerr, S. & Jermier, J. (1978). `Substitutes for leadership: Their meaning & measurement', *Organisational Behaviour & Human Performance*, Vol.22, pp.375-403.

Kets de Vries, M.F.R. & Balazs, K. (1997). `The downside of downsizing', *Human Resources*, Vol.50, pp.11-50.

Kilmann, R.H., Saxton, M.J. & Serpa, R. & Associates (eds.) (1985). *Gaining Control of the Corporate Culture*, San Francisco, CA: Jossey-Bass.

Kiluchi, J.F. (2005). `Cultural theories of nursing responsive to human needs & values', *Journal of Nursing Scholarship*, Vol.37(4), pp.302-7.

King, N. & Anderson, N. (2002). *Managing Innovation & Change*, 2nd edition, London: Thomson.

Kirkman, B.L. & Rosen, B. (2000). `Powering up teams', *Organisational Dynamics*, Vol.28(3), pp.48-66.

Kirkman, B.L., Rosen, B., Tesluk, P.E. & Gibson, C.B. (2004). `The impact of team empowerment on virtual team performance: The moderating role of face-to-face interaction', *Academy of Management Journal*, Vol.47(2), pp.175-92.

Klein, K.J. (1987). `Employee stock ownership & employee attitudes: A test of three models', *Journal of Applied Psychology*, Vol.72(2), pp.319-32.

Knaus, W.A., Draper, E.A., Wagner, D.P. & Zimmerman, J.E. (1996). `An evaluation of outcome from intensive care in major medical centres', *Annals of Internal Medicine*, Vol.104(3), pp.410-18.

Knoop, R. (1994). `Organisational commitment & individual values', *Perceptual & Motor Skills*, Vol.78, pp.200-02.

Knox, S. (2004). `Creating a centre for nursing excellence', *JONA'S Health care Law, Ethics & Regulations*, Vol.6(2), pp.44-50.

Koloroutis, M. (2004). *Relationship-Based Care, A Model For Transforming Practice*, Minneapolis, MN: Creative Health Care Management.

Koppel, I., Barr, H., Reeves, S., Freeth, D. & Hammick, M. (2001). `Establishing a systematic approach to evaluating the effectiveness of inter-professional education', *Issues in Inter-disciplinary Care*, Vol.3(1), pp.41-49.

Kotter, J.P. & Schlesinger, L.A. (1979). `Choosing strategies for change', *Harvard Business Review*, Vol.57, March-April, pp.106-14.

Kotter, J.P. (1990). `What leaders really do', *Harvard Business Review*, June.

Kotter, J.P. (1995). `Leading change: Why transformation efforts fail', *Harvard Business Review*, March-April.

Kotter, J.P. (1996). *Leading Change*, Boston, MA: Harvard Business School Press.

Kouzes, J.M. & Posner, B.Z. (1995). *The Leadership Challenge: How To Get Extraordinary Things Done In Organisations*, San Francisco, CA: Jossey-Bass.

Krackhardt, D. & Hanson, J.R. (1993). 'Informal networks: The company behind the chart', *Harvard Business Review*, Vol.71(4), pp.104-11.

Kramer, M. & Schmalenberg, C. (2002). `Essentials of a magnetism', in McClure, M. & Hinshaw, A. (eds.), *Magnet Hospitals Revisited: Attraction & Retention of 1982 Study*, San Francisco, CA: American Academy of Nursing.

Kramer, M. & Schmalenberg, C. (2003). `Securing good nurse/physician relationships', *Nursing Management*, Vol.34(7), pp.34-38.

Kramer, M. & Schmalenberg, C. (2004).`Essentials of a magnetic work environment', *Nursing*, Vol.34(6), p.50.

Krueger Wilson, C. & Porter O'Grady, T. (1999). *Leading the Revolution in Health Care: Advancing Systems, Igniting Performance*, 2nd edition, New York: Aspen Publishers.

Kuokkanen, L. & Leino-Kilpi, H. (2001). `The qualities of an empowered nurse & the factors involved', *Journal of Nursing Management*, Vol.9, p.276.

La Monica, E.L. (1994). *Management in Health care: A Theoretical Experiential Approach*, New York: Macmillan.

Lahteenmaki, S., Toivonen, J. & Mattila, M. (2001). `Critical aspects of organisational learning research & proposals for its measurement', *British Journal of Management*, Vol.12, pp.113-29.

Lapsley, I. (1994). `Market mechanisms & the management of health care', *International Journal of Public Sector Management*, Vol.7, pp.15-35.

Laschinger, H.K., Wong, C., McMahon, L. & Kaufmann, C. (1999). `Leader behaviour impact on staff nurse empowerment, job tension & work effectiveness', *Journal of Nursing Administration*, Vol.29(5), pp.28-39.

Lawler, E.E. III, Mohrman, S. & Ledford, G.E. Jr. (1995). *Creating High Performance Organisations*, San Francisco, CA: Jossey-Bass.

Leahy, A.L. & Wiley, M.W. (1998). *The Irish Health System in the 21st Century*, Dublin: Oak Tree Press.

Leavitt, H.J. (2003). `Why hierarchies thrive', *Harvard Business Review*, March, pp.96-102.

Lebor, W. & Stofman, J. (1988). `Putting management back in the middle', *Personnel Administrator*, September, pp.45-50.

Legge, K. (2002). `On knowledge, business consultancies & the selling of total quality management', in Clarke, T. & Fincham, R. (eds.), *Critical Consulting: New Perspectives on the Management Advice Industry*, Oxford: Blackwell.

Leifer, R. & Delbecq, A. (1978). `Organisational/environmental interchange: A model of boundary-spanning activities', *Academy of Management Review*, Vol.3(1), pp.40-50.

Leskin, B. (2003). `HRB case commentary: Motivating people', *Harvard Business Review*, January, pp.36-37.

Levine, H.Z. (1986). `The squeeze on middle management', *Personnel*, Vol.63(1), pp.62-69.

Lewin, K. (1951). `Frontiers in group dynamics', in Griffin, R.W., *Management*, New York, USA: Houghton Mifflin.

Lewin, K., Lippitt, R. & White, R.K. (1939). `Patterns of aggressive behaviour in experimentally-created social climates', *Journal of Social Psychology*, Vol.10, pp.271-299.

Limo-Basto, M. (1995). 'Implementing change in nurses' professional behaviours: Limitations of the cognitive approach', *Journal of Advanced Nursing*, Vol.22, pp.192-200.

Lincoln, J.R. & Kalleberg, A.L. (1990). *Culture, Control & Commitment: A Study of Work Organisation & Work Attitudes in the United States & Japan*, Cambridge: Cambridge University Press.

Linstead, S. & Grafton-Small, R. (1992). `On reading organisational culture', *Organisation Studies*, Vol.13(3), pp.331-55.

Lipley, N. (1998). `Doctors get controlling role in new primary care groups', *Nursing Standard*, Vol.12(40), pp.24-30.

Littler, C. R. (2000). 'Comparing downsizing experiences of three countries: A restructuring cycle?' in Burke, R.J. & Cooper, C.L. (eds.), *The Organisation in Crisis: Downsizing, Restructuring & Privatisation*, Oxford: Blackwell.

Litwin, G.H. & Stringer, R.A. (1974). *Motivation & Organisational Climate*, 3rd edition, Boston, MA: Harvard University Press.

Loan-Clarke, J. (1996). `Health care professionals & management development', *Journal of Management in Medicine*, Vol.10(6), pp.24-35.

Long, S. (1996). `Primary health care team workshop: Team members' perspectives', *Journal of Advanced Nursing*, Vol.23, pp.935-41.

Longest, B.B. Jr. (1990). `Inter-organisational linkages in the health sector', *Health Care Management Review*, Vol.15(1), pp.17-28.

Lopopolo, R.B., Schafer, D.S. & Nosse, L.J. (2004). `Leadership, administration, management & professionalism (LAMP) in physical therapy: A Delphi study', *Physical Therapy*, Vol.84(4), pp.137-50.

Lorentzon, M. & Bryant, J. (1977). 'Leadership in British nursing: A historical dimension', *Journal of Nursing Management*, Vol.5, pp.271-78.

Lundgren, L. & Segersten, K. (2001). `Nurses' use of time in a medical-surgical ward with all RN-staffing', *Journal of Nursing Management*, Vol.1, pp.13-20.

Lyles, M.A. & Lenz, R.T. (1982). `Managing the planning process: A field study of the human side of planning', *Strategic Management Journal*, Vol.3(2), pp.105-18.

Mackoff, B. & G. Wenet, G. (2005). *Leadership as a Habit of Mind*, Lincoln: Authors Choice Press.

Magill, G. & Prybil, L. (2004). `Stewardship & integrity in health care: A role for organisational ethics', *Journal of Business Ethics*, Vol.50(3), pp.225-38.

Mahoney, J. (2001). `Leadership skills for the 21st century', *Journal of Nursing Management*, Vol.9, pp.269-71.

Malloch, K. & Porter-O'Grady, T. (2006). *Introduction to Evidence-based Practice in Nursing & Health Care*, Sudbury, MA: Jones & Bartlett Publishers.

Malterud, K. (2001). `The art & science of clinical knowledge: Evidence beyond measures & numbers', *The Lancet*, Vol.358, pp.397-400.

Mannion, J. (1994). 'Managing change: The leadership challenge of the 1990s', *Seminars for Nurse Managers*, Vol.2, pp.203-08.

Manojlovich, M. (2005). `Linking the practice environment to nurses' job satisfaction through nurse-physician communication', *Journal of Nursing Scholarship*, Vol.37(4), pp.367-73.

Manville, B. & Ober, J. (2003). *A Company of Citizens: What the World's First Democracy Teaches Leaders about Creating Great Organisations*, Boston, MA: Harvard Business School Press.

Maslow, A.H. (1954). *Motivation & Personality*, New York: Harper & Row.

Masterson, A. & Maslin-Prothero, S. (1999). `Power, politics & nursing', in Masterson, A. & Maslin-Prothero, S. (eds.), *Nursing & Politics, Power through Practice*, pp. 52-84, Edinburgh: Churchill Livingstone.

McClelland, D.C. & Burnham, D. H. (2003). `Power is the great motivator', *Harvard Business Review*, January, pp.117-19.

McDaniel, C. & Wolf, G.A. (1992). `Transformational leadership in nursing service: A test of theory', *Journal of Nursing Administration*, Vol.22(2), pp.60-65.

McDonald, T. & Siegall, M. (1992). `The effects of technological self-efficacy & job focus on job performance, attitudes & withdrawal behaviours', *Journal of Psychology*, Vol.126, pp.465-75.

McDonald, T. & Siegall, M. (1996). 'Enhancing worker self-efficacy: An approach for reducing negative reactions to technological change'. *Journal of Managerial Psychology*, Vol.11, pp.41-44.

McGahan, A. & Porter, M. (1997). `How much does industry matter, really?' *Strategic Management Journal*, Summer Special Issue, Vol.18, pp.15-30.

McGregor, D.C. (1953). *The Achievement Motive*, New York: Appleton-Century-Crofts.

McKinnell, H. (2003). `Moving mountains, motivating people', *Harvard Business Review*, January, p.47.

McNeese-Smith, D.K. (1995). `Job satisfaction, productivity & organisational commitment, the result of leadership', *Journal of Nursing Administration*, Vol.25, pp.17-26.

Mead, M. (1978). *Culture & Commitment: The New Relationships between the Generations in the 1970s*, revised & updated edition, New York: Columbia University Press.

Meehan, T. (2003). `Careful nursing: A model for contemporary nursing practice', *Journal of Advanced Nursing*, Vol.44(1), pp.99-107.

Merriam-Webster Online, Available at: http://www.m-w.com/home.htm. Accessed September, 2003.

Meyer, J.P., Irving, P.G. & Allen, N.J. (1998). `Examination of the combined effects of work values & early work experiences on organisational commitment', *Journal of Organisational Behaviour*, Vol.19, pp.29-52.

Miles, R.E. & Snow, C.C. (1978). *Organisational Strategy, Structure & Process*, New York: McGraw-Hill.

Miller, C., Ross, N. & Freeman, M. (1999).`Shared learning & clinical teamwork: New directions in education for multi-professional practice', in *Researching Professional Education: Research Reports*, Series Number 14, London: English National Board for Nursing, Midwifery & Health Visiting.

Millman, Z. & Hartwick, J. (1987), `The impact of automated office systems on middle managers & their work', *Management Information System Quarterly*, Vol.11(4), pp.479-92.

Mintzberg, H. & Quinn, J.B. (1992). *The Strategy Process: Concepts & Contexts*, London: Prentice Hall.

Mintzberg, H. (1973). 'Strategy-making in three modes', *California Management Review*, Vol.16(2), pp.44-53.

Mintzberg, H. (1978). `Patterns in strategy formation', *Management Science*, Vol.24(9), pp.934-48.

Mintzberg, H. (1979). *The Structuring of Organisations: A Synthesis of the Research*, Englewood Cliffs, NJ: Prentice Hall.

Mintzberg, H. (1989). *Mintzberg on Management: Inside Our Strange World of Organisations,* New York: Free Press.

Mintzberg, H. (1998). `Covert leadership: Notes on managing professionals', *Harvard Business Review,* Vol.76(6), pp.140-47.

Mohrman, S., Gibson, C. & Mohrman, A. (2001). `Doing research that is useful to practice: A model & empirical exploration', *Academy of Management Journal,* Vol.44, pp.357-75.

Mok, E. & Au-Yeung, B. (2002). `Relationship between organisational climate & empowerment of nurses in Hong Kong', *Journal of Nursing Management,* Vol.10, pp.129-37.

Morath, J.M. & Turnbull, J.E. (2005). *To Do No Harm, Ensuring Patient Safety In Health Care Organisations,* San Francisco, CA: Jossey-Bass.

Morison, S., Boohan, M., Moutray, M. & Jenkins, J. (2004). `Developing pre-qualification inter-professional education for nursing & medical students: Sampling student attitudes to guide development', *Nurse Education in Practice,* Vol.4, pp.20-29.

Moss Kanter, R. (1983). *The Change Masters: Innovation & Entrepreneurship in the American Corporation,* New York: Basic Books.

Moss Kanter, R. (1986). `The reshaping of middle-management', *Management Review,* January, pp.19-20.

Moss Kanter, R. (1989). *When Giants Learn to Dance,* New York: Simon & Schuster.

Moss Kanter, R. (1994). `Collaborative advantage: The art of alliances', *Harvard Business Review,* Vol. 72, July-August, pp.96-108.

Mottaz, C.J. (1988). `Determinants of organisational commitment', *Human Relations,* Vol.41(6), pp.467-82.

Mowday, R.T., Steers, R.M. & Porter, L.W. (1979). `The measurement of organisational commitment', *Journal of Vocational Behaviour,* Vol.14 (2), pp.224-47.

Mulholland, J. (1994). `Competency-based learning applied to nursing management', *Journal of Nursing Management,* Vol.2, pp.161-66.

Muller, P.A. (1992). `Change, conflict & coping', *Journal of Post-Anaesthesia Nursing,* Vol.7, pp.54-56.

Murphy, N.J. (1999). `A survey of health policy content in Canadian graduate programs in nursing', *Journal of Nurse Education,* Vol.38(2), pp.88-91.

Murphy, K.R. & Saal, F.E. (1990). *Psychology in Organisations: Integrating Science & Practice,* Hillsdale, NJ: Erlbaum.

Narayanan, V.K. & Fahey, L. `The micro-politics of strategy formulation', *Academy of Management Review,* Vol.7(1), pp.25-34.

Near, J.P. (1989). `Organisational commitment among Japanese & US workers', *Organisation Studies,* Vol.10, pp.281-300.

Nielsen, R.P. (1981). `Toward a method of building consensus during strategic planning', *Sloan Management Review,* Vol.22(4), pp.29-40.

Nonaka, I. (1988). `Toward middle-up-down management: Accelerating information creation', *Sloan Management Review,* Vol.29(3), pp.9-18.

Norman, I.J. & Cowley, S. (eds.) (1999). *The Changing Nature of Nursing in a Managerial Age,* Oxford: Blackwell Science.

O'Hara, T. (1998). 'Current structure of the Irish health care system: Setting the context', in Leahy, A.L. & Wiley, M.M. (eds.), *The Irish Health System in the 21st Century*, Dublin: Oak Tree Press.

Oakley, A. (1998). 'The importance of being a nurse', in Mackay, L., Soothill, K. & Melia, K. (eds.), *Classic Texts in Health Care*, Oxford: Butterworth Heinemann.

Offermann, L.R. & Spiros, R.K. (2001). 'The science & practice of team development: Improving the link', *Academy of Management Journal*, Vol.44, pp.376-92.

Office for Health Management (2002). *Report on an Evaluation Study of the Leading of an Empowered Organisation Programme (LEO) for Clinical Nurse Managers 1*, Dublin: Office for Health Management.

Office for Health Management (2003). *Good Practice in Leading & Managing Change in Health Service Organisations*, Dublin: Government Publications.

Ogilvie, J.R. (1986). 'The role of human resource management practices in predicting organisational commitment', *Group & Organisation Studies*, Vol.11(4), pp.335-59.

Oh, A. (2004). 'The power of cultural influences on managerial behaviour in organisations', *Development & Learning in Organisations*, Vol.18(2), pp.13-15.

Oi-ling, S. (2002). 'Predictors of job satisfaction & absenteeism in two samples of Hong Kong nurses', *Journal of Advanced Nursing*, Vol.40(2), pp.218-29.

Organ, D.W. & Ryan, K. (1995). 'A meta-analytic review of attitudinal & dispositional predictors of organisational citizenship behaviour', *Personnel Psychology*, Vol.48, pp.775-802.

Organ, D.W. (1988). *Organisational Citizenship Behaviour: The Good Soldier Syndrome*. Lexington, MA: Lexington Books.

Oroviogoicoechea, C. (1996). 'The clinical nurse manager: A literature review', *Journal of Advanced Nursing*, Vol.24, pp.1273-80.

Oster, S.M. (1995). *Strategic Management of Non-profit Organisations*, New York: Oxford University Press.

Oxman, J.A. & Smith, B.D. (2003). 'The limits of structural change', *MIT Sloan Management Review*, Vol.45(1), pp.77-82.

Papadakis, V.M., Kaloghirou, Y. & Iatrelli, M. (1999). 'Strategic decision-making: From crisis to opportunity', *Business Strategy Review*, Vol.10(1), pp.29-37.

Parsell, G. & Bligh, J. (1999). 'Educational principles underpinning successful shared learning', in *AMEE Education Guide No.12: Multi-professional Education*, Dundee: AMEE.

Pavett, C.M. & Lau, A.W. (1985). 'A comparative analysis of research & development managerial jobs across two sectors', *Journal of Management Studies*, Vol.22, pp.69-82.

Pearson C.A.L. & Chong, J. (1997). 'Contributions of job content & social information on organisational commitment & job satisfaction: An exploration in a Malaysian nursing context', *Journal of Occupational & Organisational Psychology*, Vol.70, pp.357-74.

Pearson, A., Vaughan, B. & Fitzgerald, M. (1996). *Nursing Models for Practice*, 2nd edition, pp.2-11, Oxford: Butterworth Heinemann.

Pentland, B. (1992). 'Organising moves in software support hotlines', *Administrative Science Quarterly*, Vol.37, pp.527-48.

Pepper, G.L. (1995). *Communicating in Organisations: A Cultural Approach*, New York: McGraw-Hill.

Perrow, C. (1986). *Complex Organisations: A Critical Essay*, 3rd edition, New York: Random House.

Peters, T.J. (1992). *Liberation Management: Necessary Disorganisation for the Nanosecond Nineties*, London: Macmillan.

Pettigrew, A.M. (1977). `Strategy formulation as a political process', *International Studies of Management & Organisation*, Vol. 7(2), pp.78-87.

Pfeffer, J. & Sutton, R.I. (2000). *The Knowing-Doing Gap: How Smart Companies Turn Knowledge into Action*, Boston, MA: Harvard Business School Press.

Pfeffer, J. (1977). `The ambiguity of leadership', *Academy of Management Journal*, Vol.2, pp.104-12.

Pfeffer, J. (1997). `Will the organisation of the future make the mistakes of the past?', in Hesselbein, F., Goldsmith, M. & Beckhard, R. (eds.), *The Organisation of the Future*, The Drucker Foundation Future Series, San Francisco, CA: Jossey-Bass.

Phillips, D. (1996). 'Medical professional dominance & client dissatisfaction', *Social Science and Medicine*, Vol.42, pp.1419-425.

Pillari, R.J. (2003). `Moving mountains, motivating people', *Harvard Business Review*, January.

Pirrie, A., Elsegood, J. & Hall, J. (1998). *Evaluating Multidisciplinary Education in Health Care. Final Report of a 24 Month Funded Study*, London: Department of Health.

Pirrie, A., Wilson, V., Harden, R. & Elsegood, J. (1999). `Promoting cohesive practice in health care', in *AMEE Education Guide No.12: Multi-professional Education*. Dundee: AMEE.

Podsakoff, P.M., MacKenzie, S.B., Paine, J.B. & Bachrach, D.G. (2000). 'Organisational citizenship behaviours: A critical review of the theoretical & empirical literature & suggestions for future research', *Journal of Management*, Vol.26(5), pp.3-63.

Podsakoff, P.M., Toder, W.D. & Schuler, R.S. (1983) `Leader expertise as a moderator of the effects of instrumental & supportive leader behaviour', *Journal of Management*, Vol.9, pp.176-85.

Poggenppoel, M. (1992). `Managing change', *Nursing RSA*, Vol.7, pp.28-31.

Pollitt, C. (1993). *Managerialism & the Public Services*, 2nd edition, Oxford: Basil Blackwell.

Porter-O'Grady, T. & Malloch, K. (2002). *Quantum Leadership: A Textbook of New Leadership*, New York: Aspen Publishers.

Porter-O'Grady, T. (1992). *Implementing Shared Governance*. Baltimore, MD: Mosby.

Porter, L.W., Steers, R.M., Mowday, R.T. & Boulian, P.V. (1974). `Organisational commitment, job satisfaction & turnover among psychiatric technicians', *Journal of Applied Psychology*, Vol.59(5), pp.603-09.

Porter, M.E. (1996). `What is strategy?', *Harvard Business Review*, Vol.74(6), pp.61-78.

Posner, B.Z., Kouzes, J.M. & Schmidt, W.H. (1985). `Shared values make a difference: An empirical test of corporate culture', *Human Resource Management*, Vol.24(3), pp.293-309.

Powell, W.W. & Owen-Smith, J. (1998). `Universities & the market for intellectual property in the life sciences', *Journal of Policy Analysis & Management,* Vol.17, pp.253-77.

Power, L.P. (2001). *Competencies for Clinical Nurse Managers II in Learning Disability Nursing,* 2001, unpublished Master's in Nursing Thesis, University College Dublin.

Press, E & Washburn, J. (2000). `The kept university', *Atlantic Monthly,* Vol.285(3), pp.39-54.

Price Waterhouse Integration Team (1996). *The Third Paradox Principle: Focus Directly on Culture, Indirectly,* New York: Price Waterhouse LLP, Irwin Professional.

Pryce, A. & Reeves, S. (1997). *An Exploratory Research Project of a Multi-disciplinary Education Module for Medical, Dental & Nursing Students,* London: City University.

Pulce, R. (2002). `Organisational culture', *Seminars for Nurse Managers: Strategies for Leadership & Management* , Vol.10(3), pp.147.

Putti, J.M., Aryee, S. & Phua, J. (1990). `Communication relationship satisfaction & organisational commitment', *Group & Organisation Studies*, Vol.15(1), pp.44-52.

Quinn, J.B. (1980). *Strategies for Change: Logical Incrementalism,* Homewood, IL: Richard D. Irwin.

Quinn, J.B. (1982). `Managing strategy incrementally', *OMEGA International Journal of Management Science,* Vol.10, pp.613-27.

Quinn, J.B. (1995). `The strategy concept' in Mintzberg, H., Quinn, J.B. & Ghoshal, S., *The Strategy Process,* European edition, London: Prentice Hall.

Randall, D.M. & Cote, J.A. (1991). `Interrelationships of work commitment constructs', *Work & Occupations,* Vol.18(2), pp.194-211.

Reeves, S. (2001). `A review of the effects of inter-professional education on staff involved in the care of adults with mental health problems'. *Journal of Psychiatric & Mental Health Nursing,* Vol.8, pp.533-42.

Reeves, S. & Freeth, D. (2002). `The London training ward: An innovative inter-professional learning initiative', *Journal of Inter-professional Care,* Vol.16, pp.41-52.

Reeves, S. & Pryce, A. (1998). `Emerging themes: An exploratory research project of an inter-professional education module for medical, dental & nursing students', *Nurse Education Today,* Vol.18, pp.534-41.

Reeves, S., Leiba, T., Freeth, D., Glen, S. & Herzberg, J. (2002). `Inter-professional workshops for community mental health teams: Piloting a team-based approach', *Journal of Inter-professional Care,* Vol.16, pp.176-77.

Reilly, A.H., Brett, J.M. & Stroh, L.K. (1993). 'The impact of corporate turbulence on employee attitudes', *Strategic Management Journal,* Vol.14, pp.167-79.

Reutter, L. & Williamson, D.L. (2000). `Advocating healthy public policy: Implications for Baccalaureate nursing education', *Journal of Nurse Education,* Vol.39(1), pp.21-6.

Ring, P.S & Perry, J.L. (1985). 'Strategic management in public & private organisations: Implications of distinctive contexts & constraints', *Academy of Management Review*, Vol.10(2), pp.276-86.

Rivers, B. & Asubonteng, P. (1999). 'Hospital competition in major US metropolitan areas: An empirical evidence', *Journal of Socio-Economics*, Vol.28, pp.597-607.

Roberts, K. (2002). 'Exploring participation: Older people on discharge from hospital', *Journal of Advanced Nursing*, Vol.40(4), pp.413-20.

Robins, J. (ed.) (1997). *Reflections on Health: Commemorating Fifty Years of the Department of Health 1947-1997*, Dublin: Department of Health.

Robinson, J. & Phibbs, C. (1989). 'An evaluation of Medicaid selective contracting in California', *Journal of Health Economics*, Vol.8, pp.483-502.

Robinson, J. (1992). 'Introduction: Beginning the study of nursing policy', in Robinson, J., Gray, A. & Elkan, R. (eds.), *Policy Issues in Nursing*, Milton Keynes: Open University Press.

Robinson, L. (2004). 'BACP/FHCP strengthens its NHS presence with crucial new appointment', *Health care Counselling & Psychotherapy Journal*, Vol.4(1), pp.27-29.

Rodham, K. & Bell, J. (2002). 'Work stress: An exploratory study of the practices & perceptions of female junior health care managers', *Journal of Nursing Management*, Vol.10(1), pp.5-11.

Rodwell, C. (1996).'An analysis of the concept of empowerment', *Journal of Advanced Nursing*, Vol.23, pp.305-13.

Roemer, L. (1996), 'Hospital middle managers' perceptions of their work & competence', *Hospital Health Service Administration*, Vol.41, pp.210-35.

Rogers, E.M. (1995). *Diffusion of Innovations*, New York: Free Press.

Rosen, R. (1995). *Strategic Management: An Introduction*, London: Pitman.

Rosenstein, A.H., Russell, H. & Lauve, R. (2002). 'Disruptive physician behaviour contributes to nursing shortage: Study links bad behaviour by doctors to nurses leaving the profession - Doctors, Nurses & Disruptive Behaviour', *Physician Executive*, November-December, Vol. 28(6), pp.8-11.

Rowe, A.J, Dickel, K.E., Mason, R.O. & Snyder, N.H. (1989). *Strategic Management: A Methodological Approach*, 3rd edition, Reading, MA: Addison-Wesley.

Royal College of Surgeons in Ireland & Institute of Public Administration (2003). *Clinicians in Management: A Review of Clinical Leadership*, Discussion No. 4 Paper, Dublin: Office for Health Management.

Rynes, S.L. & Trank, C. (1999). 'Behavioural science in the business school curriculum: Teaching in a changing institutional environment', *Academy of Management Review*, Vol.24, pp.808-24.

Rynes, S.L., Bartunek, J.M. & Daft, R.L. (2001). 'Across the great divide: Knowledge creation & transfer between practitioners & academics', *Academy of Management Journal*, 2001, Vol.44(2), pp.340-55.

Saffold, G.S. III (1988). 'Culture traits, strength, & organisational performance: Moving beyond "strong" culture', *Academy of Management Review*, Vol.13(4), pp.546-58.

Sashkin, M. & Fulmer, R.M. (1988). `Toward an organisational leadership theory', in Hunt, J.G., Baliga, B.R., Dachler, H.P. & Schriesheim, C.A. (eds.), *Emerging Leadership Vistas*, Boston, MA: Lexington Press.

Sathe, V. (1983).`Implications of corporate culture: A manager's guide to action', *Organisational Dynamics*, Autumn, pp.5-23.

Schafer, D.S. (2002).`Three perspectives on physical therapist managerial work', *Physical Therapy*, Vol.82, pp.228-36.

Schall, M.S. (1983). `A communication-rules approach to organisational culture', *Administrative Science Quarterly*, Vol.28(4), pp.557-81.

Schein, E.H. (1984). `Coming to a new awareness of organisational culture', *Sloan Management Review*, Vol.25(2), pp.3-16.

Schein, E.H. (1992). *Organisational Culture & Leadership*, 2nd edition, San Francisco, CA: Jossey-Bass.

Schilit, W.K. & Paine, F.T. (1987). `An examination of the underlying dynamics of strategic decisions subject to upward influence activity', *Journal of Management Studies*, Vol.24(2), pp.161-87.

Schilit, W.K. (1987a). `An examination of the influence of middle-level managers in formulating & implementing strategic decisions', *Journal of Management Studies*, Vol.24(3), pp.271-93.

Schilit, W.K. (1987b). `Upward influence activity in strategic decision-making: An examination of organisational differences', *Group and Organisation Studies*, Vol.12(3), pp.343-68.

Schim, S.M., Zoorenbos, A.Z. & Borse, N.N. (2005). `Cultural competence among Ontario & Michigan health care providers', *Journal of Nursing Scholarship*, Vol.37(4), pp.302-07.

Schneider, B., Brief, A. & Guzzo, R. (1996). `Creating a climate & culture for sustainable organisational change', *Organisational Dynamics*, Vol.24 (4), pp.7-19.

Schulz, R., Greenby, J. & Brown, R. (1985). `Organisation, management & client effects on staff burnout', *Journal of Health & Social Behaviour*, Vol.36, pp.333-45.

Schwartz, S.H. & Sagiv, L. (1995). `Identifying culture-specifics in the context and structure of values', *Journal of Cross-Cultural Psychology*, Vol.26, pp.92-116.

Schwartz, S.H. (1992). `Universals in the content & structure of values: Theoretical advances & empirical tests in 20 countries' in Zanna, M. (ed.), *Advances in Experiential Social Psychology, Vol.25*, Orlando, FL: Academic Press.

Schwartz, S.H. (1994). `Beyond individualism/collectivism: New cultural dimensions of values', in Kim, U., Triandis, H.C., Kagitcibasi, C., Choi, S. & Yoon, G. (eds.), *Individualism & Collectivism: Theory, Method & Applications*, Thousand Oaks, CA: Sage.

Schwartz, S.H. (1999). `A theory of cultural values & some implications for work', *Applied Psychology: An International Review*, Vol.48, pp.23-47.

Schweiger, D.M., Sandberg, W.R. & Ragan, J.W. (1986). `Group approaches for improving strategic decision-making: A comparative analysis of dialectical inquiry, devil's advocacy & consensus', *Academy of Management Journal*, Vol.29(1), pp.51-71.

Schyns, B. (2004). `The influence of occupational self-efficacy on the relationship of leadership behaviour & preparedness for occupational change', *Journal of Career Development*, Vol.30(4), pp.247-61.

Scott, K.A. (2004). `Creating highly reliable hospitals through strengthening nursing', *JONA*, Vol.34(4), pp.170-72.

Senge, P.M. (1998). *The Fifth Discipline & the Infrastructures of a Learning Organisation*, video, Massachusetts: Pegasus Communications.

Shamir, B. & Kark, R. (2004). `A single-item graphic scale for the measurement of organisational identification', *Journal of Occupational & Organisational Psychology*, Vol.77, pp.115-23.

Shore, L.M. & Tetrick, L.E. (1991). `A construct validity study of the Survey of Perceived Organisational Support', *Journal of Applied Psychology*, Vol.76(5), pp.637-43.

Shrivastava, P. & Mitroff, I.I. (1984). `Enhancing organisational research utilisation: The role of decision-makers' assumptions', *Academy of Management Review*, Vol.9, pp.18-26.

Shrivastava, P. (1986). `Is strategic management ideological?, *Journal of Management*, Vol.12(3), pp.363-77.

Siegrist, J. & Peter, R. (2000). 'The effort-reward-imbalance model' in Schnall, P., Belkic, K., Landsbergis, P. & Baker, D. (eds.), *The Workplace & Cardiovascular Disease*, in Occupational Medicine: State of the Art Reviews, 15 (1), pp. 83-87, Philadelphia: Hanley & Belfus.

Soanes, C. (ed.) (2003). Compact Oxford English Dictionary of Current English, 2nd edition, Oxford: Oxford University Press.

Sommer, S.M., Bae, S. & Luthans, F. (1996). `Organisational commitment across cultures: The impact of antecedents on Korean employees', *Human Relations*, Vol.49, pp.977-93.

Sorcher, M. & Brant, J. (2002). 'Are you picking the right leaders?', *Harvard Business Review*, February, Vol.80(2), pp.78-85.

Staehle, W. & Schirmer, F. (1992). `Lower-level & middle-level managers as the recipients & actors of human-resource management', *International Studies of Management and Organisation*, Vol.22(1), pp.67-89.

Stagner, R. (1969). `Corporate decision-making: An empirical study', *Journal of Applied Psychology*, Vol.53(1), pp.1-13.

Stevens, J.M., Beyer, J.M. & Trice, H.M. (1978). `Assessing personal, role & organisational predictors of managerial commitment', *Academy of Management Journal*, Vol.21(3), pp.380-96.

Stogdill, R.M. (1974). *Handbook of Leadership: A Survey of Theory & Research*, New York: Free Press.

Taylor, N.S., Audia, G. & Gupta, A.K. (1996). `The effect of lengthening job tenure on managers' organisational commitment & turnover', *Organisation Science*, Vol.7(6), pp.632-48.

Teisberg, E., Porter, M. & Brown, G. (1994). `Making competition in health care work', *Harvard Business Review*, Vol.72(4), pp.131-41.

Thakur, M. (1988). `Involving middle managers in strategy-making', *Long Range Planning*, Vol.31(5), pp.732-41.

Thomas, D.R.E. (1978). `Strategy is different in service businesses', *Harvard Business Review*, Vol.56(4), pp.158-65.

Thomas, R. & Dunkerley, D. (1999). `Careering downwards? Middle managers' experiences in the downsized organisation', *British Journal of Management*, Vol.10(2), pp.157-69.

Thorne, M.L. (2000). `Cultural chameleons', *British Journal of Management*, Vol.11(4), pp.325-339.

Thorne, S., McGuinness, L., McPherson, G., Con, A., Cunningham, M. & Harris, S.R. (2004). `Health care communication issues in fibromyalgia: An interpretive description', *Physiotherapy Canada*, Vol.56(1), pp.31-38.

Tierney, A.J. (2004). `We need more nursing ethics research', *Journal of Advanced Nursing*, Vol. 45(4), pp.345-46.

Tizard, J. (2002). `Managing change', *New Zealand Management*, Vol.49, p.64.

Tjosvold, D. & Field, R.H.G. (1983). `Effects of social context on consensus & majority vote decision-making', *Academy of Management Journal*, Vol.26(3), pp.500-06.

Tope, R. (1996). *Integrated Inter-disciplinary Learning between the Health & Social Care Professions: A Feasibility Study*, Aldershot: Avebury.

Torrington, D. & Weightman, J. (1987). `Middle management work', *Journal of General Management*, Vol.13(2), pp.74-89.

Trice, H.M. & Beyer, B.M. (1993). *The Cultures of Work Organisations*, Englewood Cliffs, NJ: Prentice Hall.

Trice, H.M. (1993). *Occupational Sub-cultures in the Workplace*, Ithaca, NY: ILR Press.

Trice, H.M., Belasco, J. & Alutto, J.A. (1969). `The role of ceremonials in organisational behaviour', *Industrial & Labour Relations Review*, Vol.23, pp.40-51.

United Kingdom Central Council for Nursing, Midwifery & Health Visiting (2000). *Requirements for pre-registration nursing programmes*, London: United Kingdom Central Council for Nursing, Midwifery & Health Visiting.

Van Dick, R., Wagner, U., Stellmacher, J. & Christ, O. (2004). `The utility of a broader conceptualization of organisational identification: Which aspects really matter?', *Journal of Occupational and Organisational Psychology*, Vol.77, pp.171-91.

van Knippenberg, E. (2000). `Work motivation & performance: A social identity perspective', *Applied Psychology: An International Review*, Vol.49, pp.357-71.

Van Maanen, J. & Kunda, G. (1989). 'Real feelings: Emotional expression & organisational culture', in Cummings, L.L. & Staw, B.M. (eds.), *Research in Organisational Behaviour*, Vol.11, Greenwich, CT: JAI Press.

Vanclay, L. (ed.) (1997). 'Inter-professional education: A definition', Inter-professional education: What, How & When. *CAIPE Bulletin* No. 13, Summer, p.19. London: CAIPE, The UK Centre for the Advancement of Inter-professional Education.

Vera, D. & Crossan, M. (2004). `Strategic leadership & organisational learning', *Academy of Management Review*, Vol.29(2), pp.222-40.

Virgin, S., Goodrow, B. & Duggins, B. (1996). `Scavenger hunt: A community-based learning experience', *Nurse Educator*, Vol.21, pp.32-34.

Wade-Benzoni, K.A., Hoffman, A.J., Thompson, L.L., Moore, D.A., Gillespie, J.J. & Bazerman, M.H. (2002). `Barriers to resolution in ideologically-based negotiations: The role of values & institutions', *Academy of Management Review*, Vol.27(1), pp.41-57.

Walshe, A. (2003). `A critical exploration of "working together, learning together" -Does it meet the learning needs of nurses?', *Nurse Education Today*, Vol. 23, pp.522-29.

Webb, J. (1999). `Work & the new public service class', *Sociology*, Vol.33(4), pp.747-66.

Weick, K. & Sutcliffe, K. (2001). *Managing the Unexpected: Assuring High Performance in an Age of Complexity*, San Francisco, CA: Jossey-Bass Publishers.

Weinberg, A. & Creed, F. (2000). `Stress & psychiatric disorder in health care professionals and hospital staff', *The Lancet*, Vol.355, pp.533-37.

Wells, J.S.G. (1995). `Health care rationing: Nursing perspectives', *Journal of Advanced Nursing*, Vol.22(4), pp.738-44.

Wells, J.S.G. (1996). `The public & professional interface with priority-setting in the National Health Service', *Journal of Health & Social Care in the Community*, Vol.4(5), pp.255-63.

Wells, J.S.G. (1999). `The growth of managerialism & its impact on nursing & the NHS' in Norman, I.J. & Cowley, S. (eds.). *The Changing Nature of Nursing in a Managerial Age*, Oxford: Blackwell Science.

Westley, F. & Mintzberg, H. (1989). `Visionary leadership & strategic management', *Strategic Management Journal*, Vol.10, pp.17-32.

Westley, F.R. (1990). `Middle managers & strategy: Microdynamics of inclusion', *Strategic Management Journal*, Vol.11(5), pp.337-51.

Wheatley, M.J. (2001). *Leadership & the New Science: Discovering Order in a Chaotic World*, revised, San Francisco, CA: Berrett-Koehler.

Whorton, J.W. & Worthley, J.A. (1981). `A perspective on the challenge of public management: Environmental paradox & organisational culture', *Academy of Management Review*, Vol.6(3), pp.357-61.

Whyte, W.F. (1951). *Pattern for Industrial Peace*, New York: Harper.

Wickens, P.D. (1995). *The Ascendant Organisation: Combining Commitment & Control for Long-term, Sustainable Business Success*, Basingstoke: Macmillan Business.

Willcocks, S. (1994). `The clinical director in the NHS: Utilizing a role-theory perspective', *Journal of Management in Medicine*, Vol.8(5), pp.68-76.

Williams, A., Dobson, A.P. & Walters, M. (1993). *Changing Culture: New Organisational Approaches*, 2nd edition, London: Institute of Personnel Management.

Willis, E. (1989). *Medical Dominance: The Division of Labour in Australian Health Care*, 2nd revised edition, Sydney: Allen & Unwin.

Witz, A. (1995). `The challenge of nursing', in Gabe, J., Kelleher, D. & Williams, G. (eds.), *Challenging Medicine*, London: Routledge.

Wood, S. & de Menezes, L. (1998). `High commitment management in the UK: Evidence from the Workplace Industrial Relations Survey, & Employers' Manpower & Skills Practices Survey', *Human Relations*, Vol.51(4), pp.485-515.

Wooldridge, B. & Floyd, S.W. (1990). `The strategy process, middle management involvement & organisational performance', *Strategic Management Journal*, Vol.11(3), pp.231-41.

Worrall, L., Parkes, C. & Cooper, C.L. (2004). `The impact of organisational change on the perceptions of UK managers', *European Journal of Work & Organisational Psychology*, Vol.13(2), pp.139-163.

Wortman, M.S. Jr. (1979).`Strategic management: Not-for-profit organisations', in Schendel, D.E. & Hofer, C.W. (eds.), *Strategic Management: A New View of Business Policy & Planning*, Boston, MA: Little Brown.

Yasai-Ardekani, M. & Haug, R.S. (1997). `Contextual determinants of strategic planning processes', *Journal of Management Studies*, Vol.34(5), pp.729–67.

Yip, G.S. (1985). ` Who needs strategic planning?' *Journal of Business Strategy*, Vol.6(2), pp.30-42.

Yousef, D.A. (2000). `Organisational commitment as a mediator of the relationship between Islamic work ethic & attitudes toward organisational change', *Human Relations*, Vol.53, pp.513-37.

Zaccaro, S.J., Foti, R.J. & Kenny, D.A. (1991). `Self-monitoring & trait-based variance in leadership: An investigation of leader flexibility across multiple group situations', *Journal of Applied Psychology*, Vol.76, pp.308-15.

Zukowski, B. (1995). `Managing change - before it manages you!', *Medsurg Nursing*, Vol.4, pp.325-30.

INDEX

OAK TREE PRESS

is Ireland's leading business book publisher.

It develops and delivers
information, advice and resources
to entrepreneurs and managers –
and those who educate and support them.

Its print, software and web materials
are in use in Ireland, the UK, Finland,
Greece, Norway and Slovenia.

OAK TREE PRESS

19 Rutland Street
Cork, Ireland
T: + 353 21 4313855
F: + 353 21 4313496
E: info@oaktreepress.com
W: www.oaktreepress.com